# OUR
# COSMIC
# ORIGIN

OPEN YOUR EYES ABOUT
EARTH'S PLACE IN THE MULTIVERSE
AND ABOUT A GREATER ORGANIZATION
OF THE COSMOS

## ISMAEL PEREZ

# PREFACE

In the fourth century B. C., a mob of religious zealots, destroyed one of the last of the storehouse of information relating to ancient knowledge. All records about the times before the great flood were erased from history where the Library of Alexandria, the last of its keepers, was a female guardian by the name of Hypatia, who was murdered by the same fanatical religious mob. Volumes of important literature were destroyed; everything from the pre-history of our world, philosophical studies including science, and metaphysics blazed in ashes. As a result, of burning down this ancient library, all knowledge went up in flames and our world fell into darkness for about thirteen hundred years.

It was only about five hundred years ago that our western world climbed out of the long-dreaded dark ages, due to a few important records of the ageless wisdom that were secretly preserved. They survived in the secret societies of medieval times under the banner of the brotherhood of the Quest of the Great White Brotherhood, who despite their oppression, were able to eventually bring us out of the dark ages through the historical event that became known as the renaissance. The quest was the return of spiritual knowledge to mankind, which in turn would catapult us into the promised Seventh Golden age, as revealed in those ancient records. This information is not new, nor does it belong to one person, it is the ancient lost knowledge that could be traced back into antiquity and it belongs to those that seek it.

The times have changed and today mankind has arrived at a new dispensation, therefore, the age of wars and secret societies is coming to a close, for in the new era, all mankind will be initiated into the higher mysteries and given the opportunity to reach their full potential, and that era hwhererrived. This book is, therefore, dedicated to all those men and women of the brotherhood of the quest, like Hypatia, and later the legendary guardians of the Holy Grail, the Knights of the Temple, the Sufis, as well as the networks of the east in Tibet who have for centuries secretly guarded the information that is now once again emerging in the twentieth-first century. This is the spiritual knowledge of the ageless wisdom that is awakening mankind into a higher purpose and meaning of life. It unveils the information we need in preparation for the manifestation of A NEW HEAVEN ON EARTH.

The information in this book was derived from a combination of both collective pieces of research based on investigatialongong-dreaded records as well as intuitive research channeled from the higher realms. And because education has had a dual nature throughout all of history, this book is a synthesis of both, the exoteric tradition (general basic knowledge for the masses) that dominated our awareness for centuries and the other pertains to the esoteric tradition, which is the branch of knowledge that has only been taught to a select few.

Most Importantly, the information provided in this material is supported by cutting-edge science. MAY THE LIVING LIGHT OF OUR CREATOR SHINE ONCE AGAIN THROUGH ALL OF MANKIND.

This book is meant to awaken people in this time of restoration. It is not your typical book, but a revelation and message for those that are meant to know the truth. It will help you understand more clearly the flood of information that is emerging in these wonderful times. Most importantly. it is a book of initiation for the masses that upon reading this alloweditual awakening. Consider in mind each chapter, for each chapter has a clear and strong message that might trigger a spiritual awakening at any time.

# CONTENT

Copyright page     iii

Preface     iv

Introduction     viii

SECTION ONE

1   A New Science Has Emerged     1

2   The theory of multiple civilizations as proposed by our new science     9

3   The celestial connection     16

4   Our comic spiritual divine origin     29

5   The universe is bigger than what we were told     48

6   All universes and creations operate according to universal laws     74

SECTION TWO

7   A brief history of our forgotten galactic past     90

8    The formation of the galactic federation of the free world, hence their    104
     logo, galactic history part two

9    Our connection to the Pleiades, a brief history of our galaxy pat three    118

10   The real history of the earth is more than a few thousand years    126

11   The fall of Atlantis was the fall of man    151

12   Earth history from the fall of Atlantis to the rise of a new era, 12,000    157
     BC-6,000 BC

13   When kingship was lowered from (heaven) Nibiru to earth.    172

14   The inheritors and successors of the order of the essence, from about 900    192
     AD to the present

SECTION THREE

15   The rise of homonauticus the angels among us    208

16   The return of the host of heaven and the establishment of the    219
     office of the christ

17   Cosmic cycles and the precision of the Equinoxe    228

18   A vision of the two thousand years    240

19   A closer look at the coming world    254

     Glossary    259

# INTRODUCTION

We are living in what externally appears to be, troubled times, though, in essence, we are living in the most exciting times ever in the history of our world. Why? Because our world is in the process of returning to a golden age, A NEW HEAVEN ON EARTH is prophesied in all religions. Every ancient record believed in a time that the Union of Heaven and earth would come again. The signs are everywhere; the time is now, as flooding of higher information is pouring, which is the true meaning of revelation, or apocalypse. As it stands, the angels have confirmed that the work of God's glory for the earth has already been completed as it is in heaven.

However, what is important and central in the restoration process is learning to identify and adapt to the new energies, which are positively affecting and gradually, transforming our world from within as we know it. As a result, our entire physical composition is shifting therefore, it is important to understand how the universe works in terms of energy as re-discovered by our cutting-edge science. In fact, it is crucial that we get familiarized with this new higher resonating energy that is flooding our earth acting as a catalyst that is beginning to vibrate a NEW STRUCTURE, A NEW WORLD, AND NEW REALITY.

Based on our latest scientific discoveries, it appears that all manifestations are held together by vibrations, so if the vibration changes, then so do its form.

This new frequency/vibration is not only disintegrating the entire (oppressive) structure of the beast (antichrist) system from its core but is ultimately transforming our world, including ourselves into this NEW, refined, and improved reality.

In fact, there is now scientific evidence that reveals that our entire reality is held together by certain grid systems that are spread out like ley lines throughout the entire planet. It is these grid systems that resonate with the vibrations that hold together all forms, affecting all fields including our electro-magnetic and gravitational fields.

It has also been discovered that for the last thirty years a new grid pattern has been forming and that explains why HEAVEN ON EARTH is gradually manifesting as many are beginning to experience what is called a spiritual awakening. This spiritual awakening was prophesied long ago in the annals of time and all religious traditions agree to this great unfolding event that will usher in the awaited seventh golden age of enlightenment.

In exoteric terms, it is the establishment of HEAVEN ON EARTH, the Millennium. In the esoteric wisdom, it is the beginning of the fifth root-race that begins as we enter the first days of the Age of Aquarius, which is indeed upon us.

The Ancient cultures believed that in the Age of Aquarius, the earth and its inhabitants would be restored, the dark forces would be removed and the NEW EARTH (that is being shaped through by higher resonating energy) would shine like a jewel throughout the HEAVENS. It is my honor to say, that this is the process that is now unfolding in these glorious times.

One thing to understand about the shifts of the ages is that when a point of transition occurs, especially one of this magnitude that we are in the midst of (known as the great shift of the ages), everything climaxes into a boiling point where it acts as a disintegrator for the old paradigm of the old unworkable order who is desperately trying to continue to exist, and a catalyst for the new paradigm that is forcing its way into a new order of reality. Since everything is energy, then everything is recyclable from one form of reality to another.

In fact, more study into Quantum phenomena is now confirming what shamans, elders, saints, yogis, and all spiritual saints and masters knew for millenniums. What happens in the outer material reality reflects what is going on in the energy field that permeates us all (inner reality, morphogenic fields). Most importantly, what has been the greatest discovery is that we are all contributing to the collective energy field; by virtue of being a human vibrating energy field ourselves as we are also made of vibrating resonance, fields call chakras.

As a result of these positive changes, mankind, and our world as we know it, is set for a major transformation that will absolutely change the basic fabric of our existence forever.

In fact, many modern-day scientists and scholars from various fields of study are agreeing on the fact that major changes are taking place regarding natural phenomena both on earth and in our solar system. In combination with the physical changes reporting from science, there is also now solid scientific evidence that has clearly supported the idea that our reality is shaped and molded by our minds. This is the same principle that has always been known by those who understood ancient wisdom. It is this wisdom that is now making its way into the limelight in preparation for the shift into the new reality structure.

For example, what spiritual scientists (metaphysicians) can now tell us, is that for thousands of years planet earth has been vibrating in a very low-density field polarizing mostly to the negative side of the spectrum. This mass negative field produced mass negative consciousness and it is what has kept our planet mostly in the dark ages. Well, unfortunately, by not fully understanding what shapes reality (MIND) we have been contributing to that negative field, by being trapped in a negative mindset with limited belief systems about our reality. Therefore, today considering the new knowledge, we have begun to understand that as a man or woman thinketh, so shall his or her life be.

In other words, since everything is energy and therefore vibrating, our thoughts, words, actions, are also vibrating, and in understanding this, we can conclude that the vibration of our thoughts, words, and actions are attracting and creating our reality all around us in every given second in time. This is now a fact, proven scientifically through the avenues of quantum mechanics.

The good news is that we have now the collective power to end the old mass negative THOUGHT FORMS; by having enough people focus only on the positive. We the people, thus have the power to contribute to the NEW loving positive energy that is materializing A NEW HEAVEN ON EARTH.

In truth, this fallen structure or negatively polarized reality was set into motion, during the time of Atlantis, when the fallen angels took over the affairs of our planet.

Yes, it has been revealed that civilizations have existed on this planet for perhaps what the Akashic records (records in higher dimension) believe to be millions or even billions of years, as we shall soon see.

In light of this, we could perhaps understand how a new energy field (program) that is now replacing the old one, is depolarizing our world but to the positive side (light) and as a new reality sets in for those that are raising their vibrations to match the positive energies of love, brotherhood and, peace is beginning to resonating with the new incoming frequencies that are manifesting the new reality structure.

After the NEW AGE fully sets in, which is going to be precipitated by the coming of the host of heaven (beings from higher dimensions) only good people that prefer to live in a world of harmony, peace, and Sisterhood/brotherhood, will be welcomed to partake of A NEW HEAVEN ON EARTH as promised in the ancient Prophesies of all sacred traditions.

Therefore, the coming of HEAVEN ON EARTH is emerging by virtue of two things. First, since the mind creates reality, there are many people changing their personal fields into frequencies of love and compassion, peace, brotherhood, sisterhood, and cooperation since we are all vibrating little micro universes considering that our existence is now scientifically proven to be holistic. Second, is the fact that our planet and the entire solar system is being bombarded with higher frequencies (scalar waves) from the center of our galaxy that is catapulting the entire planet into a higher state of vibration, consciousness, and being, which is gradually culminating into a whole NEW WORLD structure.

Scientists have furthermore connected these scalar waves emanating from the center of our galaxy with a phenomenon known as the Photon Belt. Of course, further study of planetary, solar, and galactic cycles, which have been developed by ancient wise societies also, back up what today's modern scientists are detecting.

Today is also a defining time in which humanity can now utilize technology for the greatest benefit of all. It is the long-awaited moment where mind and Matter Bridge, science and spirituality come together, and all opposites come to a resolution by virtue of discovering the interconnectivity and oneness of all.

This is a time that mankind will completely understand and accept that we are not corporeal beings, but light beings embodied or vibrating at an exceptionally low frequency. This low frequency produces what appears as a corporeal vehicle but even that is an illusion. That is, even our physical bodies are made of vibrating strings or oscillating energy fields creating a low vibration of the electron flow in the atom, coalescing our vibrations into solid physical form, when, it is empty space.

It appears according to the esoteric wisdom that we have other subtle vehicles that we cannot see with our eyes and are as important then what we see in the mirror. In fact, the secret spiritual knowledge reveals that these other parts of ourselves are ur energy subtle bodies that we do not see, generate and hold together the construction and form of our physical body. These energy body systems, which correspond, with the planet's energy system (grids) have always been understood and known by the esoteric secret traditions of both light and dark brotherhoods. It is connected to the ancient lost arcane science of regeneration, immortality, and the development of soul power, through the integration of these subtle energy selves.

It is the core of all ancient wisdom and it must be with further knowledge of our original essence as light beings and our ability to access our light body, full awareness.

Nonetheless, if we are to survive the coming shift in energy, we must begin to familiarize ourselves with this most ancient science, as many illuminated souls on the planet would agree that the whole point of this science is to integrate our material form with the other unseen parts of our self, in order to ascend our form into higher levels of awareness (reality).

We will also come to realize that our current form is the final extension of a long process known as involution, which is the great descend of light energy substance into various forms of (matter) from subtle refined to gross physical form which is the lowest vibrational state of matter. Equally important to understand, is that change is part of the natural rhythm of the universe and should not be seen as a bad thing, for everything in the material universe is in perpetual motion always changing in order to match its shifting energy vibration. The reason being is because there seems to be a constant process of descent involution and ascend (evolution).

Therefore, instead of being upset about the coming changes as we prepare to shift ages, we should be full of joy that we are going to be the forerunners of an exciting NEW world that have for long been prophesized. Again, let it be stressed that the times in which we find ourselves today are the best times to be living in, for there is no such thing as a doomsday. The only people that are having a doomsday are the wicked of low energy negative vibration. As for the rest of us, we will ascend (raise in vibration) with our planet without tasting death, as we became translated into a new vibration, with a new modified exalted body of lighter density.

The signs are everywhere, the time is now and as we become more aware of this truth that our world and everything in it is changing, we would need to be more receptive to the new frequencies if we want to partake of HEAVEN ON EARTH that is becoming real for various people from all over the world who are beginning to experience new joy as they begin to merge with the new positive energies of Aquarius, the millennium. Those that are connecting and experiencing HEAVEN ON EARTH are those that are becoming receptacles to the new incoming energies.

These are the people tuning to the higher energies and are consequently being uplifted, inspired, and empowered with the light of our creator as more people today are discovering what born again Christians are beginning to refer to as the Christ within, which is enlightenment, atonement or becoming one with the Christ (universal consciousness).

These are the people that are becoming more whole and integrated discovering a sense of inner peace as they begin to remember the connection to source, which is light, which is represented by the Christ energies. By aligning to this higher vibration, they have adopted a better way of life, as many are beginning to achieve what is known as balance, purpose, and wholeness. Some are even discovering amazing abilities that they didn't know they had, as the gifts of the spirit begin to awaken in them. All these are but a few that are taking advantage of these transforming energies and they are doing it by choice.

They had decided that they wanted a better way of living and so acted upon it. That is the miracle that this new frequency is producing in our world for those that are beginning to believe and are acting.

On the other hand, those that are not adapting to the new frequencies that is uplifting our entire planet, are unfortunately going to leave our ascending world, due to a lack of knowledge and information.

These are those that have chosen to vibrate by the old pattern that is also at the same time disintegrating, with the collapsing of the old electromagnetic field and paradigm structure. This explains the harvest of souls, the separation of the weeds from the grass.

On another note, it is important to understand that this prison of spiritual ignorance was designed by the temporal powers of this world to rule us through our mind, emotions, and consciousness. An example of this was as we remember the dark European ages, which were brought about as a direct result of producing mass fear, through the Roman litigate.

The point is that thoughts and feelings are powerful generators of frequency; they mold and shape our reality as we begin to realize that we are co-creators of circumstances through these agencies. The powers of this world have always known this and that is why this great secret of life known to us now as the law of attraction has now recently been restored for the masses to know and put into practice. Therefore, by changing our thoughts and emotions we change our (vibrations) circumstances and that is scientific fact.

It is well known that for centuries people by default have been emotionally and mentally trapped and controlled by the Elite because they lack true knowledge of how our universe works. They have forgotten that like attracts like and that all reality is created by (MIND) and our (EMOTION) and most importantly they have forgotten their inherent connection to the divine, the source, and center of all inspiration and positive living, light, and life.

The time has come to break away and free ourselves from that old energy pattern of control through fear that only keeps us unaware and away from discovering our full potential which is the harbinger of our happiness. In other words, by taking charge of our life, we create a greater opportunity to be happy. For we are only happy when things go in the direction we want and since our thoughts and emotions are powerful electromagnetic generators that mold and shape our reality depending on where we direct the energy (our focus) we could individually begin to fabricate a happier life by will power and choice.

The dark powers of this world have not only known of these spiritual laws but have acted on them at the expense of the masses. And that is why throughout all of history they have dominated the masses by keeping them in ignorance of the great power behind their thought forms and the way we choose to feel.

All manipulation only takes place when vital information is withheld from the person being manipulated, for ignorance is the greatest weapon against a potentially spiritually awakened humanity.

In truth, it is only when the individual really begins to learn and gravitate out of the current collective negative mass consciousness and adopts his or her self to the new energy pattern vibrating at a frequency of love, peace, and unlimited joy, will they break free from bondage and become receptacles of HEAVEN ON EARTH. In other words, we must become inwardly what we want to be outward, since the energy-mind produces matter-form. As we do that, we also become less vulnerable to mind control, and instead, we become more independent self-realized which in turn leads to personal enlightenment and less dependent on external powers.

The more we adapt to the new energies, we will begin to own and control our own destiny and reality and begin to discover something within ourselves which would produce a fulfilled life and that is a personal relationship with our creator. In truth, that is the purpose of all humanity; to not only develop a personal direct relationship with the creator source but to evolve into the image of our creator.

Since our living earth is ascending now, collectively we have been given a marvelous opportunity again to take a free ride. This is the great harvest of the season when for the first time in our earth's history since the times of the fall, HEAVEN will be lowered to earth for all time and all eternity. We are living in the most wonderful age, one that is recognized as the fullness of time.

In review, let it be understood, that there is going to be a split, as a loving constructive higher energy field is replacing the low energy field that has kept our world in spiritual ignorance for ages. In so doing, only those, which are beginning to resonate with the new higher energy, are becoming more real and rooted in the NEW EARTH (STRUCTURE).

As for those resonating at the low-frequency range of fear, anger, and negativity will be removed because everything in existence vibrates to a frequency in order to remain intact otherwise it cannot exist if the pitch is not a match. This is the true meaning of the two men who are both working in the fields and one man disappears while the other men stay at the coming of the kingdom of light.

As we shift into the NEW frequency range on earth, we will be prepared to take our greatest evolutionary leap, forward into our new reality structure. A reality that will restore us back into fully functioning sovereign human beings as made in the image of God.

Now before we prepare to take this quantum leap that will dramatically change our world structure and reality forever, we must first become familiar with certain suppressed knowledge that the current powers of this world have for millenniums attempted to omit from all records.

In this next segment, a whole NEW vista of knowledge will be unveiled that will help prepare us for what is coming. And what is coming is nothing more than the prophecies being fulfilled as we prepare to not only shift ages but partake of the NEW HEAVEN ON EARTH.

It is time for all humanity to begin to know what many are discovering to be a multidimensional reality marked by boundless freedom and unlimited possibilities. It is also time for mankind to know, their true origins, and purpose as made in the image of our creator.

Nevertheless, we will also come to find out, that our universe is bigger than what we were told and most importantly, that we are not alone in what our new science now calls the Multi-Verse.

By understanding our original cosmic origin (divine ancestry) the truth will once again ring clearly for those who are beginning to know that there is more to life and reality than what appears. Most importantly as we later cover the subject matter of the photon belt, and its relationship to the coming of the kingdom of light, the book of Revelation would be clearer.

# CHAPTER ONE

## A NEW SCIENCE HAS EMERGED

One of the greatest discoveries in the twentieth century is Quantum Physics. With this new avenue of study, our scientists are slowly but surely tapping into the supernatural or metaphysical world of spirituality and higher realities. This new avenue not only opened the door to a whole new way of understanding our world and the universe we live in, but it also validates the existence of a supreme being many call God. For centuries or perhaps for millenniums, we were under the impression that everything in existence was mechanical, that life was a constructed machine and subject to decay or entropy, based on the understanding that only the tangible world exists.

On the contrary, and as now re-discovered in the twentieth-first century, the greatest and most controversial new scientific evidence is saying something else. This new evidence clearly reveals, that indeed, we live in a vast ocean of conscious energy and that we ourselves are individualized units of consciousness, therefore everything is alive and conscious, from atoms to universes, as there is nothing mechanical about our existence after all.

Scholars and scientists from various fields of study, ranging from neurology, microbiology, biology, cosmology, and physics as well as from the social avenues, are all agreeing (according to the new evidence) that our existence is holistic and most importantly that it is infinite, without beginning or end since all is energy and energy could never seize to exist.

The facts are now known that we are part of a bigger picture and that there is a purpose to everything in life. That all conditions allowing for existence in space and time are following a cosmic blueprint as if something beyond our current comprehension is weaving everything with exact precision. What is happening is that our science has rediscovered our connection with everything else, seen, and unseen and most importantly that everything is interconnected to everything else in this wonderful web or matrix of energy our new science calls unified field.

The new physics is suggesting that everything in existence operates as a unit of one and that what we thought was impossible is now possible. For instance, Einstein and other enlightened men understood that if we could decipher and figure out the Theory of Everything, then all of our world's problems would be solved because we would have access to technologies that would improve our living conditions overnight.

Ultimately, the deciphering of this grand theory of everything would scientifically and mathematically explain the existence of a universal intelligence known as God.

Furthermore, it has also been confirmed that if we tap into a field of energy known as a zero-point field, we will extract unlimited raw power from a vacuum that exists in a higher dimension.

Our science further discovered that this field of zero-point energy is not only generated by our sun but that it's also produced by all living things in existence, as we participate and interact with it. This is the field, where all energy exchange is taking place at the same time, in a dynamic vacuum that creates a vast unlimited ocean of self-generating power. In other words, it is the sum of all the energy in existence and it is equivalent to the central point of pure energy potential at its most underlying level.

Apparently, we have arrived at the holy grail of physics; without fully understanding the potential use of harnessing the power of this quantum vacuum of infinite energy potential, science calls Zero–Point field. This is the field that starts off as a singular force holding together not only the four fundamental forces (electromagnetic field, gravity, weak force, and strong force), allowing for a third-dimensional existence, but also holding together the invincible forces that shape and mold our physical reality. This unified singular force field also holds together other unseen planes of reality that are currently not measurable by our third-dimensional instruments.

Apparently, our science has now indeed reached a point in our development where spirit and matter are once again merging, and we can begin to detect this by the newfound evidence. This new developing science through quantum mechanics and Quantum gravity theory is asking for a synthesis of all fields of study and is providing evidence of a unified and a bigger cosmos. For example, the new evidence is suggesting that everything in the cosmos is operating according to some grand mathematical equation and that there is an inert universal intelligent impulse guiding all processes as it is Omnipresent, Omnipotent, and Omniscient, as described in the holy books of all religions.

The more we tap into the Theory of Everything; we may conclude that what we consider science fiction is now perhaps a possible reality. If this is the case, then we are on the verge of being propelled into a new utopian advanced spiritual, and technological age.

The NEW evidence not only provides proof of a unified energy field that confirms that we are all one, but the most disturbing discovery in our established academia is the idea of multiple universes, multiple realities, and unseen dimensions. These concepts along with others have now become the greatest taboo in the established academic community. Nevertheless, the facts are now pouring in more so than ever through the higher quantum avenues of Quantum Gravity, M- Theory, and Unified Field Theory. And through these NEW fields, it has been and as it continues in being confirmed, that we indeed live in a multi-dimensional reality and that there are multiple universes. Along with that, it has been also scientifically proven that we human beings on planet earth are only experiencing and perceiving perhaps less than one-tenth of our total reality potential. In fact, mainstream science has gone as far as stating that about 96 percent of our universe (reality) is missing, and so they have labeled it dark matter and dark energy.

Though what is more startling to the scientists, beyond the dark matter and dark energy, is that all realms intersect each other yet we are only aware of a small range of multiple intersecting planes of reality. These dimensions are apparently beyond the measurements of the subatomic world and again, are being measured through Newtonian mechanics

which only measures less than one-tenth of our total reality, no wonder our scientists cannot detect the 96 percent.

Although, some scientists had recently come up with the clever idea of using x-ray technology to pierce into the dark matter and ironically have recently detected colonies, civilizations, and evidence of life forms in the so-called missing matter, using x-ray technology.

However, nothing is new under the sun. It appears that our cutting-edge science is only rediscovering the truth about our multidimensional existence, and the idea that there are multiple universes, and endless worlds. For it has been recorded that for millenniums, saints, mystics, yogis, Gnostics, and shamans understood and experienced other unseen (spiritual) worlds beyond the five senses.

Surprisingly, this wisdom of old is correlating to the new understanding of reality as provided by the NEW scientific data. The fact that these parallel realities and universes are all existing simultaneously all-independent of themselves but through the zero point field are all interconnected with each other, at the same time in the same space is becoming more evident.

The truth of the matter and as understood in Meta-Physics is that the reason why these higher subtle finer realms of reality are undetectable to the naked eye or scientific instruments is that they are vibrating at frequencies beyond the limited range of our infrared and ultraviolet electromagnetic spectrum. According to the new physics, our perception of what we call reality is apparently one wavelength in a greater spectrum of finer and greater (realities) wavelengths of electromagnetic fields. The proposition that our reality is one small range or wavelength of a potential bigger reality (wavelength) or greater spectrum of Light frequency is evident and needs to be further examined. Perhaps this is what Plato, the Greek philosopher tried to explain to his pupils in the description of the Allegory of the Cave.

This understanding contradicts conventional physics. How can many parallel realms and dimensions exist occupying the same space all at the same time? The answer lies in the way television and radio work. If we think of how a range of different television and radio waves exist all around us, occupying the same space at the same time, then we may fathom how various ranges (frequencies) outside of the range of our own ultra violet-infrared wavelength, are able to coexist also at the same time.

For example, radio and television frequencies exist all around us yet they go right through us. It seems that the only time we interact with them is when we watch television or listen to a radio station, whicactsct as interfaces to those signals that seem to permeate the space all around us. So, if we want rock music we tune in to the rock (reality frequency-range) station. If we want classical, we tune in to the classical (reality-frequency range) station.

In that sense, we human beings also exist amid other reality frequency ranges higher than the infrared and ultraviolet range, which is one wavelength out of what science, refers to as multiple wavelengths or planes of reality. This concept of expanding reality explains why our scientists could only perceive or detect less than ten percent of our total reality potential since more than ninety percent of our reality is allegedly missing. What seems to be the case based on ancient wisdom and risen NEW scientific evidence is that more than ninety percent of our reality exists but on different frequency wavelengths or dimensions imperceptible to the naked eye or third-dimensional instruments.

Perhaps the so-called ninety percent of the missing universe (dark matter and dark energy) of our cosmos isn't as empty anymore as postulated and measured through Newtonian mechanics. On the other hand, it is more likely to be filled with life forms on different types of light vibrating matter as real as you and me.

In fact, what we call solid third-dimensional existence (frozen energy) is energy vibrating at an incredibly low frequency thus making it appear solid when it's empty space. Since matter is congealed energy vibrating at its lowest frequency, then these unseen realities are also part of the same energy field but vibrating at higher and faster frequencies, than the apparent third dimension. This notion implies that there are other purer forms of vibrating matter that are more refine and subtle. And since all is energy and whole, there is no separation for everything is a manifestation of this one energy field source, call the light.

So in that sense, we are all one and interconnected in an ocean of energy however, we are only aware of the lowest vibrational point or tuned into only one radio, television (frequency) channel-station out of what might be a greater range of frequencies-realities. It appears that modern-day science has now tapped into the higher etheric and spiritual worlds but cannot explain them using Newtonian mechanics.

With this new data, we are witnessing a coming revolution in science that will propel our world into the next phase of our evolution. For example, the concept of a universe is also being replaced by the reality of multi-universes. According to the latest discoveries in Quantum gravity theory and M-theory, our universe is one of many universes. Well by applying the NEW physics and its concept of coexisting planes to a higher level, then we may begin to also understand how many universes are also intersecting one another as they are all contained within the same space.

This multi-verse concept is slowly but surely gaining more ground and soon it should be an accepted scientific fact. Indeed, we are amid another Copernican revolution, though on a planetary and galactic scale, that would propel our world into a golden age. Nonetheless, the idea of multi universes has fascinated our cosmologists and physicist, who for centuries only held to the idea of only one single universe.

For instance, the idea of living in a multi-verse was suggested when astronomers and cosmologists discovered that space was indeed flat not curved as proposed by Einstein. This was the first clue in providing evidence that indicated that space was infinite and expanding at an extraordinary rate. The second piece of evidence came when cosmologists discovered a phenomenon known as quantum fluctuations and cosmic inflation.

This observation indicated that universes (plural) are expanding at an extraordinary rate and away from each other. Most importantly, is the revealing fact that what scientists refer to as the big bang is an event that is taking place every day. This tells us that the creation of new universes is an eternal process always taking place for what might be an eternity. This notion of perpetual infinite creation would indeed imply that our universe is one of many numbers of universes, with other universes while new universes are born every day. On a higher note, the evidence is also indicating, that all these universes are being born from what might appear to be a Mother Universe or what scientists call the Meta-Verse.

The Meta-verse or mother universe according to science has never been created. It appears to their observations that the Metaverse is infinite without beginning or end and it is the source that is causing about ten new universes to be born each day. We may imagine this mother verse to be like an umbrella unfolding and constantly expanding as it births new and new universes for what appears to be infinity.

It is now apparent that our science has rediscovered what has always been known to the illuminated seers and that is the truth that although there are multiple physical universes, there is only one spiritual mother universe that has always existed without beginning or end, exactly as explained by cutting edge science.

 With this new understanding, it is believed that every part of our cosmos operates as a unit of one, that in essence, all universes are like different parts of the same umbrella, all affecting each other as they are all different holographic fragments of the same whole, Meta-Verse.


What is sure, is that in these days to come, our scientists would have irrefutable concrete data confirming and establishing the new revolutionary notion that not only are there other unseen realities, realms, and dimensions but that our universe is one of many universes in an ocean of infinite space potential. Most importantly the underlying field of energy called by many names, (force, energy matrix, quantum singularity, Chi, Prana, Spirit of God, or just simply unified field will also be well understood as the one force in everything, which in turn will allow us to better understand the Grand Theory of Everything. At this point in our world, we are indeed at a threshold like never. A threshold that will not only ignite a new renaissance on a planetary level but propelled us once again into an upward spiral of spiritual evolution, as we evolve higher into the image and similitude of our divine creator. We are now becoming a spiritual race and culture and therefore are about to take a quantum leap like never into what some more evolve scientists are calling an interplanetary system civilization.

A NEW ERA has arrived; the seventh golden age that was not only prophesied in the ancient oracles but also in our bible is at hand, for a new reality has precipitated in our world in the greatest dispensation ever bestowed upon mankind, and it is indicated by the coming union of science and spirituality, heaven and earth.

# CHAPTER TWO

## THE THEORY OF MULTIPLE

## CIVILIZATIONS AS PROPOSED BY OUR NEW SCIENCE

One of the biggest kept secrets and perhaps a most important subject perplexing our world at this time is the idea that there exist millions of advanced space-age worlds beyond our own, which have been established as advanced interplanetary, stellar, and galactic cultures. For many are witnessing firsthand experiences of these visitors from other worlds of existence. Today more so than ever, unexplainable crop circles have appeared and mysterious UFO's sightings all over the earth are challenging people's limited belief systems.

What is happening in our world is a refusal of a lost reality that we were once a part of. Perhaps they are reminding us, that we are not alone in the universe and that we are part of a greater family (reality) of light that extends to the many multiple realms and levels of the cosmos which our modern science is now tapping into.

Based on the new controversial and suppressed evidence, the new calculations, are now surprisingly proposing the existence of multiple types of space-age civilizations.

Therefore, it is important to understand, that all space-age civilizations fall under the three categories of, population one interplanetary system, population two-stellar system, and population three Galactic Systems.

According to the new evidence, these population-advance advanced space-age systems in our galaxy are by far more advance than we are since we don't even rate them. The first one, a population one interplanetary system civilization is a planetary civilization that has learned to harness the power of the core of the planet, giving way to free energy technologies making them no longer dependent on fossil fuels oil, or the process of combustion. It is believed that type one interplanetary systems are the most common types in the cosmos and according to the new evidence; there are millions of these civilizations in our universe.

A population one-star system civilization, defines the beginning stage of space travel, because when one harnesses the energy of the core of their planet, they may develop what is known as propulsion-drive-technologies that would enable them to sour out into space, in order to begin the colonizing of other planets in close proximity, and neighboring solar systems as well. We may compare this level of civilization to the movie Buck Rogers.

The second type of civilization calculated by our new science is known as population two stellar systems and these types of civilizations not only manage to tap the power of the core of their planet but apparently also manage to tap the power of their sun. We may compare this type of civilization to the level of existence of "Star Trek" and the Federation of Planets. These types of civilizations have had thousands of years of space exploration and stellar travel and are able to interact with the entire galaxy. As mentioned earlier, with this new understanding of reality, science fiction is slowly becoming a science fact.

According to our new science, there are approximately hundreds of thousands of populations with two stellar systems in our universe. It is understood that these civilizations have mastered the theory of everything capable of space travel, greater than the speed of light. It is also believed that a stellar system is always on the lookout for pre-planetary worlds that are showing a high level of spiritual maturity, culture, and technology capability indicating their readiness to enter the space community.

Finally, the third type and most evolved of the three civilizations proposed by our cutting-edge discoveries is known as a population of three galactic systems. These civilizations not only harness the power of their surrounding suns but the full power of billions of suns. That is, they harness the energy of what is known as the core central sun at the center of their galaxy. It has been calculated that there are thousands of these types of civilizations in our universe and we may compare them to the movie Star Wars. A civilization like this who learns to tap the power of their galaxy's core can control the fate of an entire galaxy.

It appears that population three galactic systems are the most advanced intergalactic (capable of interacting with other galaxies) civilizations in our own universe and perhaps other universes. It is believed that a civilization of this type can transfer its entire civilization over to another younger universe, in the event of their universe grew old, and decayed.

The reason believed is again based on the new physics. For example, in breaking down the difference between this interstellar advanced system, it is understood that a population one-star system civilization, is in its infant stage in understanding the Theory of Everything, as we are now in this day, and categorizes its developing civilization as a first stage beginning space level which marks the beginning of the use of inter-dimensional technology.

After a few thousand years of mastering the Theory of Everything, a population one interplanetary system civilization then graduates into an intermediate space-age stellar population two system civilization. At this level, they have fully mastered inter-dimensional travel and may zoom across the galaxy in a split second, since we now know that it is possible to travel faster than the speed of light through hyperspace.

It is believed that a population two-stellar system takes hundreds of thousands of years to advance into the level of advanced space-age type three status. At which point, they have mastered the theory of everything that even the future coming death of its universe may not affect it. Galactic civilizations of this status are immortal because they can access the main stargates and wormholes that lead into other parallel new universes in a younger stage capable of supporting life forms and intelligence for billions of more years.

Only population three galactic system civilizations are at the highest level of spiritual evolution. This also proposes the idea that most if not all, space-age galactic societies are indeed highly spiritually evolve. Then the next question would be why haven't' we contacted them? First, our earth scientist is only scanning about a few hundred light-years away, while the next interplanetary civilization is a thousand light-years away according to the math.

In addition, our scientists are also only detecting radiation from hydrogen, based only on Newtonian principles. They are forgetting to use quantum mechanics, which would compel them to look inter-dimensional into hyperspace. While those spiritually oriented physicists dare to explore it, other more reserved scientists fear the possible fact of multiple realities and multiple civilizations, as they would say the impossible.

In fact, according to our new science, our current civilization rate's zero in comparison to the three types of calculated advanced space-age cultures. This has to do with our dependency on fossil fuel, coal, nuclear, and plants for energy. However, it is also understood by our new science, that the signs for our inevitable transition into a population one interplanetary system are now evident. This tells us that all civilizations here on earth have been part of a long evolutionary process and that our current phase of civilization is therefore now during the greatest transition ever. According to some scientific observations, one of the biggest indicators and signs that we have is the Internet that is a communication device used by worlds that are of a population of one space-age inter-planetary culture. Other signs are the fact that we are once again a global international culture.

Also, it is important to understand that this transit of our world into a space-age culture is a process that is unfolding throughout our entire universe, with many other civilizations as some advanced to stellar statues and others to galactic. Since there are millions of solar systems with perhaps trillions of worlds then our earth is one of many civilizations that is undergoing the same process. Not to mention that most if not all civilizations in our cosmos are populated by other beings that appear to be humanoid in appearance but are of a different nature than ourselves. It appears that we humans on earth share a common ancestry throughout our universe since all were made in the image of our ONE creator.

This validates and supports the theory of convergent evolutions, which tells us that we are not the only humanlike creatures in existence. Therefore, most of the aliens out there are people that look like you and me, some are more evolved than others. The higher the level of civilization, the more angelic in nature this humanlike intelligence exists. After all, our science has now discovered that there are millions upon millions of worlds just like our earth, and every day they come across more and more.

Based on the new understanding, it appears that other realities are not out there but intersecting our own third dimensions of length, height, and width, in a quantum phenomenon known as superposition. This, therefore, implies that those advance, stellar, galactic, and intergalactic civilizations operating on higher levels of existence higher than the third are interacting with our reality without our knowledge, like different radio and television frequencies intersect each other, at the same time in the same space.

It is believed that these advanced civilizations used all levels of reality to communicate and broadcast their signals that intersect our dimension without our knowing. It is also believed that the higher angelic humanoid intelligence is in a sense always watching over and observing us. They appear to be watching over our civilization, almost as if they are waiting for us to evolve spiritually enough, so that we may also share the rest of the infinite cosmos with them in harmony.

Considering the new evidence, it appears that we are part of a greater divine plan and that life here on the earth plane or in the lowest dimension is not the only life in existence.

Also, it is ignorance of the higher spiritual knowledge that makes one assume that dark matter is empty space without realizing that this higher intelligence are operating and existing on higher levels of reality that currently are imperceptible. This explains why we are only experiencing less than ten percent of our full potential reality. Perhaps the reason that we are currently shut off from ninety ninety-four of our full reality capacity and higher angelic bits of intelligence, is the same reason that we are not in the use of ninety-four percent of our full genetic potential, what a beautiful correlation.

The facts are obvious that intelligent life exists throughout the cosmos without our knowledge of them, until now because for thousands of years we have been in a population type zero statues. However, due to the dispensation, we are now under we are finally ready for acceptance into this greater reality. Today, however, our civilization is not only about to transition not into a population one interplanetary system civilization overnight but directly advanced into a population two system in a matter of years and we need to be ready.

The signs that we are becoming galactic (HEAVEN ON EARTH) are here. In scientific terms, we are on the verge of achieving a utopia, here on earth. Indeed, our science is now confirming all the ancient religious prophesies regarding the coming of the kingdom of God (light), the seventh golden age. However, as it's always the case, right before we transition into HEAVEN ON EARTH, there are still those factors that are preventing us from achieving such a positive transition. These factors are corruption, religious intolerance, fanaticism, apathy, wars, and global conflict.

Therefore, we as humanity representing our planet earth need to make a collective decision to no longer tolerate wars, religious fanaticism, prejudice, hatred, corruption, and anything that keeps us in a population with zero status. We need to make a collective decision to uphold and adopt a brotherlike love attitude in the pursuit of universal rights, global democracy, world peace, and tolerance by the realization that we are all children of the one God. We are on the verge of planetary transformation, as we reached the level of planetary brotherhood and partnership. It is the awakening of the masses into this knowledge, which leads to the understanding, and implementation of higher spiritual (cosmic) principles.

The fact that scientists are now beginning to see the correlation of the scientific to the spiritual is telling us, that we are true, in the midst of the biggest quantum leap ever, uniting all fields of study, under a Theory of Everything. For even in the fields of biology the genetic code has been deciphered and it has been confirmed that the supposed junk DNA is untapped potential Perhaps since we are using less than ten percent of our entire genetic material be why we only perceive less than ten percent of our total potential reality (dark matter). The math adds up and that also explains why we cannot detect all those advanced civilizations that exist in the so-called missing reality, as proposed by the new physics and backed by the ancient wisdom of the (secret) esoteric traditions.

In these next chapters, we would come to know, that everything that our NEW science is suggesting is correct. We have come a long way to reach this point of biological evolution, as we began the spiritual aspect of our higher evolution, to learn higher ideas and concepts that have been restored once again in these greatest times ever, for nothing is new under the sun.

# CHAPTER THREE

## THE CELESTIAL CONNECTION

Explain from an esoteric perspective the truth is that humanity is the final manifestation within the Angelic celestial kingdom, in a process known as the descent of spirit into matter. We have been involved in a long cosmic descent and as beings of light, we had our origin in the always-existing spheres of the spiritual realms. Our human origin is, therefore, connected to the angelic realms in the sense that all humanlike beings in our cosmos share a common ancestry known as the Adam Caedmon. And even though there are other human-like beings throughout existence that share the Adam Caedmon body (humanoids) none of them compare to the kind we know here on earth. The mankind of earth is by far the greatest masterpiece that our creator has made because we are completed beings as made in the image of our creator, and there is a reason for that.

The mere fact, that mankind on earth is connected to a long cosmic ancestry of celestial descent, proposing the theory of a convergent of evolutions. This truth is perhaps one of the most important secrets, which has been kept from us, for thousands of years. This explains why for centuries or perhaps millenniums the powers of this world (the brotherhood of Satan) had us believe that the earth was flat and that we were the only planet suitable for intelligent life.

Apparently, the earth's temporary powers (fallen angels) did not want us to know that we were not alone perhaps because this would threaten their agenda of world domination. In fact, considering emerging evidence, we can state, that not embracing the truth that life is existent in the entire universe, is likening to believing that the earth is still flat. For how can a creator who endows his life force essence throughout all of creation, only allow this life force essence to only take root in one infinitesimal portion considering the vastness of cosmos? This wouldn't make any sense, as we approach the end days of the millennial dark ages.

Today in the wonderful age of information it has been discovered that every star in our Milky Way galaxy is a burning living sun or a planet. It has been calculated that there are millions upon millions of suns in our Milky Way galaxy, so imagine out of all those millions of solar systems (star systems) how many planets are inhabited with intelligent life forms.

Furthermore, as mentioned science has also confirmed that there are multiple galaxies, clusters of galaxies, and multiple universes. This higher understanding will also open us to further knowledge as it expands our awareness and consciousness about many things that we are unaware of.

However, before we can begin to digest any of this, we must first rid ourselves of our limited belief systems and begin to really understand the true nature of our existence and the stuff that makes it up, ENERGY, as it ties into the angelic phenomena. For example, the first step in realizing the true nature of our reality is the fact that everything is vibrating.

The slower the rate of vibration or frequency, the more dense and solid matter appears, the faster the frequency or rate of vibration, the less dense and subtler, perhaps invincible to our naked eye, the matter becomes. So, by raising the vibration rate of the object to a higher octave from the third-dimensional range of vibration, it would seem to disappear in the third dimension.

This however doesn't mean that the object isn't there anymore it's just tuned in to a higher wavelength of existence that is not plugged into our limited range of perception of what we call reality in the third dimension. Remember as explained earlier, the third dimension is only one wavelength of multiple bands and planes that make up the entire spectrum of unlimited light-energy, vibrating at all different rates being different wavelengths of the same singular light, quantum singularities.

As mentioned, we are only tuned in to only 1/10 or less of the entire spectrums of our existence as we have only been using less than ten percent of our entire inherit potential. This explains the biblical veil, which is why the supposed 94 percent of the universe is missing.

So, considering this, while the object appears to be invincible and nonexistent in the lower third-dimensional frequency range of vibration, it's still existing, but at a higher pitch or frequency range within the spectrum of light. On the same note, if we managed to raise the vibrational rate of our energy field to match the frequency range of our invincible object (which is only invincible as empty space in the third dimension) then it would miraculously reappear in our range of perception again as TANGIBLE on that frequency-reality.

The only difference is that this type of solid is more of refined nature and less dense than the solid appearing in the third dimension. So, in review, all the different planes of reality differ by the rate of their vibration. The higher the frequency, the less dense matter becomes as its atomic nucleic vibrates at a higher pitch. The lower the frequency, the denser matter becomes as the vibration rate slows to match the slower rate of vibration making things more solid. Since all is energy then like Einstein RE-discovered that energy and matter are interchangeable phases of the same stuff. That is why $E=mc2$.

In like manner, there is no such thing as empty space for everything is matter in our physical universe regardless of (vibration). In fact, most matter in the universe is vibrating at a higher frequency range thereby making this matter more refined and subtler and less gross, and of course invisible to our eyes. This type of matter could only be visible to those that have raised their frequency range to a higher rate of vibration, such as in the case of those who have attained spirit and etheric perception.

In truth, energy and matter are one and the same and the only time when energy seizes to be matter is when it becomes pure light again. Then the process of the convergence (descension) of pure light back into energy-matter in its multiple bands of vibration begins again. And that is the nature and essence of our existence and why many types of angelic beings exist, on the different ranges (planes) or wavelengths of vibrations, particularly those densities higher than the third that are considered the dark matter.

In relation to higher spiritual knowledge, these higher levels of existence that have now been proven by the more evolving fields of science, are nothing more than the realms of the spirit world, astral world, and etheric worlds that the ancients have always known about. All spheres of reality are marked by different planes of vibrating energy-matter again. "In my father's house, there are many mansions." Jesus the Christ, the Bible. These higher realms are the many heavenly spheres of all religious traditions.

Considering this, we can now more clearly conclude that angelic human-like beings are as real as you and me and as physical as you and me. What separates our reality from there's, is the rate of vibration in their atomic and molecular structures. This correlates with the higher realms and parallel worlds discovered today by the various fields of study, both scientific through quantum physics as well as supported by the reemergence of ancient knowledge.

The only difference between mysticism and science is that mystics have always known what science re-discovering is now. So, for the record, it is known that the ancient spiritual cultures have known about alternative realities and angelic-like beings, so it is not new information. So how can reality be missing? It is obvious that we are the ones that are missing from a greater reality of light, for it is still there existing on higher vibrating wavelengths, as understood in the esoteric arcane tradition and as explained by all world religions.

In light of this, we may say that the beings classified as the angels of the celestial beings in our bible are the same beings described today as the benevolent human-like extra- terrestrials' beings whose numbers are present in our skies more so than ever, in this day of restoration. In contrast, the biblical demons or the fallen angels also coincidentally correspond to the negative extraterrestrials that have been the guiding force behind the TEMPORARY rulers of this world, the draconian and hydra reptilians.

This again validates the biblical concept of spiritual (interdimensional) warfare that has been taking place by supernatural forces, not of this reality. Now let's match the evidence. The biblical angels and demons were both of a supernatural nature and both have the capacity to intervene in human affairs. They could always see and pierce into the third-dimensional human reality while humans remained imperceptible to theirs. (Dark matter)

The point is that all throughout history and according to every religious tradition, we have heard of accounts of angels appearing to humans, particularly to the prophets, sages, and seers who had developed spirit vision.

These human adepts perceiving higher reality would guide the planet according to the divine blueprint of light, given to them by an angel. So in the bible, while the angels were characterized as benevolent, protectors, and helpers of humanity operating from heaven (higher realities), the demons (negative extraterrestrials) were known to be malevolent, and the forces behind the brotherhood of Satan as the oppressors of humanity. This also provides more evidence of the misunderstood biblical truth that we are not at war with flesh and blood but with powers and principalities that are not of this world (realm).

Again, it is important to know that those final editors (Constantine and the council of Nicaea) of our accepted western bible condensed everything regarding our cosmos to just one realm, one wavelength, excluding the entire spectrum of reality. It appears that those who have governed the affairs of this world had all the written records revised to fit their most rigid paradigm that only this reality exists. They omitted all knowledge regarding the higher realities to control us by default of limited reality.

With this in mind, we can begin to open our minds to the existence of these other beings that exist on higher wavelengths of light-energy- vibration (dark matter). For instance, the bible has many references to the existence of both angels and demons that completely match up with the extra-terrestrials existing in the higher densities of the reality of our physical universe.

In truth, the higher densities (dimensions) of existence are more real than this one and it is marked by multiple spheres of physical realities all-encompassing greater and greater levels of being. For example, in all spheres, the spiritual realm is the highest vibrating sphere (worlds) of matter, where matter is vibrating at its most pure and highest frequency. Most esoteric literature would agree on this to be the fifth dimension and up to where energy and matter are interchangeable and simultaneously exist in a state of singularity.

Also, by implying the concept of the holistic model of existence, we may conclude that in all the universes, the spirit is not vaporous or transparent, as it has been assumed. For instance, if we raise our vibratory rate into a higher octave (wavelength) of being, then spirit begins to take form. The higher we raise our vibration; the more solid our spirit becomes.

Now the reason why both angelic beings and demonic beings of varying grades and levels are able to travel through the different planes of existence without any difficulty is that they have learned and mastered the secrets of energy-matter manipulation, which is really energy-matter modulation. They utilize methods, like advanced technologies that instantaneously shift them from one level of reality to another level of reality by simply re-tuning their vibration at will into any wavelength that they choose to explore. For example, by lowering their vibration rate an octave or two depending on where their original frequency resonates from, they can take form in that reality, thus appearing physical to those beings vibrating at that level. Of course, in order to do that, we must obviously be using far more than just six percent of our total potential.

As revealed by the secret knowledge, at one point, our planet indeed consists of multiple levels of reality or at least it was open to those higher levels of being, before the veil set in.

According to all restored knowledge, this was during the time of Atlantis and even before Atlantis. Since the fall of Atlantis, we have forgotten this once great cosmic science, a science that at one point before our fall into the lower levels of solid reality enabled us to access the different and higher realities at will, when we were all connected to the varying realms of infinite spirit.

Another important fact regarding various intelligence that inhabits our universe is that we are all related by virtue of how much light quotient we carry in our overall being. It appears that higher evolved beings exhibit and operate with a higher light quotient. At the same time, the different types of intelligent beings fall under the three major categories.

We have the highest category known as celestial intelintelligencech equates to our creator's first extension from the top-down, giving us the various archangelic orders of angels that operate from the eternal realms down to the semi. Eternal realms. The second category of intelligence is the Eutherians, who are the offspring of the celestials and are involved in the lower part of the eternal realms operating in between the infinite eternal spheres and the finite spheres of time and space. The Eutherians are also an in-between point between the descending celestials and the ascending mortals (terrestrials) of time and space.

The last category of intelligent celestial, angelic humanoid life is known as the terrestrials. The terrestrials could include a wide range of biological organic life forms that begin their evolution at the bottom of the light energy spectrum to ascend into the higher eternal spheres. We could also say that the offspring of the Eutherians are the Terrestrials. All humanoid intelligent life forms in the multi that were intelligent design by one creator. Fall under these three overall categories.

In light of this, we could, therefore, suggest that mankind on earth today is the final product of a celestial race that eventually descended first into the level of Eutherians and then finally into the level of terrestrials being the lowest form of vibrating energy-matter.

For example, higher evevolvedeings have and utilize what is called a light body in which they use to traverse the different levels of existence. According to the esoteric wisdom, humans on earth today also have a light body, but our light body has been limited to 1/10 or less of its full capacity, by virtue of not utilizing 94 percent of our genetic material, (Eutherian and celestial DNA). In other words, the unseen levels of reality are relative to our capacity of how much (junk-DNA) genetic material we use.

Therefore, the so-called Junk DNA that scientists have discovered is the key in unlocking mankind into the higher levels of reality, for these noncoded strands connect to higher frequencies allowing humans to become multi-dimensional and begin the ascension process back into the immortal realms of the Eutherian celestial eternal spheres.

This scientific fact only implies that perhaps humans at one point in our ancient past were full conscious beings tuned with the angels of the higher realities and living for thousands of years. Perhaps this was the time when the celestials walked the earth along with terrestrial man as recorded in the book of Genesis.

However, before we rule anything out, we shall soon take a closer description, as to who was who, in ancient times. Although, what has come to light, is that descending celestial, humanity lived extremely long lives and had spiritual gifts or what science would term supernatural abilities and all of this was the result of each human having a spiritual connection to the higher spheres by virtue of utilizing more of their current six percent genetic capacity.

Eventually, as humanity regressed further and as time continued, we began to live shorter life spans, as we began to use less and less of our full genetic material, celestial and DNA. This fall (descent) of spiritual man was a gradual declining process. However, the good news is, that since we are living in a time of restoration, our light (celestial and celestial) bodies are being reactivated due to the planetary ascension of our earth. As the declining process reverses, we will begin to live for what appears to be hundreds of years without aging. With this comes a greater exaltation of the human species on earth, who have for thousands of years, been shut from the rest of the spectrum of reality, again by default of only using six percent of us inherit divine celestial) capacity.

This is why it is important to also understand, the changes that are taking place in our bodies, as we evolve into a higher state of being, like our higher evolved brethren, who are waiting for us to join them, in the greater family of light, not only in our galaxy and universe but throughout the many universe's.

Again, in order to understand the diversity of angels (celestials in existence, we must first understand the three overall levels of existence in which all dimensions, densities, and realities exist First and foremost, as preserved in the ancient wisdom, there have always been three overall major planes of existence, the celestial-spiritual, the Etheric-mental, and the physical- material. In turn, these three major planes are further divided into nine thus giving us the concept of the nine realms of heaven as explained by our biblical Paul. In turn, these nine realms are subdivided into multiple densities, degrees, and sub-planes making up the entire spectrum of light. In the spiritual plane, the highest level of being and existence, exist the highest emissions of light were only perfected light beings can reside. We can say this is the realm of the highest of beings serving and working for the light and all that is. They are the celestials and what the bible refers to as the mighty Elohim.

These beings are both luminous and androgynous one on one level as well as having a physical body (male and female) on another level. However, on the highest levels, there is a certain type of energy that cannot be contained in any form and that is the energy manifested in the highest spheres of the higher heavens, for only the light body in a state of pure energy is active there. On the same token, in order for these cosmic beings to take physical form, they would have to lower their (vibration) light quotient down into the etheric (mental) and material (terrestrial) levels of lower energy frequency vibration, as to why they are light and form at the same time since all levels exist simultaneously.

Also, it has also been unveiled, that the Elohim (celestial beings) have all been endowed with the same creative power of our prime creator, since in essence, they are all divisions and offspring manifestations of the one pure source, as revealed by the holistic model of existence. In turn, the Elohim further divides or gives birth to the multi archangelic and angelic beings that exist throughout the cosmos. This family of descending light beings, either give up their individual will to serve the will of our creator or take matters into their own hands serving their individual cause.

At this level, all descending celestials realize that they could use their inherent creative mental powers to project any world or reality they please, through their thought projections. Since all reality is a projection or manifestation of creative mental energy, then the lower extensions or material realms are reflections of the mental projections of these celestial beings. In other words, we all live (everything included) in a mental projection of descending celestial beings many have referred to as God. The only thing is, that there are many material creations or galaxies that are being projected into existence from the many descending cosmic beings that operate as the offspring of prime creator source as a family of creator Gods, the many and the one.

The celestials that give up their individual will to serve the mandates of our one creator of all that is are the good guys, while the celestials that serve their individual cause and try to play the role of god by taking matters into their own hands are the fallen (celestials) angels. Most importantly, let it be known that the benevolent celestial intelligence serving the side of life and light always maintains a perfect body of light while the fallen ones begin to function with imperfect bodies of light. This explains why the light is always on the winning side as it is controlled and generated from the highest regions.

Now let it be clear, that initially only the spiritual celestial spheres or planes of existence were the only existing spheres of light without any beginning or end. According to today's quantum research, this would be the state of pure energy where whereas different colors convert back into white light before being refracted through the prism.

It is well known in the esoteric wisdom, that in the process of the great discussion, the plans of our creator was to spread the living light into the outer regions so that which exist in the higher regions could also be anchored in the lower spheres, thus giving us a scientific explanation of HEAVEN ON EARTH. This is the great divine plan of light and playing the devil's advocate on the other side, are the fallen celestial intelligence (fallen angels) that have been since the fall from unity consciousness, attempting to block the spreading of the universal light of our creator into the lower spheres that would spiritualized matter (the terrestrial spheres).

The physical universe in which our earth hangs in its original conception was a perfect thought in the mind of our creator son (Jesus) and since thoughts become matter (form) the original thought projection of this creation was perfect. The perfection of our material creation lasted until the fallen angels intercepted and contaminate the original thoughts, by mentally projecting their own disqualified forms into existence and since we live in a free-will universe, these fallen thought patterns took shape and form thus precipitating and affecting many levels of reality.

Now it is of the utmost truth, that originally when light descended into creating the (terrestrials) physical worlds or dimensions of lower energy-matter, all matter was initially created perfect and this is what Plato referred to as the world of perfect forms which also appear eternal because they initially reflected the perfect state of both the etheric (mental and spiritual (celestial) higher planes in which all matter comes from.

Also, when the descending celestial intelligence reached the stage of refined matter in the eighth dimension, they began to take material form. And since all matter reflects thought, after descending lower than the eighth dimension, all celestials began to take gross physical form.

Now, since the physical worlds represented the outer appearance of the (inter-dimensional) higher etheric (mental) and spiritual (celestial) worlds, there was a distinction in appearance between those that rebelled against God's light and those that did not. Since mind creates matter, we can say that those celestial beings that remained loyal to the will of our creator, inherited the most perfect original angelic human vehicle, the Adam Kadmon body, which became the blueprint for all the vehicles of a subsequent generation of descending celestial humanoid beings throughout the cosmos, our ancestors.

These descending celestial beings were really the first original humans, descending children of the highest with incredible abilities that we may perceive as supernatural powers. This was the original family of light that was born into the plane of materiality (physicality) in a higher dimension than ours before they further coalesced into the third dimension.

As for the fallen celestial beings, they inherited a different vehicle that resembled their dark nature. In other words, since the lower spheres became a reflection of the higher spheres, as above so below, therefore when the fallen descending celestial beings become translated into the material plane of existence of the lower heavens (terrestrials), they become embodied in grotesque vehicles resembling their fallen state.

These fallen light beings become known as our biblical "demons" and today they are the same beings that our ufologists classify as negative E. T's. In fact, many researchers have linked this negative group of E. T., as the ancient serpent race recorded in all ancient religious traditions. The serpent beings became no other than the fallen celestial beings from the higher already existing etheric spheres (telestial) and their father became our biblical Lucifer, aka Samana as revealed in the "Yanihian", manuscript.

These serpent beings have been documented in various ancient texts from all over the world as flying serpents and dragons, and at times have co-existed with mankind. There is no doubt that these beings correspond to our biblical demons. For example, in our biblical account, their characteristics are described down to the . They all have tails, and some have horns, remembering the mythological gargoyles that have been classified as beastly-looking creatures. In fact, some shamans particularly those of the Dagon tribe in Africa, have characterized them as dark matter entities. And that is exactly what they are, for they are representatives of fallen light. Overall, our ufologists today have identified the modern-day Draco and hydra Reptilians with the biblical demons.

Now, it is important to understand also that there are different types of beings other than the positive ET's (humanoid/angels) and negative ET's (demon-reptilian). It appears, that there are hundreds of types of extraterrestrial biological alien life forms alone in our known physical universe. Most of which resemble the Descending Academic eed of humanoid beings and some the descending reptilian seed of demonic beings and everything in between, all falling under the three categories of celestials, eutherian, and terrestrials.

Another type of being that was created by our creator to work side by side with us in our world are the devas also known as the fairies or elementals, whatever you would like to call them. This group of beings work and operate to help maintain the earth's ecology as a planetary group of little helpers who are the guardians and spirits of the telluric mineral and animal kingdom. These miniature devas are another set of beings working for our creator at a planetary level co-existing with the human (terrestrial) kingdom.

The truth of the matter is that our creator has designed everything in existence to suit the purpose of the human creation here on earth. Mankind on earth is the completion of the great descent of spirit into matter and that is the reason why our exaltation is greater than all the existing species and as to why the angels were designed to serve mankind.

In conclusion of the angelic and demonic phenomena, we could rule out that for about five thousand years, we have been kept away from having true spiritual knowledge about, not only ourselves, our origin, our reality, and the true nature of our universe. It was until five hundred years ago when we finally began getting out of absolute darkness, thanks to the fifteen-century reformation and the renaissance. Since then, we've been entering a new era, therefore, the tables are turning and the truth regarding our real celestial nature and our existence has now been restored. Now on a different note: when we really consider how we have only perceived and experienced less than 1/10 of our full reality potential, we begin to see that there is nothing supernatural about the supernatural, for at those levels it's all-natural.

The bible is correct; we have been consciously imprisoned from experiencing the higher realms for about five thousand years. This is the meaning of the veil that is temporarily shutting us off from experiencing the higher realities of HEAVEN ON EARTH. Be aware that the veil has been lifting because we are under a new dispensation.

As mentioned, we live in a multi-reality existence and co-exist with beings who apparently have access to our range of reality, while we remain shut from there's. However, the time has come for our reconnection with the celestials and beings of other dimensions. Even among the fields of archaeology, there is enormous physical evidence that clearly reveals that we are not alone. All, researchers in the field of Archeology have unearthed relics of ancient megalithic structures that connect our reality with other realities inhabited by beings of other worlds. All these wonderful observations and discoveries are part of the restoration process as they remind us that we are not alone in the cosmos and that there is a greater reality and greater cosmic family that we are not aware off. In this great time of restoration, the suppressed knowledge of our planet is slowly made its way back to light.

# CHAPTER FOUR

## OUR COMIC SPIRITUAL DIVINE ORIGIN

According to the perennial philosophy of esoteric wisdom, our current humanity has fallen from a higher state of being (awareness) in forgetting our connection to source and as a result, we have been temporally sleeping in a coma-like state forgetting that we are celestial beings, that descended into the terrestrial experience. We may say that as human beings, we have existed for millions of years at least in many galaxies including the Milky Way. As spiritual beings of light, we have existed for what appears to be INFINITY.

Considering the new evidence, we may say that human beings today are powerful light beings with a major amnesia problem, forgetting their celestial origin.

We may now understand that before the existence (creation) of the physical realms (the material universe) or the lower heavens, we were light beings, all different sparks or rays of the all-powerful living light that has always existed. In fact, we are all different expressions of this infinite one light, which is the true spiritual meaning of monotheism. So, in that regard, we are infinite by nature, since light is infinite.

It is the conversion of this light that created the many different vibrational planes of reality, as they appear to be infinite in number, and out of those possible planes of reality, we happened to only know and perceive a small percentage of the entire light-energy spectrum. For in the earlier stage of existence, light existed in its purest form, as there was no matter in the pre- material realm. According to quantum observations, this light energy has never been created nor can it ever be destroyed as proven by the second law of Thermonuclear Dynamics, since energy is converted light. Therefore, LIGHT and energy are the foundation of what we call GOD and it is eternal.

The spirit of God aka in science, Unified field, or in metaphysics Universal Life Force is the foundation of all life in existence and there is nothing that exists outside of this light, for all is contained in it.

Now, even though there are multiple planes of reality in identifying our existence, they all fall under three major planes of existence, the spiritual, etheric, and physical as each major plane also consists of varying multiple sub-planes. And so due to this extraordinary nature of multiple spheres of reality; it is required to embody different vehicles that have been designing for us to exist in these different planes of light energy vibrations.

Therefore, in the highest levels of existence, we have the celestial planes, of pure energy also known as the luminal dimensions. It is where energy is a pure luminal substance and according to the esoteric wisdom, this region is beyond the confines of all space and time and it's really considered the highest level of heaven, so let's call it the always existing spheres. In these planes only, the purest light (beings) reside. This is perhaps, what the Urantia material calls the Havona systems of the Central universe or what our cutting-edge science now calls the Meta-Verse.

The Meta-Verse is the never beginning, the never-ending sphere of the eventuated central universe in which according to the Urantia material everything comes from. This cosmology will be discussed further in the next chapter.

However, it has been revealed that only perfect whole beings of light are able to exist in these eternal realms of the celestial planes.

And it is believed that out of these planes, the celestial cosmic Mother–Father first source and center become the cause of all things that extended beyond the confines of its always existing spheres of pure light emission. It is from the first source and center that all was made possible for the celestial spheres to expand out into the outer void of the cosmos thus beginning what is known in the higher esoteric knowledge as one eternal round or the expansion of light into outer darkness and its return.

However, the process is a matter of taking this light out, one outer space level at a time, for space is also infinite and therefore there needs to be organized.

We could, therefore, say that the first extension or involution of pure light into the outer and first space level, gave us the Etheric plane of existence or the middle heavens. It was in this phase that the pure light first began to step down from its pure vibration, becoming converted etheric energy filling the first space level in the outer realms that surround the divine spheres of the always-existing light, the META-VERSE. We could also say that this etheric energy became the universal matrix or universal thought-form that later precipitated into the material spheres, the lower heavens.

Now due to the never-ending surrounding infinite void of the cosmos as we exist in an Omni centric Omniverse, it was prevalent for the prime creator, the first source, cause, and center of all things, to set up a barrier or wall in a perfect circumference around the eternal spheres. This is what some in the esoteric tradition have called, the ring pass not and its purpose was to prevent the universal light from getting lost deep in the infinite void, overriding organization. These phenomena also constituted an important universal law and that is what goes out, comes back. In the natural world of nature, this is translated as what goes up comes down, or simply the law of return.

Nevertheless, this ring pass does not, allows the living light to return to its original source, thus creating a perfect cycle of outpouring light and incoming light. This continues until its entire circumference becomes marked by pure light, thus ending one round of the perpetual ongoing architectural work that is being conducted by the universal architect at the center of all that is. In this process, the light that is constantly going out is considered the descending part, or phase, which only marks half of the entire process.

And in turn, the returning light that is bouncing off this ring pas,s not a barrier is considered the ascension part of the return of light back to its pure source. Now, this process did not happen overnight although in the eyes of God it did, for all time is relevant and happening at the same time in the higher levels of the always-existing spheres.

However, from a third-dimensional perspective, it took eons and billions of what we would call earth years, for this process to unfold. In fact, it is well known now by most esotericists and mystics that the long descension process or what the eastern teachers have called the out-breath of the expanding God light is finally over. We are now experiencing the in-breath or the coming back of light as the ascension process takes effect.

This explains why our planet is ascending currently. The ascension process could also be known as the electrification (spiritualization) of matter as described in the "Keys of Enoch"; which is in progress as the earth's frequency raises into the eight dimensions.

The descent phase could be scientifically and metaphysically considered the involution of evolution, or in the higher mysteries, the descent of spirit (light) into matter (material), which is the true metaphysical meaning of the fall of light beings thus becoming man material. In fact, human beings are the resulting product of this descent of wholesome light beings into the lower levels of the material spheres.

Therefore, from the top down, mankind originated as a whole light beings in the celestial spheres, living without any concept of time, as we know it today. In fact, time is a by-product of linear limited consciousness and only exists in the confines of the third dimension. On the contrary, time is non-existent in the dimensions higher than the fourth.

Considering this, we may conclude that mankind's true origin was in the always existing spheres of pure light when we were all part of a primal singular energy field. Out of this primal energy field, we began to become individualized units of energy as the first phase of the descent occurred, when the middle heavens were formed. It was then, that we become spiritual-etheric beings, with no material form, well at least not organic. In fact, in our original state as light beings, we didn't inherit form until the creation (extension) of the lower heavens, the material spheres which are also composed of three major spheres.

Apparently, every major plane of existence is divided by the magical three all the way to the point where even man's compositions consist of three major aspects, spirit, mind, and body.

It was in the second phase of existence, that different grades of light energy came to exist as to when the light goes through a prism reflecting multiple spectral radiations. This conversion of the one light into different spectral colors is what allowed all descending light beings of light or sparks of divinity to take the form to accommodate our new environment, as we first began operating with etheric vehicles.

These were and are our energy bodies that we used in the etheric spheres when we were intelligent without yet a physical form of flesh and bones (organic) and they were five. In the keys of Enoch, they are revealed as the electromagnetic body of light, the Gemetrian body of light, the AKA body of light, the Zohar body of light, and the Over self-Christ body of light. Again, these bodies are not to be considered physical material (organic), They are energetic vehicles, to be used in the higher (realms) worlds of the Etheric spheres.

In the aftermath, of the conversion of pure light essence into the ether, the material planes finally came into being as the lower heavens were formed into existence. It was during this phase that the descending light-etheric beings (us) needed a material vehicle. This vehicle has been revealed through the restored knowledge as the perfect embodiment (Adam Cadman). It became the last energy-matter manifestation for the descending light beings that had their origin in the always existing spheres of the central universe, thus correcting our true origin as made in the image of God.

We may now state that the first Adam (our ancestor) was a light being a full conscious spiritual being who first existed in the EIGHTH dimension of the perfected material form of refined manifested nonorganic matter. This refined manifested non-organic matter being superior then the organic matter was originally made eternal as explained in our bible.

The point here is, that we humans of the earth today, were and are light beings, that descended from the highest spiritual realms gradually condensing into organic form.

Therefore, it is important to begin to understand that modern man; today's human beings are all children of the one God, the primal light source of all existence. So we could now begin by reconditioning our minds to see each other as one and the same; not mentioning our environment as well, for everything in existence holds within itself the life essence (universal life force) of the light source, which is the same everywhere.

Also crucial to understand, is that before the extension (creation) of the material universe when we existed in our original habitat and original essence, the celestial spheres, we were all aligned and connected with the great central source and everything reflected universal unity (sisterhood/brotherhood). We are all thought of as a collective hive mind. Considering this, we need to correct our limited invalid belief system that believes mankind is a descendent of the animal kingdom. Mankind is not a descendant of the animal kingdom from the bottom up as explained through Darwinian evolution. On the contrary, man is a descendant of whole light beings that originated in the higher spheres of the always-existing meta-central universe. The animal kingdom was but a phase in the gradual development of the organic vehicle that eventually played a role in the final descent of spiritual beings descending into frozen condense form, the organic vehicle of flesh and bones, homo sapien-sapiens, which will be explained in greater detail in later chapters.

It is important to distinguish us; as the true essence of light spiritual substance inhabiting a temporary mortal physical organic vehicle in order to experience the lower dimensions of congealed dense form, known as the third dimension. We are pure conscious awareness, not our organic body. However, it is equally important to understand that our spirit essence needs to descent into an organic vehicle (body) in order to successfully complete the ascension process. For true ascension, as we shall see is the integration of spirit and matter, HEAVEN AND EARTH.

So in the correction of the jaded misunderstanding of our origin, we humans on, the other hand, have always existed as whole light beings of the highest light that descended into the matter so that we may infuse the light into the lowest spheres of lower vibrations in order to spiritualize matter.

Unfortunately, we have mistreated our animals, our earth and that is why they had become so beastly in nature, whereas before the fall of man, which is the fall of unity consciousness into separative (dual) consciousness, man and the animals living in harmony, communicated among each other and shared collectively as keepers of our planet. For the record let it be known that Jesus the Christ attested and proclaimed that all of us were sons and daughters of the living God not just himself.

The fact that we are celestial beings capable of ascending like Christ is well understood in the eastern tradition of India, Tibet, and China.

For millenniums, we have been locked into this linear rigid dimension, and have only perceived our physical body, and unfortunately have been conditioned to believe that all we are is physical bodies when in essence, we are the fire life spirit that gives substance to both our energy vehicles and physical body.

To make a correction, in the lowest point of creation in the lower heavens, (the material spheres) light-energy matter was initially intended to vibrate at no lower than the fifth-dimensional planes werewhererergy and matter are in a perfect balance. In this phase of being, the matter is more refined and easily able to be manipulated by the power of our light body.

The imbalance of this type, however, came about when the fifth-dimensional non-organic matter further coalesced into the fourth-dimensional semi-inorganic matter and then into third-dimensional organic matter, which is the densest.

At its densest, it appears to be an extremely solid reality thus losing its fluidity, connection, and balance with the subtle world of energy. This condition has caused many philosophers and scholars to believe that the world of apparent organic matter is an illusion and that it traps our spirit in our organic body of flesh and bones.

Now yes and no, because from a higher perspective descending into the lowest vibrations equals a greater ascent into even higher levels of vibration, expansion, and growth, which is the reason for incarnation and reincarnation.

It appears that in this limited third dimension where organic matter seems to be at its most dominant over energy; we are in a fallen state, however as we ascend into higher levels/densities, then our energy vital self dominates our material form.

Maybe that is the reason why for centuries we have only identified ourselves with our physical body while forgetting our original nature as celestial beings of light energy vibration.

However, let it be clear that in the higher dimensions, life is more eternal and timeless, because of the constant flow of universal life force coming from our light body into our subtler organic form, giving our organic form ageless living for thousands of years, making us appear immortal. On the other hand, in the third dimension, life is less than a hundred years, because the organic form is receiving less than ten percent of the entire universal life current that flows through our chakras (energy centers). It is this universal life force that flows through us that determines our life span.

According to the esoteric wisdom, our light body is broken off into nine energy vehicles, all different vibrations of the same energy field with the lowest vibrational vehicle being our physical organic shell, which is the only one we see. Perhaps this correlates with the three overall planes of reality that are also broken off into nine sub-dimensional planes of existence.

These other bodies are as real as our physical body and exist in the higher vibrating states of energy-matter beyond the third-dimensional range of dense organic matter. Therefore, since our real composition as humans involves vehicles and aspects of ourselves that exist in the higher dimensions, our goal then would be to integrate those other aspects of ourselves so that we may become whole light beings with a perfected and ascended organic form. This would not only integrate but ultimately ground the higher vibrations with the lower ones thus re-uniting HEAVEN ON EARTH as we shall see soon.

In truth, we are powerful celestial beings of light, with a major amnesia problem and as we take up ascension with our planet into higher dimensions, we will begin to access those vehicles and realize how truly powerful and unlimited we are. This is not science fiction; this is the truth of the matter, WE ARE MULTIDIMENSIONAL BEINGS, ITS TIME TO WAKE UP.

We will begin to understand this more as we began to awaken spiritually, or as our other ninety percent of our genetic material becomes re-activated.

In fact, the best way to imagine a whole being of light or soul is a core extension, extending from the great central source of all that is at the center of all existence, which is pure luminal light. Or we could say that we are all individual sparks of the one light resonating at the center of everything, containing within ourselves holistically the same attributes and elements of the entire light source, since our existence is holistic. From its center, we could conclude that this light in its pure state is the prime source of everything that exists, God. For instance, in terms of our latest scientific breakthroughs, it is energy in its most pure state or highest vibration.

Therefore, we could scientifically affirm that before we inherited organic physical bodies, we were considered intelligent because since the universe is holistic and living, we were all perfect functioning aspects containing the same nature of the whole in us. For example, our light body acted as a Tran's vehicle enabling the soul, the real you, and me to experience and sojourn on the multiple planes and sub-planes of the overall celestial realms of the higher light spectrum (dark matter).

In truth, the light body was our original and first vehicle as our souls extended from the central core, celestial spheres. It was this vehicle the ancient Egyptians referred to as the Ka body and the ancient Hebrews refer to as the Merkabah. There is also reference to this vehicle in the ancient Chinese, Indian, and Tibetan text as well. Unfortunately, this knowledge regarding our original vehicle, the light body, was omitted from our records, by the dark brotherhood and only preserved in the esoteric literature of the brotherhood of light and their various benevolent secret societies of both east and west.

Again all of these energy vehicles are different aspects of the overall light body that sustains the soul (ray of light) the real you and me, existing in the multiple planes of existence, all the way from the core in the highest vibrating spheres of pure energy, to the lowest heavens in the material universe were light-ether is converted into different grades of energy-matter, from the most subtle to the grossest organic.

It is also important to understand, that some of the beings who descended first in their light bodies to scope the new conditions of the lower material spheres, had become disconnected from pure spirit and began to take things into their own hands acting for their own individual cause, as free will has always been honored as a universal cosmic law.

This was the beginning of separation as some of the light beings began to see themselves as individual beings separate from everything else. So, the beginning of pride ensued the original first deadly sin. In this sense, these souls were the first ones to descend as a result of separating themselves from the unified state of a singular consciousness, which is today known as Christ, or universal (cosmic consciousness). This is the consciousness that unites us back with the whole of existence or primal source.

Even though duality is represented by a separation of the one into two, therefore giving everything a dual sense, good vs. evil, female male-malec., Duality also serves its purpose in the descension process, for it allows all souls involve in this process to realize their oneness and interrelation with all others while appearing separated. This allows all opposites to integrate as they were in the celestial and etheric spheres, before the descent of material duality. In truth, we began as celestial beings with a pure body of light then we proceed in becoming intelligence operating with etheric bodies, then to finally descend or coalesced into a physical organic body as a final condensing of our energy field. Also, it is important to understand that when we whole light beings enter the final phase of our descent, embodying a vehicle of flesh and blood we become only a portion of our total self. And since we are the first spirit, we must descent into matter, and then bring down our divine spirit into matter or ascend our matter back into spirit, thus completing our perfection as made in the image of our creator, who has also in a previous creation cycle gone through the same process as we all are in this current creation cycle.

Each cycle is known as one universal round and it is a process every spirit being takes in order to achieve the greatest experience and the highest degree of exaltation (ascension). This allows for each soul to explore and experience all levels and facets of the overall spectrum of the unified energy field, with the result of re-uniting our individualized unit of consciousness with the all universal (Christ) consciousness. The whole purpose of the universal round is so that all the sparks of light (children of God) may evolve like our creator God. That eventually man may ascend and go out there in new cycles of creation into the never-ending realms of cosmos as creator gods, as done so by our creator God in our current round. After all, our cutting-edge science has now confirmed that there are multiple universes and that the creation of more universes appears to be happening every day as an ongoing eternal process.

In other words, since our creator is all perfect, he/she provides the same grounds of experience so that all his/her children (sparks of light) may follow in the same footsteps (blueprint). This explains why the cosmos operates according to divine laws and why there is a set system or what esotericism and mystics call a patterned blueprint in the unfolding of everything. It is the same system of involution (descent) and evolution (ascend) that serves to create universes and worlds beyond number, all fallowing and being fashioned by the same universal principles of the always existing and expanding mother universe.

Therefore, since we are all evolving together, we all follow the same universal cosmic blueprint of descension and ascension, as we are all subject to the same universal laws and principles. Except that in the descent, we tend to lose our oneness with all that is (which serves a purpose) to eventually rediscover what we have lost, reconnect and in the process inherit a spiritualized physical vehicle as we reunite with our spirit self, consciously and by our own volition, allowing our light body to spiritualize organic matter.

In truth, the middle heavens became the exact replica of the higher heavens and the plan was to also bring this same blueprint into materiality (AS IT IS IN HEAVEN SO SHALL IT BE ON EARTH) that completes the last phase of this grand cosmic unfolding. Therefore, it is important to know that each time the light frequency lowered its vibration, a new layer or vehicle was needed to envelop our soul (core being a ray of the one light) so that we may further explore the lower realms of vibrating energy to the point where the non-organic matter was born with the precipitation of the twelfth, eleventh, tenth, ninth, and eighth dimensions.

As mentioned, the light beings that served the light and maintained connective (unity) consciousness with the prime creator become the most beautiful beings in the first phases of the lower heavens, particularly in the eighth and seventh dimensions where the descending light being translated into a human angel, the Adam Cadman.

As revealed in the previous chapter, at this point of the descension all descending beings become enveloped in a material vehicle that would secure their existence in the lower vibratory planes of the lower densities. On each level of the material plane, matter vibrates at different rates. In like manner, the vehicles that enabled us individual light rays to experience the different realms also vibrate to match the frequency of the surrounding energy field within the various electromagnetic fields.

It is equally important to understand that even though our light body at this point has had several layers of denser vehicles covering it up, it has always been our prime vehicle, the highest vibrating one, and responsible for transferring our individual universal life force (life currents of our soul) into the lower densities.

The light body also carries with our entire life's blueprint, for it generates our etheric vehicle and our material vehicle as well, as the Adama thus making us a fully conscious being. Our light body is the electron force that is generated by our soul when we are fully connected with universal Christ consciousness and the blueprint of our untapped crystalline DNA.

For example, in the celestial spheres; our light body is at full light quotient potential. Meaning it assimilates the entirety of the living light of the great central source of all that is. Therefore, through the full operation of our light body, we are capable of manifesting divine qualities. For the most part, it is the light body that maintains the high frequency of pure light and holds that vibration until it descends into the lower heavens, the material planes.

In like manner, since the lower heavens also consist of three major planes, it is important to state that the highest region of the material planes of existence; (lower heavens) are considered the celestial spheres of the material planes perhaps occupying, the twelfth to ninth densities and the etheric part occupying the ninth to the sixth densities were energy-matter becomes more solid and the lowest part occupying the sixth densities to the lowest point of vibrating energy-matter, all the way to what we experience as the third density which is where energy-matter condenses to the point that it becomes frozen (coalesced) energy still, however, being the same energy fields vibrating at its lowest oscillation.

Nonetheless, in the material levels of energy matter, a perfect balance exists all the way up to the fifth-density where we once existed as pure energy beings projecting a perfect etheric meta material form. In other words, in the fifth-density and up of the material spheres our light body is operating at full capacity, or our current DNA is in its full use.

Apparently, as we descend lower than the fifth density our light body becomes less operative as we begin to assimilate less and less of its entire light quotient and thus use less of our DNA potential, which for the most part is a crystalline substance. Therefore, our so-called junk DNA is spiritualized substance that exists in the subtle realms of vibrating higher realities.

We may also correlate the use of our light body with the spinning of our chakras or energy vortexes as revealed through eastern metaphysics. For instance, in the second aspect of our material universe (lower heavens) our light body is less dominant as our etheric self becomes the most dominant aspect of our lower material self. This is the phenomenon known in the Urantia material as the Morontia worlds of spirit personalities, with a humanoid form. For the most part, this has been misunderstood for thousands of years, though today in the greatest dispensation ever, which marks our planet's initiation into the seventh golden age, more people are beginning to understand this truth. Since the higher spiritual knowledge is making its way back into the limelight, many people are beginning to understand our true composition as made in the image of our creator and that we are more than just gross beings of matter.

For instance, the higher understanding has restored the knowledge that each human being is a composite of seven major vehicles, technically twelve. Though in terms of seven, four of them are the lower vehicles and three of them are the higher ones. So in truth, we are composed of not only our visible physical body

but our emotional/astral body, our etheric double energy body, our intuitional body, our high mental casual body, which marks the four lower ones, and finally our spirit body which in turn is divided in three. This is the true composition of a human being. We are indeed MULTIDIMENSIONAL and have other vehicles that currently we don't know exist except for the lower ones, physical, emotional, and mental.

Our light body even though currently not in its full use is what maintains all our other vehicles in operation, including our mental and etheric ones and in turn, our mental and etheric vehicles generate the physical vehicle.

Our, chakras exist in our etheric-energy body. This doesn't mean that their existence begins there, it only means that since the etheric vehicle is the in-between point between the physical body and the light body, it is the conduit vehicle that acts not only as a generator for the physical body but as its blueprint as well. On the same note, the more subtle like vehicles cannot be seen with the naked eye but seen under certain energy reading technologies, such as the one that takes aura pictures known as Kirlian photography.

In fact, the aura is the energy field that envelopes and is generated by an individual and corresponds to the seven, nine, or twelve vehicles that make up the human being. In like manner, our chakras correspond to each of our seven subtle energy vehicles, the lowest being the gross physical vehicle of ur body, the highest being our light body, and everyone in between. Imagine each vehicle denser as it vibrates lower and more subtle and lighter as it vibrates higher with the light body being the finest or the highest vibrating vehicle. All bodies exist on different frequencies of the same light energy spectrum.

In light of this, we may postulate that we are more than just human, that we are more than just what we see in the mirror, and that we are able to return to our exalted state of divinity as made in the image of our creator. This understanding would bring mankind extraordinary healing and enlightenment.

Since our true origin was in the celestial realms, then we are indeed descended celestial beings with great abilities that are waiting for us to harness as we remember our oneness with the cosmos.

This great truth is what all the spiritual and religious masters (spiritual adepts who have to achieve enlightenment) have always taught. In fact, all diseases and illnesses known to man have been the result of mankind ignoring and not bringing into account the spiritual proponent of existence. It is only when we deal directly and become involved with the spiritual, the source of all existence, could we begin affecting life in the most positive way.

Since everything that exists consciously or not (beings or things) has its origin first in the spirit realm and then in the etheric realm before it finally manifests in the physical realm and that is the process of descension or what science calls light precipitating into the matter. In light of this, it is well known today that when we suffer from any physical, emotional, or mental turmoil is because one or more of our chakras are misaligned or not spinning correctly and therefore not processing the proper amount of universal life force into the organs that are causing the disease. This means that all illness begins at the energy level as quantum physics and metaphysics would mutually agree. In other words, when the subtle bodies (invincible to the naked eye) are affected, the damage is shown in the densest of all vehicles, the physical body. So, in this case, any illness whether it be mental, physical, or emotional, begins to ripple first in either the astral body affecting the emotions or the etheric body affecting the physical or the mental body affecting our minds.

All our vehicles are interrelated and function as one and that is why materialistic science could never find real cures in chemically man-made remedies like the pharmacy. While they are busy tackling the problems examining only the gross most dense aspect of our total being, our physical body, which is ineffective, the real root and cure of all problems lays in the energy subtle bodies, and there are seven spinning wheels, the chakras. If science considered and began to explore the spiritual side of things, we would have a perfect understanding of how the physical world works, thus solving all our problems.

Each subtle body has certain responsibilities and functions and at the same time, they all operate as one, the physical aspect being the only one we see. Picture our physical body as one layer of various layers that make up our entire being and at the core lay the true self, which is our soul, PURE CELESTIAL essence. In addition, each chakra (spinning wheel of light) corresponding to each of our seven vehicles carries a ray color tone and vibration liken to the prism of light.

As known in eastern metaphysics, these colors are red, orange, yellow, green, blue, purple and indigo, pertaining to the seven major rays. It is the chakra's colors that determine its function, purpose, and energy. For example, the first or root chakra which is characterized by red represents survival, willpower, and our ability to be well-grounded into the earth. The second Charka characterized by orange is also known as the sacral or sex chakra which represents our pleasures and governs our emotions, it is the seat of our ability to selfheal because orange is the color of healing.

The third chakra is known as the center of our power, corresponding to our solar plexus and yellow characterizes it. This chakra is also known as our inner sun and its function governs our individual power and how we relate to others. When our bowel, spleen, and liver are in good condition, it is because our solar plexus chakra is facilitating the right energy needed for those organs to work. The fourth chakra is in our heart area represented by green and it governs our cardiovascular system making sure all our blood flows properly throughout the entire body. This is also the seat of compassion that gives way to the understanding that we are all one. The fifth chakra is in our throat, marked by blue signifying, truth, and our ability to communicate properly. The sixth chakra is located in the middle of our eyes, its color is purple and it is known as our third eye which gives us a spiritual vision to see into other realities as it is connected to our pineal and pituitary glands that govern our higher mental faculties.

When this chakra is fully functioning, we began to see with our third eye and acquire extrasensory perception, capable of piercing the veil into the higher levels of reality. It is unfortunate that this chakra has not been in full use. But then again, all our chakras are not in their full use as to why our physical bodies age and die eventually. If our seven seals as described in the book of Revelation, (chakras) processed the full potential of our light body we would become immortal. If we learned how to properly clear and align all chakras we would never get sick and never age.

The last Chakra is known as the crown chakra and it's the most important one. This chakra if counting from the top-down would really be the first chakra for it connects us to our light body in the higher spiritual realms as it pours down universal life force into our other chakras in order to maintain all of our bodies functioning properly and in harmony. Its color is indigo and if it was fully opened, we would become great spiritual giants. As spiritual beings, we must realize and take care of our subtle vehicles by clearing and balancing out our chakras through proper diet, exercise, positive thinking, and good motives. Our chakras are our channels to those vehicles and only when all seven chakras are spinning and functioning the way they're supposed to, we will be completely healed on all levels of our existence.

As we learn more about our cosmos in the next segment, we will come to find out that our light bodies are connected to what is known as the great central suns. And that is why at a solar-planetary level, all lower vehicles are sustained by cosmic energy that is being transmitted by our sun, which in turn gets the energy universal life force from the great central sun at the center of our galaxy. Also, we would soon come to find out that our solar system is an entity on a macro scale of evolution just like our earth is also a living being. In fact, the Great Spirit that animates our solar system is known as Helios Envesta who was originally born with a family of twelve planets. In fact, as revealed through the new science, that everything in our cosmos is alive and that we humans on planet earth in a sense are like cells in the greater body known as our solar system. In turn, our solar system with other solar systems form organs in a greater body or being known as our galaxy which is a macro being known as Melkior, hence the MILKY Way Galaxy who is a being that holds and exist in twelve dimensions all at once.

The beauty of this sequence in the holographic concept of reality is that no matter in which direction we go everything is interconnected as the trillions of cells in our individual bodies are, all working together for the total functioning of our physical body. In like manner, we may say that all universes are all different organs and aspects of the greatest macro being in our existence known as the Central

Universe/mother-verse or META-VERSE as referred to by our cutting-edge science.

Again and for the record, let it be clear, that all life-sustaining nourishment is facilitated to all of our entire beings by our light body and since all life is energy and in turn, all energy is converted and refracted light then our nourishment comes directly from the light source the same substance that we are made out of which again is generated by our sun, the physical source and symbol of our creator's power on the lower material spheres.

In fact, it is now understood that if it wasn't for the existence and the energy that comes from our sun, there would be no life in any of the planets in our solar system. There is more to our sun than just a burning giant gaseous ball of hydrogen and helium. The sun has spiritual significance and its role is greater than what we have been led to believe. The sun obviously has a direct relationship with all our light bodies, as it also transmits energy through its own chakras, from the central sun at the center of our galaxy.

In truth, it is crucial that mankind begins to understand the true nature of our existence in relation to our entire composition as made in the image of our creator. Therefore, in spite of the materialistic one-sided view of linear reality, our evolution was never meant to be just operating on a physical level but rather a long spiritual process since in essence, we are light beings expressing a human experience, so that we may become more like our creator. So let it be established, as we prepare to take up our new evolutionary route, our origin began in the always existing celestial realms, and as the process of descending (involution) occurred, we began to take form and shape until we become human, which is the lowest point of light condensing into a material being. This was no accident order of course; it was the divine plan of our prime creator to facilitate further expansion of the always-existing Grand Central META-VERSE, which is expanding one space level at a time.

In addition, we can also conclude that mankind was God's ultimate masterpiece in the grand scheme of things as to why our creator decided to make the material realms. In other words, to be human is to be a divine celestial spiritual being in matter and that is why every single one of us is a manifestation of divinity in the flesh. WE ARE GREAT SPIRITUAL BEINGS OF LIGHT projected out from the point of pure energy, pure light which is the essence of all that is.

THE FACTS ARE THAT WE ARE ALL SONS AND DAUGHTERS OF THE LIVING GOD, THE SOURCE OF ALL EXISTENCE, WITHOUT END AND WITHOUT BEGINNING.

In the scriptures, Jesus the Christ states, perhaps two of the most important yet misunderstood meanings in the bible. In the book of John, Jesus states, "For isn't written in your own language that ye are gods (that is different aspects of the one eternal light that burns inside us all as the Christ within which is our original divine self.) "For all of you are living daughters and sons of the living God".

Secondly, "for you shall do the same or greater works than me", said, Jesus. In truth, Christ taught and demonstrated ascension (integration of light body and matter) he came to show us the way to ascend back to the father's universal mind, which sees no difference. "I and the father are one as I and you are one", said Jesus, implying that we are all celestial beings' different aspects of the great central source.

The Christ with-in or cosmic universal consciousness is a concept we all must come to know, understand, cultivate and implement for us to achieve our full divine inherent

 potential.

In conclusion, we originated as pure light beings that gradually descended into this limited experience. The hour though has come for mankind to take their rightful place in the universe as made in the image and similitude of God all mighty the source/light of all that is. We have been in spiritual darkness for thousands of years about who we really are as children of the highest God (light). Wake up to your divinity for the time is at hand.

# CHAPTER FIVE

## THE UNIVERSE IS
## BIGGER THAN WHAT WE WERE TOLD

In the vast creation of our cosmos, there are many levels and realms of existence. Today it has been postulated particularly in the realm of particle physics that there are many universes that are evolving parallel to each other and we only perceive, know, and understand only one. According to the esoteric wisdom, all evolving spheres are different aspects of the one Omni-verse that is broken off into multiple universes with evolving multiple galaxies and worlds.

Well, in a sense they are both correct. For there are multiple universes as there are many existing realms and planes of reality. However, all the universes that are evolving side by side are part of a greater omniverse or what cutting-edge science calls the Meta-Verse, proving the esoteric wisdom correct. Therefore, all the universes are different parts of one all existing big META-VERSE. At the center of this META- VERSE there is only one source from which everything springs from and nothing exists outside of this source, THE LIVING LIGHT. Even though there are many perhaps infinite numbers of ways in which this source expresses itself through different wavelengths and frequencies of its own singular light essence, it is all part of the same whole.

As mentioned, the greatest discovery in human existence is that everything is energy and therefore everything is light, because even energy, is a stepped down frequency of pure luminal light. In Fact, there exist many ongoing refractions of this one light, although it appears as if there are many different reflections, universes, planes, and worlds. So yes, there are innumerable parallel universes as well as there are innumerable stars, galaxies, and planets, and the beauty is that they are all existing as one body, therefore let's call it the OmniVERSE, the ONE and the MANY, the MANY and the ONE all different parts of the same whole. Now in a closer examination of our cosmos let's re-emphasize the fact that there are billions of stars (suns) in our galaxy, as our science now calculates. Now since there are billions of suns (stars) then there are probably a few trillion world's/planets, like our own or different, just as how there are different types of planets in our own solar system. So just alone in this galaxy, there are innumerable suns and planets. Now as we stretch beyond this concept, it is important to know that there is more to our cosmology than just a few billion bundling galaxies, for our universe is much bigger than that, as has been re-discovered in the last fifty years or so.

As the multi-verse concept gains more ground in the scientific community, there was a revelation in the late fifties that allegedly came to us from heaven in the form of a book called Urantia. Urantia is considered the fifth epochal revelation for earth the bible being the fourth and some of the information ther, supports not only the scientific evidence regarding our multiverse but also the fact that we are not alone and that we are part of a system of about a thousand organized worlds that in turn is organized in a larger constellation body of 100, 000 systems.

However, before we dive into the Urantia papers, let's continue revealing what the new scientific data is indicating. As mentioned, since about ten universes are being born every day due to cosmic quantum fluctuations then galaxies and solar systems are also being spawn into existence every day.

This idea of constant endless creation is directly related to the Central Sun Theory. According to the Central Sun Theory, universes and galaxies are being spun out from a central focal point generating cosmic energy in a centrifugal manner. This is fascinating because this theory proposes the idea that at the center of every galaxy and universe there is a heartbeat pulsating universal life force (central sun) emitting its life force in a circumference manner administering its light rays to all its galaxies, stars, and worlds providing them with the universal life force energy needed to sustain all life.

For example, one level of cosmic source in the material spheres lies at the center core of every universe. This central core acts like a giant sun in which many galaxies are revolving about as in the case of a giant nucleus. It is this great hub that administers and controls all the galaxies in perfect formation around its source, the light at its center, which is known as the great central sun for our local universe.

It is this core central sun of a universe that brings into being the first level of manifestation from the pure etheric realms. The second level of manifestation is the central sun at the center of each galaxy that is sub-divided universes within each universe. In the case, of our own local galaxy, the great central sun is known as hanab-ku-tzolkiin, as revealed by the Mayan scholars, Kolob to the latter-day saints of the church of Jesus Christ and Tula (Ophyocus) as known by the western mystics.

In fact, this pattern continues down to the solar systems of galaxies. For example, there is a cosmological phenomenon regarding greater revolutions of systems being restored by modern scholars and that is what the ancients called the precision of the equinoxes, which is, the solar alignment of our sun with the central sun of our parent sun known as Alcyone that occurs every 26, 000 years. (More on this later).

The lowest manifestation of light in the lower heavens is our local planetary star system or local sun in which our local planets revolve about. So on behalf of the higher divine plan, creation is an ongoing process as it corresponds to the ongoing impulses of the one light that is forever sending its light rays outward from the center of the Omni Verse, sending its life force to all universes, all galaxies, and all solar systems.

Another way of seeing the Centropic Model of cosmology is by adopting the most correct esoteric axiom that correlates all existence as one, from the micro to the macro. For example, since we now have a better understanding of the nature of our existence, we find a common pattern that repeats itself over and over in never-ending swirls. That is, just as the electrons revolve around its nucleus so do the planets around the sun, the solar systems around the galactic center, and the galaxy around a greater universe, and so on.

In a way, our existence is like a never-ending spiral of circles within circles. To our surprise, we can identify this pattern of swirls with all physical manifestations, including the composition of man.

For instance, all glands, muscles, bones, etc. everything in our physical body is governed by the center of man's being, the soul's true light essence. In the esoteric tradition, this is known as the inner sun and the heart is the physical organ that represents this pulsating light as blood is its physical correspondent circulating universal life force that gives physical life to our body's biological components. Now in an examination of these facts, we may conclude that our entire creation is based on the revolution of bodies around its source.

In the more evolved circles of higher knowledge this postulation is characterized as the laws of entropy, as opposed to the entropy model that has dominated our world under the control of the dark brotherhood, whose time is up, according to the entropic model of existence, there is neither ending nor beginning, we exist in a circular condition with never-ending cycles within cycles.

On the contrary, in the entropic model, all existence is characterized as from point A to point B in a linear form and this kind of condition is, therefore, subject to entropy, since there is a beginning point and endpoint. On the other hand, the entropic model states, that since everything is configured as cycles within cycles, with never-ending cycles then we are indeed infinite.

If we add the now confirmed scientific evidence that all is energy and since energy is neither created nor destroyed, then we can safely conclude that the entropic model is the correct one because everything is energy and it's being held together by some central focal point from the microcosm to the macrocosm. This eternal infinite pattern of our cosmos, "the entropic model" of existence also provides evidence that our existence is holographic.

Another example of the entropic model was seen in the dark ages when people held the idea that the earth was flat and that it was the center point in which everything revolves around, the sun's planets, etc. This medieval fallacy kept mankind trapped in the limited pattern of the entropic model, compelling them to a linear subjective reality. In truth, this fallacy continued up until today holding on to the idea that this is the only planet with life and that our sun was the only sun/star with planets.

However, by adopting the entropic model we can conclude that our local planets revolve around our local star/sun, and since there are billions of stars/suns in our galaxy then according to the entropic pattern, they too are revolving around a single source at the center of our galaxy. This emerging truth should shatter the last breath of believing in the entropic model, which indicates that everything has an end, when in fact, in light of correct knowledge there is no end to life because life is light and light is the eternal source. So, if there is always light there is always life.

What is even more disturbing is that no matter how much this new data makes better sense than the old, there is a perpetual resistance against the new evidence, taking place within the scientific community by those who don't want to reform to the new concept of existence and those trying to unite all theories into a unified theory of everything.

For example, in modern accepted mainstream science, this great truth has been buried under the false assumption that at the center of most galaxies lays a black hole that sucks everything up, thus meaning the end of physical life as we know it.

On the contrary, and based on the higher restored knowledge, it is the other way around. It appears, in light of the new evidence, that there is a constant pulsating (light) life force that is continually emitting its light ray's outward from the center of our galaxy, not inward or sucked into a black hole, favoring the entropic model.

Therefore, based on the new data, the entropic concept has always been invalid and false. For it is well understood that black holes happen as a result of only two things. The first is when a star or planet implodes it creates a massive black hole sucking up everything in its immediate surroundings. The second way a black hole is produced is when a universe reaches old age and it collapses into a point of singularity. Overall, the entropic concept is one of many inaccuracies like the flat world concept that ruled our minds for thousands of years till about five hundred years ago. Since we are correcting commonly accepted inaccuracies, let's remind ourselves that in our material universe there is no such thing as empty space. All is energy-vibrating-matter even in the higher realms of the spiritual spheres, that are not perceptible to the naked eye, or the 94 percent of the so-called missing matter in our universe. Until recently our earth scientists have failed in measuring anything outside of the range of the third-dimensional frequency, the lowest vibrating field of energy matter.

However, it was brought to my attention that earth scientist has recently modified there detecting technologies using Xrays to measure the realm of dark matter and to our surprise have detected colonies and life in the realms of dark matter. At least now our earth scientist has registered energy emitting from the so-called missing reality thanks to their Hubble x-ray satellite.

As revealed earlier, dark matter is a higher reality vibrating at high frequencies, so it appears to be dark or empty to our naked eye. So, with that said, let's correct the material approach and reinstate the fact that at the center of all galaxies lays a colossal sun, a central sun that is equivalent to the power of billions of suns. All central suns at the center of all galaxies have such a high level of energy vibration that unless we step up in frequency or dimensions

higher than the low third-dimensional rate of vibration, it would appear dark, of course, logically speaking (left-brain) assuming it to be a black hole at its center.

As a reminder, our scientists have been only measuring 6 percent of all existence and so have based their facts on incomplete data. Though in truth, it is the great center hub in which all billion stars/sun systems revolve around that cultivate the grounds for accepting the entropic model of existence. Therefore, by readopting the entropic model of cosmology, we can now begin to see that our entire galaxy is being held together in a perfect circular fashion the same way the atom and our solar systems are. In truth, the central sun of our galaxy is like a gigantic nucleus sun or power generator that sustains all the billions of suns/stars.

In fact, all the life force that is being generated to our planet via our sun is essentially coming from the central sun of our Milky Way Galaxy; through what higher evolved scientists call scalar and Gamma waves. This applies to all the living suns/stars in our galaxy, as they are all sustained by the life force emanating from the center hub of our Milky Way galaxy.

Now since there are innumerable galaxies as revealed through NASA and as we continue applying the entropic model, we can begin to understand that our own galaxy, with other galaxies, is iso making a greater revolution around a perhaps even greater source of the energy center. Therefore, we may conclude that a great number of galaxies together would make up one universal body or one universe.

Since there are multiple universes as postulated by the new evidence, we can now begin to see how there could exist multiple universal bodies each a composite of revolving galaxies around a greater source, thus validating what our new science is now confirming.

As mentioned further evidence in support of this claim is also coming from the emissaries (higher intelligence) hailing from the higher planes of existence. This higher intelligence is now coming in the numbers, to assist our creator in the restoration of our planet.

IN THIS NEXT SEGMENT WE WILL UNCOVER INFORMATION FROM HIGHER SPIRITUAL SOURCES THAT CONFIRM THAT WE INDEED LIVE IN A MULTI-VERSE -SYSTEM

According to the Urantia material, a compilation of higher valuable information that has been transmitted by celestial beings, revealing the existence of many of universes, composites of billions of galaxies that are evolving side by side but yet remain connected through a greater universal cosmic body in which all universes are revolving about. In the Urantia material, this central body in which all universes are revolving is known as the Central Universe of Havona. Could this Central Universe of Havona revealed in the Urantia material, parallel what scientists are referring to as the Meta-Verse, or Mother Universe?

Therefore, the Metaverse that has been proposed by the new scientific evidence, leading the way towards a theory of everything while also being supported by the Urantia Papers. Let's examine this restored body of knowledge known as Urantia, also known as the fifth epochal revelation, that is to unite science, spirituality, and philosophy.

According to this revelation, we have a central universe, which is eternal. This eternal central universe is divided into what the Urantia material calls the seven Super Universe spheres, which altogether comprise the Grand Central Universe. The seven Super Universes are seven segments in which the Central Universe first breaks into, as it begins, the arcane process known as involution or the great descent/divide. As we will begin to see, that from the beginning of the descending/division or expansion, there was organization.

These seven Super Universes are also known as the space-time creations or extensions of the Central Universe which according to Urantia, are considered eventuated without beginning or end, as its spheres are eternal. This fact of always-existing eternal spheres correlates with the NEW scientific evidence regarding the eternal metaverse. Also, it is supported by the esoteric ancient wisdom of all traditions. According to the ancient arcane wisdom, it is the meaning of the great cosmic birth of the true Immaculate Conception. Every spiritual source has testified to this fact of a primal Immaculate conception.

Furthermore, Urantia reveals that each of these seven super universes that comprise the Central creation is divided into ten major sectors, giving us a total of 70 major sectors.

Each major sector has one hundred minor sectors, giving us a total of 7,000 minor sectors. Each minor sector contains, one hundred thousand organized local universes, calculating about seven hundred thousand local universes and growing every day. In turn, each local universe contains approximately one hundred constellations, giving us roughly about seventy million constellations and growing by the second.

Each constellation contains a hundred systems giving us a total of seven billion systems in the grand central universe. Finally, each system contains 1,000 worlds. Now if we add this up not considering the eternal spheres of the central universe periphery, we end up with approximately seven trillion organized evolving planetary worlds in our cosmos and growing by the second. As mentioned, every day new universes are being born and organized daily into the domain of the mother central spheres as the central universe forever continues its expansion into the eternal void of infinite space.

Very interesting, now there is more, at the center of the Central Universe of Havona, there is the eternal isle of paradise which itself consist of seven sacred spheres or the seven mansion worlds of the universal Father-Mother, the absolute. Urantia also reveals that in addition to these seven sacred spheres there are about two hundred architectural world spheres that are inhabited by both descending beings that had their origin in the eternal spheres and ascending beings that had evolved from the bottom up as creatures of the time and space experience.

The always-existing eternal spheres of the central universes are known as eventuated realities with no beginning or end. On the other hand, the realities from the super universe level and downward are known as experimental realities, design to overall work for the eternal growth and continued expansion of the eternal spheres of the central universe.

Now in understanding cosmic divine personalities, it is believed that at the center of this central sphere there exists the universal Mother-Father the absolute, who are also referred to as the first source and center.

The first source and center together with the Eternal son, make up the first trinity known as the Paradise Trinity. In this original Paradise Trinity, we have the Universal Father, the Eternal Son, and the Infinite Spirit.

The universal father represents the source of all gravity personality, while the eternal son represents the spirit gravity circuits and the eternal spirit acts as the universal mind of the trinity, which is translated as the container of existence, or the great Mother.

Furthermore, during the great descent, it is believed that this primary cosmic trinity divides into what is known as the seven master spirits who dwell in the seven mansion worlds or sacred spheres of the central system.

In turn, each master spirit rules over a super-universe segment with its own trinity. The celestial order of the Eternal of Days has always been the first celestial administration acting on behalf of the Paradise Trinity, the primary central core of all existence.

Now it is important to understand, that in this eternal sphere only celestial beings of pure light live there. Perhaps these were the first souls that were born from the family of the first source and center, the trinitized sons and daughters of the Paradise Trinity. The Urantia papers refer to them as the firstborn of the central spheres. It is also revealed that these divine personalities later act as the descending sons and daughters of light, (creator gods and goddesses of the local universes) in the experimental architectural spheres of the Seven Super Universes.

Following the celestial order of the Eternal of Days, which administrates the affairs of the Central Universe, is the order of the Ancient of Days, which is the administration that governs all seven super universes all within the domains of their respective spheres.

It is the overall cosmic divine plan that sets the ground for the perpetual divine guidance and celestial administrations, that appears on all levels of existence, all the way down to the order of beings known as the Faithful of Days that oversee the spiritual councils of planets themselves. In this way, all of creation

is dancing in tune with the great divine plan that stems from the great central hub of all that is, the central isle of paradise, which is, by the way, the Great Central Sun of all universes as we integrate cutting-edge science with higher restored knowledge.

What we see here is divine order represented on all levels of existence. The order of the Ancient of Days as the second cosmic order was designed to govern the entire Havona system from the level of Super Universe downward. It is this great order that works with endless groups of Seraphim and Supernaphim hosts that were assigned to the service of the orders for the fulfillment of the great cosmic divine plan.

So, from the top down again we have the Order of Eternal of Days who oversees the affairs of the central spheres, of Havona. Next, we have the order of the Ancient of Days that oversee the development of the time-space experiential worlds of evolutionary potential, all within the periphery of the seven super universes Then as we descend further to the ten major sectors, we have the celestial Order of the Perfection of Days who administrate the major sectors and minor sectors on behalf of the order of both the Eternal and Ancient of days.

Further down, we have the celestial order of the Union of Days and this order administrates the affairs of all local universes, within the minor sectors. Now within the domains of local universes, in the lower levels of the constellations, we have the celestial order of the Recent of Days and further down to the star system sovereigns, we have the celestial order of the Faithful of Days.

In further examination, we can also correlate the Urantia material with the idea of the three levels of heaven, (the celestial, etheric, and material), mentioned earlier. In this comparison, we could line up the Havona central spheres with the eternal celestial spheres that have always existed as the most purified levels of light. As we descend into the second heavens, then we match the organization (extension) of the Seven Super Universes corresponding to the middle heavens of the etheric realms which extended from the already eternal existing spheres of light, the celestial planes, or as Urantia puts it, "the Grand Central Universe".

The creations of the local universes could be considered the lower heavens of the material spheres, where all the galaxies exist. Now on a galactic level, if we can further correlate these three levels of existence, to the postulated three types of advanced population planetary, stellar and galactic civilizations proposed by our new science, then we are on the verge of the greatest scientific and spiritual revolution ever, which only comes with the re-establishment of HEAVEN ON EARTH or a UTOPIA GOLDEN AGE

According to the Urantia material, we live in the Local Universe of Nebadon, which is one of the multiple evolving universes within the seventh segment of the known super universe of Orvonton. However, the Urantia material does not mention the other Super Universes, other than Orvonton, nor does it mention anything about any other local universe other than Nebadon. Perhaps, those other super- universes with their respected local universes have been completed and are waiting for the completion of Orvonton, the seventh segment we belong to.

Urantia also revealed that the central universe of Havona is expanding its periphery one space level at a time in support of the entropic model of existence and in the overall scheme of things we are barely in the stage of completing the first outer space level, out of four others that are awaiting further organization. In other words, all creations from the central universe (celestial) to the super universe level (etheric) and down to the local universes (material) with their trillions of planets exist within the periphery of the first space level in circumference to the always existing spheres of the Havona system. This tells us that the organization of energy-matter is taking place one outer space level at a time. This is the same esoteric concept regarded as the ring pass not, which is equivalent to one universal round of Involution (Descending) and evolution (Ascending).

As revealed by Urantia, we are at the completion of the first space level and are waiting to once again begin the next round of extension in the second outer space level from the ALWAYS EXISTENT grand central universe.

As far as the three outer space levels are concerned, they are waiting to be organized and inhabited by intelligence that is ascending in this universal round. As for now, those three outer space levels are unorganized with no life forms, however upon the completion of Orvonton the last of the seven super universes, we will begin a new universal round as everything begins again from the purest levels in a new cycle in the second outer space level surrounding the always existing spheres of Havona and all its sanctified worlds of evolutionary completion.

Now since we are barely in the end stage of completing our first outer space level, then we are perhaps in the beginning phase of a process that will probably be infinite, since there is no end to numbers. Even the completion of the first level seemed like an eternity. This cosmic expansion is an infinite process, as we further expand into the outer levels of the infinite void, what an adventure. It is absurd to think that this world, galaxy, or universe was it and that there is a black hole at

the center of all galaxies. Only now as we enter a new age with a new understanding, will a higher cosmology emerge through the synthesis of spirituality, philosophy, and science which would promote eternal life, HEAVEN ON EARTH.

As a reminder, and for the correction of facts, modern-day human beings are descendant immortal light beings, which have always existed in the celestial spheres of the Great Central Sun. And since our entire existence is eternal, for it has never had a beginning nor will it ever have an end, it would only evolve into greater and greater manifestations of itself as we continue to further expand outward taking with us the infinite light of our creator onward. What is important to understand is that we are all connected and part of the same universal body of light and everything from the universal, to the human, to the atom, has a focal point of energy, a central sun. The human being, in fact, is the ultimate middle point, between the manifestation of the grand macro cosmos and the small micro, particles, thus uniting both sides of the spectrum. And since there is no end to light, then there is no end to energy-matter. For as long as there is light energy, there will always be matter. Now, since we are on the topic of better understanding our cosmos, it is my honor to also share another restored higher spiritual cosmology that will help us understand the meaning of the number twelve.

In the Urantia material, all universes and divine orders of sonship are signified by the number seven. Also, it is vital to understand, that the Urantia material was commissioned by a collaborated group of higher bits of intelligence or divine personalities that exist and operate from the central universe of Havona, the super universe levels, and down to the higher worlds that oversee the development and evolution of the lower planetary worlds. In addition, it has also been brought to my attention that the Urantia material is only 49 percent accurate, however, the concept of cosmos is correct.

Therefore, let it be understood that according to the guide of the high spirit, the information revealed in this material is only pertaining to the true aspect of the Urantia papers. The other 61 percent that is incorrect is not shared in this material.

In this next account of cosmology, the information revealed was restored to the earth by the overseer and divine administrator of our own local universe, Lord Michael.

In esoteric scriptures, Lord Michael is one of five COSMIC LORDS and one of twelve celestial adepts. According to his restored record, the Yanihian script, he is adept at the Klusian solar ray of power and rulership that oversees the twelfth universe of God.

According to this cosmology, our earth exists in the twelfth major universe extending from the central core universe known as the universe of the godhead, which has always existed without beginning or end.

The Universe of the Godhead is an eternal existence like the grand central universe, without beginning or end. It is the abode of our celestial parents.

The first universe that extends outwards from this central core is known as the universe of beauty, and it's attributed to the first of five cosmic lords the first solar adept, the firstborn of Heaven our eldest brother, and the greatest of the sons of God, Lord Jesus. As the firstborn in heaven, everything came through his ray essence. He is the adept and holder of the first cosmic ray known as the Atruhm silver ray of unconditional love and beauty. It is this cosmic ray that permeates and holds all other cosmic rays by virtue of unconditional love and purpose.

It is also the most powerful ray in existence, for it is the first ray to extend from the core as the essence of all unconditional love. In this universe, only planets of exquisite beauty exist. There is only one solar system and it is relatively a small universe with only a few hundred inhabited worlds. By virtue of being adept at the first cosmic ray, Jesus is the Lord of all the first solar planes in each succeeding universe. He is also known as our oldest brother and king of all celestial beings.

The second universe extending from the God source, surrounding the central core is known as the universe of women. The overseer and adept of this universe is known as Mariya the second born of heaven and that is why this universe was attributed to women only. Mariya is also known as God's eternal companion who acts as the focal point of power for the sacred divine feminine and it's governed by the second cosmic ray of wisdom (Sophia).

In the universe of women only, the love side (feminine) of God exists to its fullest degree. In the "Keys of Enoch," this is known as the Shekinah Universe, which also corresponds to the Bride of Yahweh our heavenly father according to the Kabala (the secret knowledge of the western mystics).

The third universe is known as the universe of men; it is the universe of intellectual pursuits, for only the masculine aspect of God exists there. The overseer and ruler of this universe were known as Lord Samana before he fell from grace and became the father of all historical Lucifer-like beings. It was this prideful son of God that rebelled against the ongoing creation of the Godhead and therefore became the universal archetype Lucifer, the adversary of God. According to the "Yanihian" manuscript, Samana became the catalyst of the darknoncosmicc ray of Colodhon that streamed throughout all creation, causing the fall and destruction of many worlds. Nonetheless, in the fourth universe, both the feminine love aspect of the godhead and the masculine intellectual aspect of the godhead come together as one. It was in the fourth universe where both the feminine and masculine or the love and intellectual aspects of the godhead first came into balance and balance is really at the root of all democracies as it is governed by the fourth cosmic ray.

The fifth universe is known as the great silent universe and it was governed by the fifth cosmic ray. There were no sounds only thoughts and everything was conducted by the power of pure thinking in this creation. For instance, in this universe, everything a person thought of instantaneously manifested and that is why it was known as the great silent universe. The next universe is known as the universe of the little people. It was in this universe, that all fairies, gnomes, and salamander aka nature spirits had their origin and it is governed by the sixth cosmic ray.

The seventh universe, known as the universe of mathematical science, was given solely to the pursuit of all universal mathematics as to why math is a universal language across all universes and is governed by the seventh cosmic ray. Then came the eighth universe, which was known as the great laboratory of God. It was in this universe, that all the cosmic rays were put into experimentation. It was also recorded that Jesus the firstborn in heaven and greatest adept of all, had visited this universe in order to console the people, due to the tremendous experimentation of the cosmic rays that were taking place there, making it extremely challenging for the intelligence that lived there.

In fact, everything we have come to know about all sciences, from the superluminal to the metaphysical and physics derived from the experiments and observations conducted in this universe. This universe was one macro experimentation of the cosmic rays and was governed by the eighth cosmic ray. Let it be known that we see a pattern here unfolding in each and succeeding creation.

By observation of this formation, we can conclude that everything has a harmonious order to it. For instance, the first cosmic ray laid the fundamental essence, for all the creations. This essence was unconditional love. So, in a chain of creations (extension), or expansion universal love was the primary ingredient that sustained and acted as an underlying field (essence) behind all the other rays. With the second ray, the experience is only concern with universal unconditional love that is all nurturing as the feminine aspect of the godhead or the feminine side of the great silver son Jesus the Christ.

In the third universe, we see only the development of the mind that corresponds to the development of the male side of the silver son represented by Lord Samana. Then in the fourth universe, the birth of democracy, we see the two aspects come together in perfect balance as the feminine and masculine begin to coexist as two aspects of the same whole. So now that we have a balance and coexistence of the Love's heart (feminine) and mind (male) intellectual of the one ray, then we begin to understand the power of thoughts as they deal directly with what we experience. From exploring the power of thoughts, we realize that everything in existence, all shapes, patterns, and geometries that make up existence, begin in the mental plane.

In the sixth universe, we experience life on a micro level as we learn to work together in order to maintain the beauty of all nature, as we blend with our environment. Now in the seventh universe, we can begin to explore the mathematics of the patterns created in the universe of thought-forms. After we understand the precession and laws of these creations, through mathematics then we begin to experiment with all its properties in the great laboratory of God in the eighth universe. What we are seeing here is an unfolding that takes place one step at a time.

After the creation of the eighth universe comes the ninth universe in which all of creation is devoted to the worship of its creator. This universe is governed by the ninth cosmic ray. The Tenth universe became known as the universe of theology where everyone becomes ardent students of the God subject and this universe was governed by the tenth cosmic ray. After the universe of theology fallows, the eleventh universe is known as the universe of mechanics where all technology had its origin and it is governed by the eleventh cosmic ray. The final universal creation in this cosmology of twelve is known as the twelfth universe of compassion and it's governed by the twelfth cosmic ray.

According to "The Yanihian script", all universes have returned to the great central core of their origin. That is all universal extensions from the first universe of Lord Jesus to the eleventh universe have returned (ascended) back to its parent source and the only one left is the vast universe of compassion, which is the twelfth universe we belong to. Nevertheless, the last unvastse of compassion is now ready to ascend like the other universes and that is why the last battle, or may we say, the final resolution between duality is now coming to an end here in our world, as revealed by the higher bits of intelligence and as confirmed by the ancient prophesies.

It is important to understand that every single universe contributed to the existence of its successor. For instance, in seeing this unfolding as a building construct, we could say that the essence and existence of the first universe gave birth to the next universe as if the first universe acted as a layer to the second one. This in turn occurred for each succeeding universe as each one inherited the cosmic ray of the previous one and every new universe inherited its own cosmic ray as well. Every universe had the same solar planes and solar systems of its indicated number.

For example, our universe the last creation inherited all the cosmic rays prior to its creation, however, its primary ray was known as the Klusian ray of power and rulership. According to this revelation, our earth's sun is known as the twelve solar planets within the Twelve Universe of Compassion containing all the essences and properties of every existing universe prior to its creation. This explains why our solar system and our planet earth have been a source of great value in the entire twelve creations. The twelfth major creation known as the universe of compassion has a purpose and it is to achieve the ultimate compassion within every living soul who resides in it. Also, it is important to add that every living soul that came to live in the twelve universes had its origin as it was born out of the breath of God in the second and third universes.

In retrospect, the first universe was dedicated to the great silver son; the first-born in Heaven, (Jesus), and all beings were as pure as his essence. The living souls which were born of the breath of God in the second and third universes were the same souls that proceeded in their involution (descent) in the following universes as each universe was governed by its own particular ray, which provided all of God's descending children with a new experience each time they would come into a new creation under a new ray as each ray would afford them the opportunity to explore a different (aspect) wavelength of the ONE pure light essence.

According to this cosmology, all souls came to be born out of the breath of their parents for sex did not exist until the last creation, the twelve universes when the vibrations lowered into the eighth, seventh, sixth, fifth, fourth, and eventually third dimensions.

This was primarily since all beings from the first universe to the eleventh were etheric and were capable of reproducing by combining essences, coupled with focused thought-form and collectively intending the child of their union into existence. This is the same way each universe and all our creator's original children (us) were firstborn in spiritual essence. In addition, in each universe, all souls become endowed with the same creative powers of the Godhead, as we were made in the similitude and likeness of our creator, thus validating the modern-day concept of the holographic universe as postulated by the latest research in quantum physics. Eventually, as each universe returned to its prime source as the ascension process took effect, the souls would graduate from that ascended universe and continue in their experience in new creations until they reached the last creation, the twelve universes, thus completing their total descension, in the revolutionary and evolutionary process.

It has been revealed by Lord Michael, that the twelve universes being the largest of all the other universes is ready to come home and the last one to ascend and that explains the resolution coming into fruition in our world in these glorious times, where heaven is scheduled to materialize on earth. The process of creation, however, does not end there it only marks the completion of the seventh super universe as revealed by the Urantia material. And for the record, let it be known that all souls born into the last creation (extension) of the seventh super universe were endowed with all the twelve cosmic rays as to why we have twelve overall chakras systems or energy centers. Each major chakra (energy center) is in direct relation to one of the twelve living major universes.

We have seen two different cosmological accounts of our cosmos. According to the Urantia material, we live in the local universe of Nebadon. In turn, the local universe of Nebadon is one out of a multitude of local universes existing side by side within the domain of the seventh super universe segment WHICH IS 1/7 of the entire Havona system, or Meta-Verse Grand central universe. In comparison to the cosmology account of "Yanihan Script", which reveals the existence of twelve universes all emanating from the central core universe, which one would be the most accurate one? In order to understand the sacredness of the seven and twelve, we must understand the patterns that shaped our world. Looking at within the records of all sacred traditions it has been known by most adepts, mystics, and saints, that the numbers seven and twelve are the most sacred numbers, as they are related to one another.

We can see this repeating pattern in almost everything. For instance, God created the heavens and the earth in seven days. There are seven days a week, as there are seven levels of initiation in the ascension process as there are seven major chakras. Not to mention according to the secret doctrine there are seven evolutionary cycles of civilizations, corresponding to the seven evolving root races of our planet. Now for the sacred number twelve, they're our twelve astrological houses in our galaxy known as the Zodiac. There are twelve tribes of Israel. Jesus had twelve apostles. There were twelve Knights of the Round Table in the courts of Camelot. Etc. Not to mention in our original makeup, we had twelve functioning chakras as there are twelve strands of DNA, however, the other five chakras are located outside our body.

In a comparison of these two cosmologies, seven and twelve are sacred numbers, as they pertain to the overall creation of the Godhead.

Although, let's not forget about three which is perhaps the most important number. One thing to understand is that our OMNIVERSE operates in perfect order, and that order is reflected in all things, as there are different aspects, extensions, and manifestations of the one God-source, all functioning together as different parts of the same whole. Therefore, we may say that perhaps in the great beginning, there was only one single undivided whole as there still is at the highest point of existence or in its primal state. This state of existence could also be classified as the unqualified absolute or primal virgin birth of the cosmos.

So, in the expansion of this whole unqualified absolute, the first step was to first divide into three as three become the first underlying pattern to all creations. This was the initial step in the creation, expansion, involution, and evolution of all universes.

This first division also gave us the concept of the trinity or as stated in the Urantia material, the Paradise Trinity was born in which everything comes from, including our Christian trinity.

In this process, as the one became the three, we begin to see this pattern first in the three major planes of existence, celestial-spiritual: etheric-mental and material physical. From a macrocosmic level, we see the trinity as the central universe, the super universes, and the local universes. From a local universe level, we see it as, galactic, solar and planetary. At a personal level, the spirit,t, mind, and body make up the human being, which is the last and final extension of the Godhead. First God the (whole) ONE becomes the three, and then it divides into seven. The seven mighty Elohim, the seven archangels, the seven super universes. Etc

So bear in mind that this is the same substance (unqualified absolute) now divided into seven aspects of itself. Most importantly let it be understood as validated by both quantum physics and metaphysical science, that there is only one immeasurable force with innumerable parts, as a photon is both a wave and particle at the same time. So in tracing this back to the great beginning at the time of the great unfolding, first there was God the one fold and then came God the threefold as the trinity, and then God the sevenfold, and since everything is divided from the one, there is no separation only expansion for we are dealing with the same energy field, same light energy expressing itself in different forms and parts, the MANY and the ONE, the ONE and the MANY.

Also, as the trinity divides (involution-descent) into seven parts, it preserves the trinity in each part, for each master spirit in each super universe is also composed

OUR COSMIC ORIGIN

as a trinity as there are three ancient days for each of the seven super universes.

After the expansion (division) into the seventh super universes the great godhead (unqualified absolute) from the one to the threefold, to the seventh fold, was now ready to begin its experience in the outer realms of the first space level to become God the twelve-fold thereby explaining the twelve major universes perhaps emanating from each super universe, each acting as one-seventh of the whole Multi-Verse-Central eventuated always existing spheres.

From a holographic perspective, we may now safely conclude that each super universe is an exact replica of the already existing Central Universe-Meta-Verse. That indicates that each Super Universe extension acted as its own central core evolving twelve major creations and innumerable minor ones, down to the billions of galaxies. At twelve, in each super universe the one immeasurable source, which is one-seventh of the whole, has now broken off into twelve separate aspects of itself. And as the three is inherited in the seven and as each seven carries the property of three, then this means that in the twelve, there are also properties of three's and sevens as there are three overall planes of existence, seven major chakras in our body system and five minor ones, thus making it twelve, all interrelate with one another.

Let's sum it up. The one first divides in three, and then into seven then twelve, as each further dividend, carries the whole of the entire central original universe. This tells us also that the inherent property or blueprint for all life that exists is generated from the inner core of all that is. Just like our own cells in our bodies follow a genetic blueprint based on a central control program, known as DNA-RNA. This tells us that everything in existence is propelled by an inert intelligence that by far exceeds our comprehension, as we use only 6 percent of our full capacity. According to the new findings, the entire cosmos is influenced by a cosmic DNA central control program. Considering this we may conclude that everything in existence is dancing to the tune of our UNIVERSAL ARTICHECT (GOD) who is always in control of all things and in all its extension (creations). Most importantly, this concept validates the idea that everything in existence has a purpose and that there are no accidents.

After viewing that three, seven, and twelve are inherent traits in all creations, we

68

can now comprehend why the new physics suggests that indeed everything is holographic in nature as every aspect of existence is reflected in everything else. So we can conclude that all of existence is orchestrated by the same patterns which all stem from primal sources that first dividing into three, then seven, and then finally the twelve or at least in our universal extension and that explains why our galactic systems within the twelve major creation are further divided by twelve parts, the Zodiac.

Now in an attempt at bridging the two different cosmologies that have been restored back to our world by the higher emissaries, we may conclude that there only exists, one great overall central universe (Meta-verse) with no end and no beginning, as proposed by the new science. Second, by applying the analogy of the primal sacred number, this great cosmic universe is first divided into three levels of itself. This is known as the peripheral, nether, and upper paradise of the celestial spheres, as indicated in the Urantia material. Then the great central universe becomes seven central universes all reflecting seven parts of the one grand central one. So, thinking in terms of a holographic picture, if we cut it in seven pieces it becomes seven entire pictures, all reflecting the same whole perhaps in different positions. That means that each super universe reflects as a central universe with no beginning or end just as in the case of the already existing Central/Havona spheres.

Since we are part of the seventh aspect known as the sexes even supervises of Orvonton and since the twelfth is the next dividend, this seventh central universe (Orvonton) now begins to divide into twelve. So perhaps could it be that the Twelve Universes of God revealed in the "Yanihian Script", are part of one of seven central core creations, all different components or segments of the grand central core of all that is. This implies that each super-universe creation has its own central core and Godhead.

So, to integrate these two cosmologies, we could say then that we are one major universal creation (extension) of seven super universal creations, each with its own core center and twelve major creations. Each core center is like a cosmic central sun to each extending creation as to why there is a central sun on every level, all the way down to the solar systems of planets. In turn, each cosmic sun is one of seven expressions of the one grand central cosmic sun that acts as a nucleus that lies at the center of all that is. This central hub is known as the Isle of Paradise.

It's equally important to know that it is only at the level of super universes that the great experiment in time and space begins. For it has been revealed, that at the highest level of the grand central universe, there is no time or space. This condition has always existed for the grand central universe and of course, it continued to exist even after the grand central universe first divided into seventh segments, becoming the central core of the seven super universes.

Now in remembering the descending and refraction of pure light substance, it was at the point of first dividing into seven, where the extension of the light source of pure energy began its experiment into measurable time and space. In quantum physics today, this is like how the singular white light is refracted through the prism to reflect the seven colors of the rainbow. So in the case of our creation, time begin (the great descent) at the moment the central core universe became the seven fragments of seven cosmic rays, thus beginning its experiment into the great void, therefore creating alpha and omega into a completing cycle that became known as one universal round.

In the case of our creation round, it was the twelve major universes of compassion that marked the end of this experiment in the cosmic grand time cycle, of the seventh super universe of Orvonton. According to the Urantia papers, the super universe of Orvonton is incomplete. Perhaps, the ascension of the twelve major creations marks the completion of the super universe of Orvonton.

So in review of the Urantia material with the "Yanihian Script", we can postulate that there are twelve major universes in our seventh segment, however only pertaining to the seventh super universe of Orvonton, but in actuality, there are a total of eighty-four organized major universes (12 times 7) in number with millions of local minor universes existing in different segments of the grand central omniverse.

This cosmology of higher evolution is now evidently being confirmed by the revolutionary scientific concept of a multi-verse cosmology, which slowly is now been accepted in our scientific community. In fact, LISA (laser interferometry satellite antenna) has concrete data scientifically confirming the existence of multiple universes. As mentioned, in our world these days, the concept of multi-universes has become a hot topic within the leading scientific discoveries, particularly in the realm of M- Theory, Superstring theory, gravity quantum theory, and Unified Field theory.

As mentioned, Urantia only references the seventh super universe of Orvonton, without much information on the other sixth super universes. Maybe we are only to be concerned with our own super universe until its completion, which is underway. As for

the other super universe, have their own celestial host of creator sons and daughters of light, who are by the way the celestial family, brothers, and sisters of our creator son, Lord Michael. These other sons and daughters of light govern and direct the cosmic force of universal power for our UNIVERSAL father of the grand central spheres at the level of local universes within the time-space continuum.

They are collectively known as creator sons/daughters and are the descending sons and daughters of light. According to the Urantia material, they originated in Paradise and were the offspring of the first union experience of the universal father and universal mother, who produced the first family of light, beginning with the five cosmic Lords and their offspring before the beginning of any time as we know it.

These descending sons and daughters of light were given absolute power and dominion over their time-space creations, the local universes, which there are millions of them in the entire grand central spheres. When the time came each creator's son/daughter was endowed not only with the same divine attributes as their parents in paradise but were descending in pairs providing a balance between the feminine and masculine aspect of the universal God force. It turns out that each creator's son had a wife or twine flame that reflected the feminine aspect of the paradise trinity within the local domains of the local universe since each fragment contains the essence of the whole.

For instance, in our last major creation and particularly in our local universe of Nebadon, Lord Michael has a complementary partner that governs our creation with him. According to ancient esoteric studies, it is believed that Lord Michael's heavenly concert and feminine side is known as Michaella or Faith. This lady Goddess is the loving side of Lord Michael and at the highest level of existence, they are considered one androgynous being, as all twin flames are. All creation reflects both duality and singularity. It just so happens that living in the lowest vibration of the spectrum we only perceive the duality state.

In conclusion, let it be known that ultimately there is only one universal source known as the supreme absolute (prime creator) and that everything has stemmed from this one source. The Omniverse or as science now calls Meta-verse is one body animated by one great macro spirit, and by virtue of its holographic nature, it is important to know that everything in existence is an extension and part of

this great living universal force that many call spirit. It is everywhere at once (unified field) and it is in everything. For nothing will ever and has never existed outside of this all-encompassing energy source. It is the true spiritual meaning of monotheism, as this one spirit source permeates all of existence as it is omnipresent (everywhere at once) omnipotent (all-powerful), and omniscient (all-knowing) existing in everything all at once.

Whether we see it as the force of "Star Wars" or the unified field theory of everything in science, or chi-prana in eastern metaphysics, or the Holy Spirit in western theology, it is describing the same phenomena, that we are all a part of, the living spirit of God, or primal source.

In review, we have witnessed that there is a great cosmic pattern unfolding throughout all of the existence celestial, etheric, and material. With this in mind, we can therefore conclude that the great central Godhead of all creation has endowed all his creation with the same creative abilities and characteristics of its original self in each single one of us. Mankind in general is the final extension (descension) of our creator's light and our purpose is to reflect the entire whole within us, therefore making us co-creators with our creator source. The time for us to recognize who we really are draws near.

This is the opportunity that is being offered at this time in our world as our planet ascends into higher dimensions of refined spiritual matter.

We live in an Omniverse or Meta-verse, holographic existence which is first divided into three than seven, then twelve, and then one hundred and forty-four, and so on. And even though there are multiple universes and worlds all evolving parallel to each other, we must remember that they are still connected and part of the Grand Central spheres, like different aspects of the whole cosmic umbrella. We are all part of one grand cosmic experience all inter-connected and all evolving as one macro living entity at the highest level. In fact, based on the new evidence, human beings are like trillions of cells coexisting together in these omnivores as cells are in our human body, FOR ALL EXISTENCE IS ONE.

# CHAPTER SIX

## ALL UNIVERSES AND CREATIONS OPERATE ACCORDING TO UNIVERSAL LAWS AND ARE GOVERNED BY MULTIPLE, CELESTIAL, ETHERIC AND MATERIAL ADMINISTRATIONS (councils) OF LIGHT THAT HAS BEEN SET UP BY THE GREAT GODHEAD (primal Source) OF ALL CREATION

Since we are now familiar with a higher understanding of cosmology and the different levels of its expression, we can now begin to understand just how there have been planetary governments in our third-dimensional world, there have also been, cosmic and celestial governments in the higher realms (worlds) dimensions which in fact are more effective than those governments in our third-dimensional world.

In fact, these cosmic-celestial councils are multileveled operating from the always existing realms of the mother central spheres, which is one. Its celestial organization is manifested on all levels of the cosmos down to the many organized universes and their galactic domains.

For the physical universes which occupy most of the material realms, including some of the 90 percent of the dark matter, there have been established divine orders at the center of all galaxies validating the central sun theory. AS IS THE CASE WITH EVERYTHING in the grand central spheres (Metaverse).

Therefore, all organized galaxies that are part of the grand cosmic organization of our prime creator are being governed from the great central sun where the galactic council of guardianship resides. From the great central sun of all galaxies, the great councils of light expand their protection to all the billions of solar systems by establishing smaller councils of light that oversee constellations, multiple solar systems down to planetary systems.

Everything in existence whether in a state of spirit, mental or physical embodiment, is governed and controlled by the great Godhead of the paradise trinity. It is the first source and center which acts as the grand council control center or COSMIC DNA PROGRAMER in which everything follows. That is why the Godhead as supreme absolute, is forever pulsating its light source to all its creation initiating its divine order in which the cosmos expands. This way, everything down to the material creations would dance to the tune of our Universal architect.

The great cosmic celestial councils (government) as revealed, is manifold because it encompasses all dimensions, all realms, all realities, and all levels of existence. At the highest levels, it is one great functioning vehicle that operates in harmony at every level down to the planetary spiritual councils because it is all driven by the same universal principles. For example, it is the structure in which the great universal architect is able to experience and administrate to all of his/her creation all the way down to the planetary worlds in the material realms in a way a president in a corporation, is able to administer his organization by setting up different men to act

on his behalf all the way down to a manager of a store. Now it is important to know that, unlike a closed hierarchy that resembles that of a dictatorship, the cosmic celestial hierarchy was designed for all its creation, including all beings to ascend and reach higher and greater levels. That is the difference between a closed dictatorial hierarchy and one that is based on the equality of all in the different levels or planes of existence.

As mentioned, in the previous chapter, the highest celestial order of existence is known as the Eternal of Days, which governs and controls all operations of the Grand Central eternal spheres and its nucleus is the isle of Paradise.

Together and acting as one body, the paradise trinity acts as the core nucleus to all existing hierarchies (councils) of all universes within the great Omnivore, Meta-Verse by setting up the cosmic archetypal blueprint of the Holy Trinity for all heads of councils to follow. In fact, every hierarchy (celestial administration) or council is an exact replica of its previous one and acts in unison as if it were the previous hierarchy governing that realm. So, in that regard, we may say that the isle of paradise is the core body of the Eternal of days, the first celestial administration that has always existed. Following the rule of the Eternal of days comes the order of the Ancient of Days. The order of the Ancient of Days is administrated by the seven master spirits or the seven mighty Elohim as revealed in our bible. Each master spirit makes up the core of the order of the Ancient of days who represent the order of Eternal of Days at the etheric super universe level.

Also, it is important to understand that each master spirit is one-seventh of the godhead and therefore each one inherits the same cosmic duties and attributes of the first source and center as if each master spirit was the great Godhead, providing even further proof of our holistic existence.

Therefore, each supreme master spirit acts as an exact replica of the supreme deity source and administrates its segment super-universe domain as if it were the great architect God the absolute, the one-fold, or three-fold. Perhaps each master spirit is a holistic representation of prime creator source, on seven distinct levels. In this case, it goes from God the threefold to God the seven-fold as each master spirit with his own trinity continues the great divine plan that originated with the supreme creator at the center of our always existing central spheres.

Therefore, from the moment of the great descend, the great divine plan was meant to reach, every level of existence or kingdom down to the lower dust worlds where it was intended to culminate in our times today as our planet ascends into higher dimensions, HEAVEN ON EARTH. In light of this, it is important for the human kingdom (us) to represent and anchor the great divine plan of divinity into the lower dimensions in order to bring the kingdom of eternal light to the lower regions, as planned in the higher spheres. The whole purpose of our collective celestial descent into matter, was so that we light beings could anchor the living light of our creator into the lower regions as each and every single one of us carries the entire essence of the creator source in the lower dimensions.

Also, within the establishment of the celestial administrations of light, there are innumerable celestial personalities that are assisting the great cosmic divine plan without going through the process of incarnating into lower-dimensional vehicles. It is believed that there are multiple orders of seraphim in the cosmos.

At this point, we may begin to conceive the existence of the many cosmic, archangelic, and angelic beings and the multiple levels and aspects of their service. The highest level of known angels is known as the supernaphim who are considered the highest order of servers, perhaps serving within the orders of the Eternal and Ancient of days.

We also have the Seconaphim, the Seraphim, and Teritariphim, the Ophanim, the list goes on. Just as there are many levels of existence there are also various levels of angelic services all working together to bring about the plans of the one celestial architect, prime creator. It is important to also understand, that all supernaphim and seraphim are functionaries of the second celestial order of days, the Ancient of Days. In truth, it is important to distinguish between the two categories of descending light beings.

According to the higher knowledge, it is revealed that the original beings became known as children and offspring of the paradise trinity, the great family of light, the forerunners of all human ancestors. However not all descending light beings partake in the incarnational process some, in fact, remain in the etheric realms in order to assist those of us who might have forgotten unity consciousness when we so choose to participate in the incarnation process of encasing in a physical form.

Therefore, the Supernaphim, Seraphim, Seconaphim as well as the high trinity celestial personalities were design to assist us, the descending sons and daughters of light, involved in the involution (incarnational) process. Those of us that did incarnate in the material realms are known as free will descending light beings. Those that didn't incarnate gave up their free will to serve our creator as guardians and servants of the many realms. There are those who watch and there are those who experience. Nevertheless, whether we incarnate or operate from the higher spheres, we are all children of light that descent from the grand celestial spheres into lower realms (worlds) of ether and congealed energy-matter and are all working together for the greater good of all that is.

Equally important to understand is that at each level of existence, each creator logos operates with the same creative powers as its parent logos. In this case, the great Ancient of days who resides at the center (core) of our super universe of Orvonton is known as the great central sun (supra universal logos) in which the main twelve experimental universes spring from evolving out of the twelve great cosmic rays which are generated by our super universe creator in Uverse, the capital sphere of Orvonton.

U-verse according to the Urantia revelation is the core sun and capital headquarters of the entire super universe domain of Orvonton and it is the nucleus producing all circuits and conditions required for the development of our super universe segment. Now if we take this further down to the level of material realms local universes, we may say that our creator son Michael is known as one of the twelve logos (creator sons) and is the logos of our local universe domain.

Further down, each galaxy in Nebadon has its own logos correlating to its central administration with its own nucleus (central sun). In each galactic system, we have a galactic logo or council that administrates the affairs of our galaxy from the central sun. In each galaxy, there are billions of local sun logos (solar systems) with planets revolving around them. Not to mention all the trillions of planetary logos, that exist in the entire cosmic domain of our Central mother spheres.

At the planetary level, the logos and physical representation of planets is known as the iron crystal core or the inner sun at the center of all planets. From the bottom up, all planetary logos are in turn working and dancing to the tune of their respective solar logos. In turn, all solar logos dance to the tune of their respective galactic logos who in turn dance to the tune of their respective universal logos, who then in turn dance to the tune of its super universe logos, who finally dance to the tune of the Grand central Logos.

In this case, all administrations act in unison and are connected to each other through their central suns (through the law of resonance) who are of one universal body and core. Now bear in mind, that these suns or inner sun of planets are only physical representatives of the actual planetary administrations or spiritual hierarchy who are known as the masters of light. They operate from the 12 dimensions down to the seventh as in the case of our planetary spiritual hierarchy of ascending masters, (earth angels). In this regard, all suns and cores (inner suns) are just focal points of pure energy emission fostering and administrating the cosmic rays, which these light beings from the unseen realms use to direct the affairs of any planet or any given star or galactic system.

We may conclude that within the domain of our super universe of Orvonton, Lord Jesus in tandem with his other eleventh brethren collectively makes up what is known as the grand council of twelve. The council of twelve is an existing body of twelve creator sons/daughters who work together as a cosmic administration guiding everything towards the divine upward spiritual evolution of all in the twelve living universes, including all of its galaxies who are evolving into the image of the higher cosmic evolution, grand central eternal spheres.

The celestial command known as the council of twelve operates on behalf of the cosmic paradise trinity, the order of Eternal of days and the Order of the Ancient of Days, of the super universe governments.

As mentioned, the first creator son in the twelve-universe system is Lord Jesus who was the firstborn from our Ancient of Days becoming the administrator of the greatest cosmic ray, the first ray known as the Atruhm (Radium) ray.

As mentioned in the previous chapter, this ray under the sonship of the Great Silver Son the firstborn of heaven is the sustainer of the first solar plane which came forward at the emanation of the first major universe creation. This explains why all great Christian mystics and adepts have referred to Jesus as our eldest brother, the firstborn of heaven, and the king of all angels.

The next overseer and adept of the council of twelve and adept of the second ray is known as, Lord Ahmenhah ruler of the Bhamba yellow ray of sight. Lord Ahmenhah is the second born of heaven and is also lord of the second solar plane. Next in divine birth is Lord Ithuriel who is adept at the third cosmic ray, known as the Gloinhiam ray controlling the green Crisneth power of natural growth. After Lord Ithuriel is Lady Mariya the fourth born, overseer of the universe of women and adept of the Sekht solar plane, the fourth solar plane, controlling the Hakhanh Scarlet Ray of Mysticism. Notice that each cosmic ray is characterized by color as in the chakra systems. After Lady Mariya comes Lord Makhumsih, adept of the Granhisiam solar plane, the fifth controlling the golden ray of creativity.

Then comes Lord Mlyhyhia adept of the Corb indigo ray of cosmic knowledge and lord of the sixth solar plane. The Next Lord serving the cosmic hierarchy of the council of twelve is Lord Arhura controller of the Amethyst ray of Perfume and serves as Lord of the seventh solar plane.

After lord Ahura comes Lord Rahaal who is adept and keeper of the Numhiam solar plane, the eighth. He is Lord of the Lukhanic Ray, aka the medical ray, which is the roots of all medical sciences, he is also known as Archangel Rafael in religious lore. After lord Rahaal comes to lord Aahnahtah, adept and keeper of the Motsumh ray of magnetism. This ray is characterized by the deep royal blue color and it deals directly with heat, electricity, and magnetism.

The tenth adept of the great council of twelve is lord Kahana of the tenth solar plane known as the Kransha plane that controls the Grinhilam Ray, a pale blue ray that deals directly with all records and keeps track of everything in all the universes.

This lord is known as the recording lord and therefore deals also with foresight and is the central pillar for the restoration of the office of the Christ and eldership at the coming of the celestial council of twelve. He is the overseer and protector of the great akashic records of all time.

The eleventh adept is lord Azrahaehl of the eleventh solar plane controlling the Bakh solar plane which is the dark green ray of art, music, and color. The final adept and member of the great council of twelve is Lord Michael who controls the twelve Klusian solar planes known as the Facnic ray of power and rulership.

These great adepts," the twelve", are the celestial board of directors who operate under the guidance and direction of the great ancient of days, our creator mother-Father of the super-universe administration known as U- verse, the core capital of the Super universe of Orvonton. Also, the administrative body collectively known as the council of Twelve or the celestial hierarchy consisting of twelve major universes is also known as the order of the Union of Days, which makes up the third great celestial order stemming from the previous two, Eternal of Days and Ancient of Days.

After the Order of the Union of Days, the council of twelve comes the universal council of the twenty-four elders who according to the Keys of Enoch, "Book of Knowledge, surround the throne of grace, of the Twelve and one. The council of the twenty-four elders is also known as the Order of the Perfections of Days, as described in the Urantia revelation which administrates the cosmic rays to all galaxies within all their local universes. Now according to the "Keys of Enoch", this order was set up by a cosmic being operating at the level of the Ancient of Days who is referred to as Lord Metatron.

This cosmic being is also known as the facilitator and engineer of the outer light (outer space circuits) in the outer realms of the outer space levels and works in tandem with the council of twelve as an Ancient of Days. In fact, he is part of the cosmic administration and works directly under Yahweh/Shekina, our Ancient of Days who are our universal parents within our super universe of Orvonton. After the twenty-four elders come lesser celestial orders like the council of 144 thousand who operate under the council of the twenty-four elders.

These lower orders under the council of 144 thousand have been assigned to administrate the lower heavens or material galactic systems, on behalf of the higher orders and collectively they are known as the great white sisterhood/brotherhood.

In general, all these ruling celestial bodies are known as the councils of light or councils of Elohim, plural for the many light beings and many offices of light.

In review, each major universe was given and co-created by one of the twelve sons and daughters of Yahweh, with Lord Jesus being the firstborn and the main chief architect in providing the purity of unconditional love power for all the universes of universes. It was his Atrium ray of silver light that set the foundation that began the entire twelve major universes and the twelve major solar systems and planes that act as power centers to each major universe, as chakras do for our human energy bodies (aura). .

Therefore, in understanding the spiritual administrations of the universal father-mother, the great ancient of days we must also understand the fall of Lord Samana who came before Lucifer. As mentioned earlier, the fallen angels disagreed with the plans of the great celestial architect, by opposing the expansion of light into the outer realms.

According to the restored "Yaniahian", manuscript, the battle to oppose the great divine plan didn't take place until the eleven universes of the mechanism were in progress. It was lord Samana who once was a great son of God overseer of the third universe of men that fell from grace. The story reveals, that lord Samana fell from his position as one of the original twelve, and apparently, he has been replaced by Lord Franchela Gabriel.

As revealed in the "Yanihian Script" this fallen lord become extremely disturbed when God who upon seeing two lads experimenting with natural growth in the underground without any solar rays, saw the ugliness of the fungi it produce, thereby declaring for the first time, something not of beauty and therefore not of light. According to the "Yanihian Script", this occurred in the third universe of men.

Since everything is made up of light (cosmic rays) we can see how, all living things, plants, animals, humans, celestials, etc. need to be nourished by the cosmic-solar rays, for they are the living light rays from the creator source, that provide us with nourishing universal life force energy. Apparently by, experimenting with growth with no sunlight, a fungus was born and that apparently didn't go well with our creator. The lads were reprimanded but this left Samana stained forever. Even, though this incident occurred in the third universe of men, it didn't take effect, however, until our Ancient of Days breathed in the eleven universes of mechanism.

As a result, it appears that all wars had their origin in the eleventh universe. Prior to the eleventh major universe, all universes from the first to the tenth universe of theology were peaceful and were all well settled in life and light. This means that Lord Michael had to deal with the outbreak from the moment God created the last universal extension in the seventh super universe segment. This incident is what is classified in the Urantia material as the Luciferian rebellion.

The concept of a high-ranking fallen light being is confirmed by all esoteric traditions, including all the great world religions. In Urantia, Lucifer became the leader of a group of fallen seraphim known as the Nonondedeks.

A Nonondodek son is one of three groups of descending light beings. The highest ranks are the Melchizedeks, and then comes the Lonondodeks who operate under the direction of the Melchizedeks, and finally the Nonondedeks who operate under the direction of the Lonondodeks. (See Urantia material for more info on these three orders of sonship).

As revealed by Urantia, not all the Nonondedeks rebelled but many of them did. The premise of the Luciferian rebellion was founded on a lie. A lie that Lucifer imprinted on the minds of the weaker angels (light beings).

The deception was the belief that Yahweh, the universal father, our great ancient of days was not real and therefore the plan to follow in his footsteps as laid down by his son Lord Michael was not worth working for.

This postulation aborted the ascension plans of all living sentient creatures and beings who were created to evolve in the image of our celestial parents. According to biblical scripture, Lucifer took one-third of the angels as followers.

At this point, it is important to understand that everything that occurs in the previous universe translates into the next one. So if fallen lord Samana began his exploitations in the eleventh universe (the universe of mechanism), then Samana's plan could have been translated directly into the last of the universe, the one that was to become the culmination of all twelve living universes.

What we do know, is that it has been recorded in our bible, that the battle against the forces of darkness has been led by archangel Michael without mention of the other previous universes. Since the rebellion against our creator's plan took effect at the beginning of the twelfth universe, it was Michael who challenged Lucifer and his legions in favor of God's plan, our universal father. For that reason, Michael became overshadowed by God's unlimited power and so he became the lord of the Facnic ray of power.

As overseer and adept of the twelfth creation, it was Michael's duty to secure the descension process of Man (descending spirit beings) and therefore was given the job and duty to restore the last major universe completing the grand masterpiece of the super universe of Orvonton.

This Facnic ray is the composition of all the other cosmic rays and its power comes from the point of pure compassion. It is Michael with his Klusian Facnic ray of power that protects and has been cleansing and restoring our creation, therefore capable of defeating the black non-cosmic ray of Colodhon, the dark stinging ray that becomes born at the onset of fallen Lord Samana.

For the record, we are part of the universe of compassion, the last of the twelve major creations and since the great cosmic trinity is seen in everything, we also see that everything is divided in three within this creation. So, as we take this and apply it to the universe we are a part of, we can say that our universe of compassion has an upper celestial region, middle etheric region, and a lower physical region where our earth hangs. We may also say that within this last creation, the biggest out of the twelve, there are sub universes and local galactic systems that we have come to know as galaxies and clusters of galaxies.

As revealed in the "Yanihian Script" there are twelve solar planes in the last major creation all inherited from the previous major universes. With this in mind, we may say that twelve is the patterned number of our current creation.

Celestial organization and heavenly administration did not stop there, however. There are lesser orders of days that are serving under the order of Lord Michael in each of the sub-local universal systems and galaxies.

Initially, each system was generated by love, willpower, and compassion as this reflects the characteristics and nature of the last major universe.

According to the Urantia revelation, the Luciferian rebellion only affected what is known as the system of satanic (please) which consists of a thousand worlds in which our earth is a part. Yet according to other revelations, the war against the forces of darkness encompassed our entire universe and many galaxies. The Urantia revelation also revealed that there were other rebellions again the light prior to the luciferin rebellion.

However, it doesn't mention rebellions in other local universes as there are about seven hundred thousand organized local universes.

Perhaps fallen Lord Samanas non cosmic ray of colophon set the grounds for certain lower orders of principalities to rebel against our creator source in multiple universes. This information was not revealed in the Urantia material. Therefore, it is my belief that fallen Lord Samana was the original Lucifer in a chain of many fallowers that also became rebellious against the living light.

Apparently, the great councils of creator sons and daughters, the twelve, agreed with the order of the Ancient of days. They all joined Michael and agreed that Lord Samama (Lucifer) was not to fully contaminate and plunder all the surrounding local universes and systems pertaining to the last major creation of compassion. So, they planned to limit the influence of Samana's scorching black non-comic ray from affecting the entire last major universal creation.

Therefore, the great order of the Union of Days, also known as the order of Melchizedek, was given the duty of repairing and securing our region known as Nebadon, which is a cluster of multiple galactic systems within the last major creation. However, after defeating fallen Lord Samana from the higher spheres of Nebadon, they extended this order further down reaching the galactic systems thus culminating in the great wars in heaven in our local region. Therefore, from the beginning of the celestial revolt, the armies of light known as the celestial command established themselves at the center of every galactic system within our local universe that had become contaminated by the non-cosmic dark scorching ray of Samana. This high celestial command, operating under the order of Melchizedek and under the direction of Lord Michael was conceived and so our epic cosmic battle of good and evil was born at which point the forces of light, initiated a plan, known as the Seal Of Paladar. The Seal of Paladar was a celestial covenant established by the descending armies of light that was used to restore the light in every aspect of the contaminated fallen galactic systems. The great universal order of Melchizedek under the leadership of Michael has collectively been known as the host of HEAVEN in our bible.

According to a higher intelligence that is now coming forward, the order of Melchizedek (the Union of Days) restored each galaxy one at a time beginning with the galaxies closest to Salvington, the headquarter sphere of our local universe of Nebadon in which our galaxy is a part of.

Due to the various galaxies that were affected by the non-cosmic black scorching ray of Colodhon-Samana, the restoration has been going on for about 38,000,000 million years (earth time).

It is believed that this battle ends in our current time, which marks the end of a grand cosmic cycle. This entire period was classified as the first celestial wars and they were fought for the control of our entire local universe of Nebadon. Not to mention other local universes, that joined the rebellion.

In a review of this segment, following the cosmic rebellion, it was imperative for the cosmic order of Melchizedek, the restorers and repairs of universes to establish certain galactic commands and councils that would maintain divine order in all of the galactic systems within the periphery of our local universe.

According to higher sources, the last of the galaxies to be restored before our own was the galactic system of Andromeda that also happens to be the closest one to our galaxy, the Milky Way.

In fact, some believe that the galaxy known as Andromeda has acted as a parent galaxy to our own Milky Way Galaxy. Our brethren from Andromeda are among some of the forces of light that have been helping in the ascension process of our galactic system, who according to the higher intelligence, is in the process of ascending now.

This means that the hosts of Michael have finally arrived and are preparing our planet (earth) for the restoration of the Office of the Christ (light) as it exists everywhere in the higher dimensions (heaven).

Furthermore, when the time came to seed our galaxy, the order of Melchizedek under the direction of Michael set out to establish their settlement of light in the star system known as Sirius.

The star system, Sirius, happens to be the closest star system to our galactic center, our galactic central sun (hanub-kub tzolkin, Kolob, (Ophyocus) which is where the original guardians of our galaxy were stationed as indicated in the movie Thor.

So by establishing their headquarters in the central sun of our galaxy and its chosen sector Sirius, the guardians of our galaxy were able to harness its power which is equivalent to the power of billions of suns, and in turn, overall control the fate of our galaxy as described by our cutting edge science. This was a smart move and a secured victory for the forces of light.

It is important to also understand that the entire cleansing has been conducted from the highest levels down to the lower levels within our own galaxy, as to why Sirius occupies the highest vibrations (dimensions) in our galaxy.

Therefore, the entire restoration of our galaxy has been one of a gradual process that has taken millions of earth years but really about a few days in the eyes of God.

In support of this information, according to all esoteric knowledge, it has been confirmed that in the early history of our galaxy, the Sirius Star system was where the great divine plan was stationed in order to be carried out through to the entire galaxy.

According to science, the Sirius star system has been known to be the brightest star in our Milky Way galaxy, its color being lapis blue. This is the color depicting the Klusian solar ray used by Lord Michael to restore light and life into the lower planes of our entire local universe. It has also been revealed by the higher knowledge that the origins of mankind in our galactic timeframe began around Sirius particularly in the star system of Vega, in the constellation known as Lyra.

It was there where Lord Michael planted his seed, his offspring that became known as the original line of all human races, in which the entire early human family originated before we began colonizing other parts of our galaxy. Now bear in mind that currently there is no record of this on earth yet but believe me in the records of other planets and in the records of the great central sun this information is public galactic knowledge. In addition, it has been revealed in the Keys of Enoch, The Book of Knowledge, that the office of the Christ which is the office of the everlasting kingdom of light (God) was first anchored in Sirius and so the great plan to restore our galactic system began there.

The office of the Christ is another term describing the overall command of the entire celestial administrations that originated

with Knowledge, that the office of the Christ which is the office of the everlasting kingdom of light (God) was first anchored in Sirius and so the great plan to restore our galactic system began there.

The office of the Christ is another term describing the overall command of the entire celestial administrations that originated with the order of the Eternal of days (the central eternal spheres) and the Ancient of days springing from the celestial spheres of the higher spiritual worlds that have eternally existed.

In summary, the order of Michael has also been known as the Union of Days and combined with all his brethren known as the cosmic order of Melchizedek. It is this great cosmic brotherhood/sisterhood, that consists of various celestial orders all working in tandem with the varied angelic orders who are all collectively called the great white brotherhood/sisterhood of the celestial, etheric, and galactic material commands.

Nonetheless, these great spiritual councils are orders that work simultaneously on the multiple planes and dimensions of the celestial, etheric and physical planes of all local universes. All these commands are set up on all levels and are organized by the overall command of the cosmic order of Melchizedek serving under the guidance and direction of the order of the Ancient of Days.

Now as we descend from refining matter into grosser materiality within our local universe there exist what is known in the secret knowledge as Galactic Confederations or Federations of planets. These have been developed by the order of Melchizedek to operate in the lower levels of reality within the galactic spheres, which are still realms higher than the third dimension. These galactic Confederations have been set up in every galactic system by the celestial councils to protect and serve the many galaxies and star systems. They are known as the galactic peacekeepers and in all cases, they have protected and served the mandate of Lord Michael for the galactic spheres of the material universes.

Therefore, it is my honor to reveal that our planet earth is being monitored and protected by what is known to some as the Space Command of the Galactic Federation of free worlds, or the Galactic Federation of light. And even though we have no knowledge of them yet, they have always monitored and intervened silently in our world affairs, throughout all history. Do remember they exist in a higher wavelength of light (reality) and even though we can't see them, they can see us. At times this higher intelligence has lowered their vibrational range to the third dimension and has allowed being seen by certain people. After all, according to the new scientific evidence, there exist millions of advanced space-age cultures, planetary, stellar and galactic systems known as populations one, two, and three.

One way in which these higher evolved beings make themselves known to us is through UFO sightings and crop circles. These are signs that the hosts of Heaven (galactic federation) are here preparing our planet for the ascension and restoration of the office of Christ as it exists everywhere now throughout our galaxy.

If you thought "Star Wars" was a fantasy make-believe story, well guess again, for there is a forgotten history regarding our connection to the multiple stars interplanetary, stellar, and galactic systems in our own galaxy and beyond.

Remember every star system is a sun with encircling planets. There are billions of burning suns alone in our Milky Way galaxy, one of the multiple galaxies, in multiple universes. We could say that we have been quarantined and isolated from not only the rest of our galaxy but from other galaxies as well. However, according to the great galactic prophecy of our Milky Way, the earth will return to its original galactic status as part of the great restoration that began 38 million years ago, by Lord Michael. As for the fallen angels (negative extraterrestrials) that intercepted the divine plan in the days of Atlantis, they have finally been dealt with by the galactic confederation, and now the time to clean up the mess here in our planet is at hand. In all the religious traditions there is a universal accord depicting a time when our own earth would be restored to its original glory and shine like a jewel in the entire cosmos; states the universal prophecies.

# SECTION 2

## CHAPTER SEVEN

## A BRIEF HISTORY OF
## OUR FORGOTTEN GALACTIC PAST

Long ago in the records of our forgotten stellar lineage, there lays a story that pertains to the real history of our Milky Way Galaxy. If you thought "Star Wars" was fiction, then guess again. Perhaps this is one of the most kept and secured secrets preserved by the forces of light and suppressed by the dark forces.

For some this might be a bit farfetched, for others, it will trigger lost memories of an ancient forgotten past that has been stored up in our DNA as we have all existed prior to this planetary round. It might be important to re-assert that we are eternal spiritual beings that originated in light. Most importantly, we have existed in many dimensions prior to becoming temporarily stuck in the third dimension, which is the lowest condensing point of light-energy– vibration.

The creation of the original biological man came as a result of the formation of all galactic systems, which embody dimensions twelve to one. The original humans or rather, us back then were of an etheric nature with functional light bodies that allowed us to exist in multiple levels of reality simultaneously.

This type of existence included all dimensions. From the higher ninth dimensional frequency to the sixth-dimensional frequency where ether began to take on more solid substance reaching the fifth dimension, where it becomes refined matter.

It was, however, at the vibration frequency of the eight dimensions when we descending spiritual-etheric beings began to inherited etheric-material physical bodies, or rather our energy bodies just become denser.

The only difference between those vehicles and our third-dimensional organic vehicle is that those of the fifth and fourth densities were of a more refine matter-based substance, also known as morontia matter.

Nevertheless, it is in the fifth dimension, where energy and matter have a perfect fluctuating equilibrium. This is where the spirit of the individual may freely manipulate matter instantaneously to convert its physical substance back into pure energy or light body. This allows the individual to travel to other dimensions and back into gross physical dense form. With that have said, the condensed version of the war in heaven as explained in our bible is more detailed to the effects of this version.

From the onset of the celestial Luciferian revolt, there was a cosmic battle that had contaminated the local universe of Nebadon among other local universes. The first galaxies to be restored were the ones that were revolving around Salvington (the headquarters and capital of our local universe of Nebadon).

That is the abode of Lord Michael and the Elohim lords and ladies of light. According to the records of Nebadon, it has been believed that the last galactic system to be restored was our local galaxy, the Milky Way which is one of twelve galaxies within our own local universe domain.

In fact, some sources believe that our galaxy acted as a depository (for the un-purged intelligence that didn't want to accept the light) by taking refuge in our Milky Way galaxy. This type of situation also occurred to our own planet when the forces of light won the battle of Orion, as will be revealed.

According to restored galactic history and backed by esoteric ancient records, our current earth originally belong to the Sirius system, which is the system that encircles the great central sun in the periphery of the first concentric circle extending from the center of our galaxy outward.

It is where the light of our galaxy's central sun first anchored the covenant that became known as the Seal of Paladar, which is equivalent to the agreement known as the covenant, that God and Abraham established here in our world. It was therefore in Sirius, where the seed of light and life begun during our galaxies infant stage. From Sirius, the great quest to spread and secure the universal light force that emanates from the center of the galaxy was anchored.

Now let's say that George Lucas did an excellent job in writing Star Wars. Some mystics and initiates of the secret knowledge believe that Mr. Lucas tapped into the Akashic Records if not of our own galaxy then perhaps another, as an adept of the "Secret knowledge". In fact, in order to understand our own ancient galactic wars, it is almost a prerequisite to first watch the "Star Wars" trilogy as a trigger to our own galactic history.

As the true story of our long-forgotten galactic history unfolds, there indeed was a time in which the earth and our entire solar system were positively interacting and connected to the other colonized interplanetary, stellar, and galactic star systems in our Milky Way Galaxy.

Emergent facts that our planet was part of galactic culture, have been revealed by the ancient artifacts and confirmed by the new science.

In esoteric literature, it is disclosed that our local sun-star system (Helios Envesta) was revolving about and part of the Syrian trinary systems. As revealed, the earth we inhabit, was part of the Vega Solar system located in the constellation of Lyra in the galactic sector of Sirius B. It was from this constellation, agreed by both esoteric and modern revelations, that humanity began the colonization of our Milky Way galaxy particularly from the Lyra- Vega system. In support of this, our science is now suggesting that our earth and the solar system could be part of a trinary star system. In fact, thanks to telescopes, our scientists are postulating that most stars in our galaxy are part of multiple star systems.

This concept proposes the theory that most worlds in our galaxy are part of a convergent of evolutions, where human- beings exist in other solar systems and worlds within our Milky Way. The theory of convergent evolutions validates the fact that we indeed share a common ancestry throughout the cosmos.

To further understand this, let's go back to our story about our cosmic descent. Since our galaxy is one of the billions of galaxies, perhaps a younger one, then we may now understand how the concept of mankind as a materialized being of light has been involved in a long descending process known as involution. Therefore, we may assume that intelligently advanced humanlike beings (celestials) not only crossed over into our galaxy from other colonized galaxies but also primitive life forms were produced organically in new planets from within new forming galaxies as hominids (terrestrial).

So, what we have here is descending celestiaintelligencees from the top (central spheres) down to the material spheres and ascending newly organic terrestrial mammalian creatures moving up from the bottom up.

According to esoteric thought, it is believed that the celestial descending children of light of the Central Universe spheres seeded all material realms in all galactic systems. They planted the angelic/humanoid seed, the "Adam Cadmon" not only in our galaxy but also in all the other existing galaxies and they are in the billions considering the entire periphery of the expanding central universe spheres. So, in the case of our galaxy in the local universe of Nebadon, it was Lord Michael with his twine flame faith/Michelle that gave birth to the entire human lineage.

Also, to understand is that in our galaxy, humanity was not the only descending spirit being that was seeded in physical form, for we also had to deal with the followers of fallen Lord Samana. Unfortunately, the followers of Samana had also planted their seed in our galaxy, from the moment they escaped the purification of the Andromeda galaxy.

As revealed earlier, these fallen light beings became translated as the Reptoids and Dinoid species, the extra-terrestrial group of negative E.T.s that have been identified by today's ufologist and secret space programs. It has been held that the reptilians existed before the humans in our galaxy, however, it has been brought to my awareness that humanity's original form was celestial in nature and therefore in that form, we existed prior to the seeding of the fallen celestials. Although some sources believe that the Reptoids and adenoids had condensed further into the lower fourth dimension for they only operated out of the lower chakras, while the original descending celestial humans (mankind in its original make- up) operated mainly from their higher chakras. It is believed that the fallen light beings followers of Samana, originated in the eleventh major creation, "the universe of mechanism". As a result, they had to depend more on exterior technology rather than their natural light body. Therefore, they are always polarized to the extreme of technological capability as confirmed by restored information.

These reptilians were also known as the ancient serpent race in the more mystical traditions of the various world mythologies. They were the product and children of the non-cosmic black ray of lord Samana, our historical Lucifer. Samana created them with the intent to populate our entire galaxy in order to prevent the spreading of the universal living light force by obstructing it and thus ending all life forms in our Milky Way.

From their inception, the fallen angels translated as serpent beings and were given several directives or what is known as creation myths. The first directive was to destroy all humanoid species because Samana's new humans were bio-conductors of the living light the central sun, through there Anta Karana (a vertical line that connects all humans with the central sun of their galaxy and the center core of their planet). The second directive was related to the first directive and that was to subdue and enslave any species that they encountered because they were told that the galaxy was theirs to control and do as they wish.

Their final directive was that in the end, after succeeding in the first two directives; they were to bring the entire galaxy under their absolute power and control in order to destroy all twelve dimensions and our galaxy as we know it. The reptilians were designed to accomplish these three directives as encoded in them by, fallen lord (Samana). That is why it is important to relate the concept of world domination and absolute power invested in one person as Luciferian in nature, as it originated with the fallen angels.

Collectively they become known as the children of darkness, as described in the

Sephiroth Hebrew text of the Kabala. It appears that the formation of the Reptilian bipedal vehicle was no mystery for fallen Lord Samana who needed to create or rather biogenetically engineer vehicles for his fallen legions to exist in the lower planes of reality.

The reason behind biogenetically engineering fifth and fourth-density vehicles was because, by divine decree, it was prohibited for any fallen light intelligence to inherit the Adam Cadmon body, (angelic/human form) for going against divine protocol. This was forbidden by the order of the Ancient of Days acting under the direction of the highest of the Central eternal universe spheres.

Therefore, throughout all cosmic history, the children of Samana were marked as the abomination of light. In our world, we may trace this mark of the beast, back to our biblical Cain, Ham, and Nimrod. As this personage carried the highest concentration of reptilian DNA in their genetics (More on how the reptilian DNA was transferred to our earth becoming the abomination of desolation of the biblical text, will be explained later in chapter 11).

So, from the initial fall, Samana's plans were to bring our universe under his control, and since our galaxy is part of our local universe, it became targeted for two reasons. The first and most important one is that in our galaxy there exists a specific planet that was originally set up by the prime creator to be the culmination of all revolutionary and evolutionary and evolutionary cycles from the creation of the first major universe of Jesus, to the last creation of Michael.

This meant inheriting the best qualities of every prior universal creation that existed prior to the formation of the last universal creation known as the Twelfth Major universe. The chosen planet for this final masterpiece is our current earth. Since then, the original purpose for our present earth was to become a showcase planet in all the cosmos not only in the last universal creation but in all Orvonton the seventh super universe which is one-seventh of the entire grand central omniverse. Therefore, since earth inherited all the qualities of the entire evolutionary potential of all Orvonton, the seventh super universe, it was always coveted by all descending celestial intelligence. For since the beginning, our earth was set apart in order to bring in the divine plan of the highest and still is, that is why the last battle takes place here according to all prophetic traditions. It has also been revealed that at the end of linear time, (third dimension) our planet would be restored and become the showcase world it was meant to be. This prophetic vision has continued and echoed through all eons in our galaxy for millions of years and it's now coming to fruition in our times as our planet ascends.

In addition, higher evolved human- beings (our parent race) collectively known as the Pleiades (who were recorded to be the angels or sons of God in our bible), are coming forward revealing their connection to our world. The Pleiades are also confirming the fact that our planet indeed was set up as a living cosmic library containing everything in creation.

Now in uncovering the history of our galaxy, we could now begin to compare the Sith of "Star Wars", to the serpent reptilian race of our ancient galactic past, that became known as the Dragons, the biblical demons. This is what ancient manuscripts have documented to be the ancient battle between Celestial Man (ANGELS) and the fallen angels, the (demons) Draco-reptilians.

It was revealed that the fallen celestials upon incarnating in fifth-dimensional vehicles lost their connection to the higher chakras, and thus were operating with an imperfect body of light.

Now as far as the real "Star Wars" that took place millions of years ago, was known as the wars of Orion. It was a battle between the celestial humanoid family of (light inhabiting upper Orion and the reptilians (dark) of lower Orion. It was this battle that determined the outcome of our galaxy.

According to various independent researchers and benevolent extraterrestrial celestial sources that are now coming forward, have all confirmed that the fallen celestials upon incarnating into their grotesque vehicles settled first in a region far from the center of our galaxy where the light was overwhelming for their fallen light bodies. This region became known as the lower belt of Orion.

Thanks to our galactic logos Melkior who heads the council of the central sun operating from the center of our galaxy, the fallen celestials could not inhabit regions that were in proximity to the great central sun at the center of our galaxy. Apparently, their light bodies began operating with less light quotient forcing them to settle in a region that would allow for their fallen light energy to exist.

Of course, in an act of intelligence, they settled in lower Orion, for the purpose of gaining control over the biologic programming center of our Milky Way galaxy. This allowed the dark forces to control population stellar star systems in the third concentric level in reference to the central sun. The dark forces knew that it was impossible for them to gain control over the higher regions of the first and second concentric levels surrounding the central sun, due to the higher radiation of light at the center of our galaxy.

However, Samana (Lucifer) understood well that he who controlled the Orion region of our local galaxy would rule all the other regions from the third concentric circle, as well as the fourth concentric circle, where our earth hangs today in the outer rim of our galaxy.

IAs confirmed, in the "Keys of Enoch", Orion was revealed to be the mission control center that allowed access to any part of our Milky Way galaxy beyond the second concentric ring. This allowed access to all the systems and worlds in the third and fourth concentric rings.

Fortunately, the higher stargates of Orion were secured by the forces of light for the very reasons that these stargates access other galaxies and other universes. In fact, Orion was known to the ancients as Kesil, as they recognized it as an important integral sign in the heavens. This explains why the ancient Egyptian pyramids were constructed in alignment with the stars EL, AN, and RA of Orion. It has been revealed that from these systems, the forces of light administer control of our fifth fourth, and third-dimensional universe.

Considering this, the war in heaven has been a perpetuated war that involved a battle that has been affecting many worlds and galaxies. At one time it involved our entire galaxy until the forces of light began to establish themselves in Orion approximately 4.5 million years ago. But before the heavenly war affected our galaxy, the Order of Melchizedek, hailing from Salvignton, established an advanced spiritual etheric civilization at the center of our galaxy. These would secure the victory of light by harnessing the power of our central sun.

As a result, the Sirius trinary system was quickly inhabited by etheric beings that had secured the stargates from the first concentric circle.

This move prevented any dark force from accessing the systems that were in proximity and connection to the central sun where the etheric/guardians of our galaxy were stationed.

At this point, our galaxy split into two sides. On the one side, we had the descending human family of light that was led by Michael becoming the first spiritual incarnated being that planted the seeds of divinity in our local galaxy. Many esoteric sources are now confirming that Lord Michael was the first solar being to incarnate as the first fifth-dimensional human Adamah. This took place millions of years ago in Lyra, before the accepted biblical account of Adam that was distorted by the fallen celestials.

In like manner, Samana (Lucifer) become the first Dracon reptilian to incarnate and plant his seed in our galaxy in the lower Bellatrix system of Orion, on a solar system known as Regal.

As mentioned, both groups were given a creation myth to abide by. The reptilians creation myth held that they were entitled to ownership of the entire galaxy and that if they encountered other sentient beings regardless of the level of development, that they were to subdue and conquer them in the name of Samana-Draco their leader, the first Sith.

This was the draconian creed and creation myth, as laid down by fallen Lord Samana (Lucifer) and his followers. On the contrary, the Adamic/celestial/humanoids had another creed and universal standard to abide by. It was to bring peace, freedom, universal cooperation, and most importantly to spread the light of a loving creation to the entire galaxy. The first Adamic angelic/humanoids in our galaxy (our ancestors) were taught that everything in existence was sacred and that everything was interconnected and alive. They also believed that everything functioned as a unit of one as to why they have always been referring to as the children of the one. On the contrary, the reptilians held the idea of separation and so began to initiate the first acts of conflict by plundering all other sentient life forms that got in their way of achieving absolute domination of our galaxy.

The forces of darkness first settled in the star system of Rigel that became their first galactic stronghold in lower Orion, next to the Bellatrix system. They expanded into other regions as well, settling in the Bellatrix system including Alpha Draconis, and Sigma Draconis, known as the Draco star systems, which become their second stronghold. Eventually Zeta Reticuli 1 and 2, in the Rhombolla system also joined, as did Epsilon Boots, the Altar system, the Cappella system, and the Bernard system.

From the Rigel system, the dark forces began a long military expedition of conquest bringing many planets and star systems on their side of the galaxy under their absolute control. The fact that they harnessed the power of several local suns made them a population of two-stellar space-age civilization.

The fact that they were extremely technologically inclined, allowed them to traverse the galaxy before the original celestial//humanoids did. The celestial/humanoids, on the other hand, were more inclined spiritually as they used their natural light body for inter-dimensional travel.

After a couple of million years, the seeding of our galaxy was underway as millions of planetary systems within the periphery of the second and third concentric circles had already evolved to the level of space travel population one interplanetary and stellar system. At which point, we also had many life forms springing forward throughout the second and third concentric rings of our galaxy. Perhaps some of these star systems were inhabited by other sentient beings not necessarily humanoid that might have been the Dragon's first successful accomplishments.

According to the higher knowledge, the Dracos did bring many worlds and systems under their control. And in some cases, they implement horrific suffering with their advanced technologies of death. For example, from the various technologies of death and destruction, in one case, they had genetically altered certain species creating mutant races as well as implanting them with nanochips to control their thoughts, by remote control. Talk about absolute mind control.

This galactic horror perpetuated until the Draco reptilians reached the region of the original human colonies, in the Lyra system. This span of distance gave the original celestial/humanoids enough time to exist in peace, brotherhood/sisterhood, and freedom for a couple of million years, before the encounter with the Dracon reptilians.

Knowing that this might happen after securing the highest regions of our galaxy, the forces of light established their first stronghold in the Sirius-Lyra system creating a coalition of light that eventually spread beyond the first concentric circle bringing other advanced worlds into the alliance.

This coalition of light was carried over from other restored galaxies as the Seal of Paladar, as mentioned. It was there in SiriusLyra were the descending celestials/humanoids (as they were then known) first begun colonizing other planets. One became known as Avalon, which became a harmonious spiritual civilization.

It resembled the first advance human society known as planet Avon, the original eight-dimensional Earth. Eventually, the early humanoid family spread to other star systems in the surrounding areas of Lyra, spreading the light of a loving creation to other sentient evolving terrestrials from the planets encircling in the outer rim of the galaxy. Everything went well until the celestial humanoids encountered the Dracos.

The interaction with the Dracos caused the first Star Wars in our galaxy as they were both at population two (stellar) level space-age statues both acting upon different creation myths. As mentioned, the original celestial/humanoids were mostly inclined spiritually. This meant, they utilized a spiritual technology commonly known as Merkabah, to traverse the different dimensional planes of existence.

Merkabah would allow the celestial/humanoids to materialize anything they needed including a spacecraft by the power of their own thoughts as they did in the fifth major universe dedicated to the Power of Thought. Therefore, in Lyra, all humans were telepathic and forse of the direct royal line of Lord, Michael was the most advance and was considered the highest adepts in understanding and mastering the energy forces of the entire light spectrum. In other words, they accessed the full power of their light body, capable of manipulating the elements and energies of the universe. Liken to the Jedi knights of "Star Wars".

The Lyran celestial/humanoids led by an incarnated version of Lord Michael became fully aware of the intentions of the Dracons. They sensed the attacks through their clairvoyance and prepared for their first galactic battle in defense of their original habitat and home star system. As descending intelligence of the central universe, they also received guidance by the spiritual hierarchy and the celestial order of Melchizedek who operated as their overseers and spiritual counterpart from the higher etheric and celestial spheres, which always control the outcome of everything.

Luckily, it is believed that the celestial hosts of non-incarnate beings (celestials) also hold power over and controlled what has become known as the dark side. Therefore, good and evil are ultimately controlled by the highest good and that is why evil, or darkness is always on the losing end.

The victory of our first galactic war in our Milky Way was won by the great support and assistance of Lord Michael as Amelius/Adam of Lyra. Amelius/Adam established an awesome plan that would initiate the restoration process for our entire galaxy springing from their galactic headquarters in the sector of Lyra/Sirius. Thanks to Amelius the first incarnating version of Michael, the forces of light won the first battle in Lyra, however, this cultivated the grounds for many battles to come that would involve our entire galaxy for the next millions of years. Due to these ancient advanced civilizations, we may then conclude that our galaxies version of Star Wars occurred in our distant past and perhaps might have ended twelve thousand years ago at the sinking of the world'srlds last advanced civilization is known as Atlantis. Initially, after securing Lyra, the forces of light began extending the office of Christ "the Seal of Paladar" to the region of Orion. There is Orion, they immediately settled in the Upper systems where the light was much for the fallen light beings to withstand but just right for the forces of light.

This move not only secured the stargates to other galaxies and universes, but it also secured the central control programs that allowed access to other star systems in the third and fourth concentric rings. The fourth ring is where our earth hangs and where many new worlds were coming into being. These moves prevented the forces of darkness from extending our galactic war to the rest of our galaxy, which was the other 80 percent.

Therefore, from the upper systems of Orion, the great plan was initiated to begin the liberation of systems and worlds that had been controlled by the fallen celestials, Dracos. The wars of Orion lasted for millions of years. Almost all the star systems in Orion were involved in this battle. This event was a galactic war of colossal proportions, destroying many worlds and in some cases solar systems as well. But after millions of years, it's now come to an end in the victory of the light.

The fact that the forces of light secured the Ra stargate, the Horse-head region, and the EL region gave the light the eventual victory not only in Orion but also for our entire Galaxy.

Other regions in our galaxy that become inhabitable by the early descending celestial/humanoid family were of course the Pleiades star system, which is considered the cradle of human consciousness, according to the Keys of Enoch. In fact, Enoch revealed that the Pleiades anchored and carried forward the seed of the celestial humanoid family to the many solar systems within the Pleiades including our solar system.

For it has been confirmed by all esoteric literature, that our local sun in which the earth revolves about is the eight missing sisters or the eight stars of the Pleiades.

Other humanoid star systems that participated in the battle on the side of light and life led by the forces of light in pursuance of the Seal of Paladar, were the Hathor system, the Betelgeuse system, the Arctuarian system, the AN system, the Alpha Centauri system, the Epsilon Eridani system and the Tau Ceti system, to name a few.

It is believed that this conflict between our galaxy's humanoids and the Dracos lasting for millions of years creating a galactic Star Wars in the early history of our galaxy. However, it is my honor to reveal that this conflict is now ending with the ascension and restoration of the earth.

Apparently from the initial unfoldment of our galaxy, the forces of light managed to narrow this galactic horror to a single planetary affair here in our world.

The concept, that a long time ago, we earth humans were part of a greater galactic community, supports all the latest theories in cutting-edge science regarding our multidimensional existence and the idea that we are one of many civilizations. In fact, it has been confirmed, that the earth on which we live was once a member of the organized galactic confederation of free worlds under the leadership of Lord Michae.

It appears that our planet earth has been quarantined since the Draco's (fallen angels) took over during the times of Atlantis. It is also known that upon our planet's ascension, we will have open contact with the Galactic Federation.

For the record let it be known, that out of the billions of star systems that exist in our galaxy, less than 20 percent of them became inhabitable or occupied by all descending celestial intelligence existing in stellar communities. It appears that about eighty percent of our galaxy is waiting to be colonized and that takes effect after the ascension/restoration of our earth. This provides more evidence that our existence was first in the stars and before that, it was in the always existing spheres of the central universe- metaverse.

Again, it is important to understand that the great galactic prophecies profess of a time that when our planet earth ascends, its livestock will repopulate the rest of our galaxy. This means that the rest of our uninhabitable galaxy (which is 80 percent will be seeded by all the earth's life forms. This also tells us that the current human species on earth carries the greatest genetic diversity in our galaxy, which in a way makes us the culminating master peace of all creations, within the super universe of Orvoton. Therefore, in the aftermath of our ascension, our earth would be operating at all three major population systems, as it was before our planet earth became quarantined and isolated from the rest of the cosmos.

# CHAPTER EIGHT

## THE FORMATION OF THE GALACTIC FEDERATION OF FREE WORLD, HENCE THEIR LOGO, GALACTIC HISTORY PART TWO

Since the forces of light began to repair fallen regions from the highest levels down, they needed a galactic vehicle of some sort that would enable them to protect the many evolving terrestrial worlds. So it was decided by Lord Michael and the celestial order of Melchizedek, who is likened to the Jedi Order in the movie "Star Wars", that a Federation of free worlds is initiated in order to bring protection and freedom to the rest of the galaxy, on behalf of the Great Divine Plan, the Seal of Paladar.

As revealed, this covenant known as the Seal of Paladar was carried over from other restored galaxies to our own. So, from a higher multi-galactic level, it operated as the Intergalactic Federation of Free Galaxies. All of which have been under the direction of Lord Michael. It appears that every galaxy in our local universe now thanks to the Confederation of Free Worlds, Aisin alignment once again with the governments of the great central sun, of our local universe, our super universe, and our central eternal universe.

In our galaxy, the Galactic Federation of free worlds was first established 4.5 million years ago in the higher regions of Orion. It was an alliance of many civilizations of population two- stellar statues that honored the great Seal of

Paladar. What has been also revealed by the higher intelligence, is that the Galactic Federation of free worlds is comprised of different galactic species (benevolent extraterrestrials) some human, some not. It was this diversity of species that enabled this organization to co-exist under the banner of universal brotherhood/sisterhood with the celestial/humanoids leading the way fulfilling their creation myth of Co-existence.

Nonetheless, with the establishment of the Galactic Federation of Free Worlds, in pursuant to the covenant of Paladar, the great divine plan to restore our galaxy was a success.

However, as mentioned these conflicts lasted millions of years because, in response to the Federation, the dark forces formed their own alliance known as the Orion Empire led by the Draco leaders of the reptilian forces.

The Orion Empire is like the galactic Rakata Empire of the Sith in the movie "Star Wars". This dark alliance recruited as many species of lower biological genotypes, in their controlled regions. Among this species was the infamous Grays, a group of degenerate humanoid species that became genetically altered to suppress their emotional body, which led to their conversion to the dark side. As a result of suppressing their emotional body, they only operated from their intellectual mental body.

Other groups that followed the Draco's reptilians were unsectarian in nature and some even resembled the dinosaurs of old, known as the Droid race. Perhaps, these species were a by-product of the scorching black noncosmic ray of (Colodhon) of fallen Lord Samana.

On the other hand, the species in favor of the light of non-human origin were also benevolent beings that reflected divinity, as they were different strands of the same light body DNA that made the humanoid race. For instance, the lion people were known as the Felines and in some instances, they acted like parents and benefactors to the humanoid races, particularly in our galaxy.

It appeared that the felines came from a different galaxy that settled in light (ascended) long ago. Other galactic sentient beings were the bird people, (Carians) who are nine-dimensional beings that are also assisting our humanoid family. The Whale and dolphin people who are commonly known as Cetaceans are among the most loving beings in our galaxy that also came from another ascending galaxy to assist us. Some sources have said that many of the Cetaceans that originated in Sirius, have been on our planet since the beginning of its first great galactic civilization, known as Mu.

Nonetheless, as mentioned these early galactic battles affected many planetary systems and star systems, by the dark ray under the actions of the Reptoids, droids, and grays, or simply just biblical demons. For instance, millions of years ago earth time; it was revealed, that some inhabited planets and star systems in other parts of our galaxy had become one hundred percent controlled by the dark side of the Orion Empire. These worlds tasted like a full-scale global dictatorship falling under the galactic Draconian empire.

The good news is that after millions of years these worlds have been liberated by the Federation of Free Worlds and are waiting for the removal of the last residue of darkness from our planet in our current times. In most cases, except for the systems that were saved and restored by the Galactic Federation, most invaded worlds ended up in total destruction, because eventually worlds that get completely shut off from the universal living light for a long period of time, begin to lose their life-force and everything, therefore, begins to die out.

Universal life force is another term describing the light source that sustains all life forms in all dimensions. Again let it be understood, that the central aim of the Draconian agenda was to bring all power to Samana for the very reason that he did not want the creation of the celestial/Humanoid (Adam Cadman) to prevail since they were the light carriers of the complete universal life force of the twelve major universes. Instead, Samana intended to populate our galaxy with the Reptoids, droids, greys, and other insectoid species that were under the rule of the Draco reptilians exercising only the lower chakras, thus separating the higher dimensions from the lower ones.

By eliminating the descending celestial/humanoid family, the dark side would have achieved its goals of not allowing the universal life force that emanates from the great central sun at the center of our galaxy to anchor into all parts of the galaxy thus connecting all spheres with light. Without this process, the lower material spheres would eventually cease to exist. It appears that this universal life force is constantly being transmitted to all levels through the twelve chakras systems within all Adamic/humanoid races.

According to the great galactic prophesy, the last battle is to take place here on our planet and once this comes to pass, will our entire galaxy be restored and settled completely in light and life, for eternity. Perhaps upon the restoration of our galaxy, our material universe will have become eternal, like the spiritual and etheric spheres, which is part of the great divine plan of investing the material spheres with eternal light. As it is above so shall it be below, HEAVEN ON EARTH.

Furthermore, in revealing further information regarding the history of the Federation let's refer to Anu, a member of the Federation of light serving under Lord Michael as a direct descendant of the Michael /Amelius bloodline. Serving in the Pleiadian star league particularly as the former commander of the Nibiru battleship planet, commonly known as planet X to our modern scientist and the planet of the crossing (Nibiru) to the ancients. After all, it was Anu who played perhaps the most important role in our world's ancient history as the leader of the Anunaki gods (descending celestial/humanoids) in the mythologies of old.

Due to the restoration, he has now come forward to share information with us regarding our stellar galactic roots. This information sheds light on the work of ZachariaStitching, validating the ancient astronaut theory.

All world ancient mythologies speak of immortal celestial inteintelligencet have interacted with this planet since times immemorial. In the bible, this information was condensed to the sons of God or the Elohim, which is plural for the many celestial humanoids that cohabited with evolving terrestrial primitive man in pre-flood times. After years of intensive research and considering today's new evidence, we could now say that those ancient Elohim who came down to earth were our ancient descending celestial human ancestors that biogenetically engineered today's human species, known as Homo sapien-sapiens.

Now for the record and correction of facts, our parent race were not gods as portrayed in mythology. They were descending celestial humanoids of a type two population stellar star system space-age civilization and had a full functioning light body, enabling them to access many levels of reality, allowing them to live for hundreds of thousands of years. They came as a celestial fifth-dimensional family as to why the bible refers to them as Elohim, plural. Although some believe they came down from the Pleiades with an agenda of their own. Others believe, they were the ancient reptilians that mated with the early celestial/humans in Lyra during the first galactic war.

Now according to Anu, a full-fledged descending celestial angelic/humanoid a true Syrian-Lyran-Plaiedian of royal celestial descent, revealed that some Anunaki were indeed benevolent while others were of a malevolent nature, this explains the later biblical condensed translation of angels and demons.

According to the restored Nibirian Council author and extraterrestrial Pleiadean walk in, Jellaila Star", revealed that Nibiru was an isolated planet that evolved out of the debris left behind from the first great galactic war in Lyra and was chosen by the Federation high council of Sirius to become a battle-star planet.

This was due to the great elliptical orbit that Nibiru followed across the galaxy reaching many star systems. Most important, the Galactic Federation believed that this battle-star-planet Nibiru would be a watcher for the newly evolving life that was scheduled to exist on our current earth during our planet first seeding two million years ago.

In fact, the history of Nibiru is tied to the history of our planet. If this was the case then the line of control of Nibiru has been attributed to the celestial angelic/humanoids of pure Lyra and now Pleiadean descent, not Reptilian.

However, it has been revealed that out of the line of celestial angelic/humanoids, Anu was the last chosen commander of the Galactic Federation's battle-star planet, (Nibiru) until around 2024BC, when his nephew Marduk took it by force.

Indeed, Anu, the former commander of the Galactic Plaiedian Nibirian battle-star planet, did confirm that the first celestial angelic/humanoid colony in our galaxy was known as Avon, which was in the Vega star system in Lyra-Sirius.

Now the way Anu explained it, was in a form of a universal game known as polarity integration. According to this version, the celestial angelic/humanoids represented the light and a feminine spiritual way of life. Also, since the etheric/angelic/humanoids descended from the higher spiritual spheres, they represented the higher chakras, which relate to the higher dimensions of spirit and etheric realms. On the other hand, the reptilians represented the lower chakras and so their nature was masculine and represented the opposite of spiritual evolution, which was pure materialism. So, the whole purpose of this duality was to achieve polarity integration allowing both groups to fuse as one, thus integrating the higher chakras and the lower chakras as one.

In this case, the goal of the descending celestial angelic/humanoid family was to become as physical as possible by adopting the lower three chakras and this was not possible without the aid of their Reptilian counterpart. For instance, since the descending celestial etheric/angelic/humanoids polarized only to ascend back into the higher etheric and spiritual spheres of pure light, the Reptilians only polarized to the material lower realms without any desire to ascend. It is also important to understand, that without the lower three chakras it would be impossible to exist in a sixth-dimensional sphere and downward where etheric matter begins to become material gross dense matter.

According to this perspective, the Reptilians in turn needed to understand and acquire the higher chakras in order to ascend back into the spirit which would free them from their grotesque beastly appearance into a beautiful Adam Cadman (human angel). Overall, it was a matter of descending for the celestial angelic/humanoids and ascending for the Reptilians and the integrating point was the bridging of dimensions, higher etheric matter, and lower dense material matter. This postulates that everything in existence has a purpose and that everything is heading in the direction it is supposed to, no matter how it appears. This makes me want to state firmly and with confidence that the cosmos makes no mistakes. All is in divine providence, no matter what it seems like.

Equally important to understand is that the reptilians are our fallen sisters and brothers who did their part of playing the role of the antagonist in this universal game of polarity integration. For in the ETERNAL central SPHERES- before the experimental creations of time and space (the seven super universes) we were all one celestial family remembering that Lucifer or rather Samana was also a celestial son of God, and still is for he was also fulfilling his part.

Again, the entire fall from heaven was a metaphor indicating the fall of (light) spirit into matter ( for everyone) for both angels and fallen angels. Nonetheless, the experience in duality would provide further spiritual growth and an opportunity to unite the light and the dark back together as one family as we were, before the great descent.

In this duality, the light is represented by the higher worlds of spirit and the dark represents the lower worlds of matter. All other dualities such as negative-positive, female-male are just reflections of the ultimate primary duality since everything is holographic. So, in understanding this, we can now envision that the ultimate alchemical marriage is really between spirit and matter, as primary and secondary would be the union of male and female within oneself by achieving balance, as revealed through the esoteric wisdom.

It is however great when all polarities find their common ground as they unite and that is true love. Despite this, let it be clear that every soul has its ying and yang, male and female aspects that they need to balance. The point is to integrate both spirit (light) and body (matter) as is the case of the ascension process of ascending our body and at the same time allowing our Great Spirit over self to descend into the matter. In other words, the matter could only be eternal if it's spiritualized. Perhaps from a higher level of existence, this fall into duality was orchestrating as a perfect game allowing opposites that at one point existed as one, to eventually resolve their differences and find a middle ground, and thus learning to embrace both the higher and the lower dimensions but to bridge them together. In this sense, we begin to see matter and spirit as one and the same, two different vibrating realities of the same all-pervading light source.

It is this extreme polarity that would provide the perfect education in order for all souls of both light and dark to eventually evolve and learn that all conflict ends when the two become the one again, rediscovering the oneness that connects us all, spirit. For in spirit we will always be one and information we will always be many.

Today it is well understood that compassion is something we humanoids had always had, and it is our strongest defense mechanism against our reptilian counterpart. Humans must love their enemies because it is through compassion that we convert our fallen brothers back into the light. Overall, both sets of descending beings had lessons to learn, for the whole purpose of this existing opposition, was to unite both groups of descending beings back together as one in the physical realm and this would mean that the humanoids would learn how to be more physical material developing lower chakras while maintaining their high spiritual connection. As for the Reptilians, theirs was to learn compassion and love (which is the opposite of their creation myth) so that they may redeem themselves and inherit their long-awaited physical vehicle the Adam Cadman, humanoid light body.

So, in the end, there exists only one universal angelic humanoid family as keepers and representatives of the entire material spheres and live happily ever after, what a beautiful galactic ending.

It is my honor to reveal, that we are at the close of this cosmic drama in our current time, as all prophetic traditions confirm it. However, in the early history of our galaxy, the game of polarity integration was only in its initial stage. Let's go back millions of years ago in standard earth time, as we explain the version given by Anu.

As revealed and confirmed by Anu, the first spiritual humanoid colony was seeded by the spiritual councils of light in the Lyran star systems in a planet known as Avon. According to various celestial sources working with the Federation, this was the fourth planet in the Vega star system in the Lyran constellation.

Apparently, the humanoids existed in the fifth dimension and everything was fine. The lower dimensions lower than the fifth were all integrated and in tune with the higher realms. Some believe that the celestial angelic/humanoid vehicle was gradually condensed from its energy counterpart.

When the humanoid vehicles were ready for high spirit embodiment, a group of Etheric beings from Sirius which were the first descending souls incarnated in those celestial humanoid bodies to proceed with the process of descending into the fifth dimensiowherere matter and energy is in perfect equilibrium.

The only problem was that the new incarnated celestial angelic/humans were still geared towards the higher realms of light, not fully grounding into the lower chakras in the third, second, and first dimensions.

Anu of the restored Niburian council believes this caused them to automatically block their opportunity of inheriting the lower three charkas that they needed in order to exist in the lower dimensions, to integrate spirit and matter. So, the game now is commonly known as polarity integration began when their counter opposite, the reptilians began to travel into their proximity. Anu revealed that this set the stage for the first opportunity of polarity integration between these two beings, uniting the higher chakras with the lower ones. This was known as the first earth grand experiment since planet Avyon was considered the first incarnation of Earth in our galaxy.

According to Anu, the royal house of the humanoid family become known as the royal house of Avon name after their first home planet and whose animal emblem is the lion, which corresponds to our planet's tribe of Judah of messianic descent. As mentioned, humans are only polarized to the feminine spiritual way of life acting out from the higher chakras, without external technology. This made the fifth-dimensional humans semi-etheric in a world that was condensing into the fourth and third dimensions. So, it came to pass, that for the first time, these two different sets of beings met, and to our surprise things were initially peaceful.

According to Anu, the reason why the reptilians were not hostile to the galactic humanoids upon arrival, was because the spiritual councils of the higher etheric and spiritual spheres were bombarding them with frequencies of love and compassion, thus transforming their negative nature. This proves that anything could be transmuted or transformed with pure unconditional love at a very high frequency. So immediately, the reptilians introduced the

humans to their material external technology as the humans introduced the Reptilians to meditations and spiritual practices. For the most part, it appeared as if the first universal game of polarity integration was going to be successful.

However, it was the great influx of light and love by the non incarnated higher-ups that allowed for the peaceful co-existence of these two species, which endured until a group of high-ranking Dracos, heard of the co-existence. Upon hearing of this co-existence, the high-ranking Dracos deciding it was time to pay this healthy planet a visit. The Draco generals left their home planet Aln in the Rigel star System of Lyra to aggravate the situation. Their home planet, the house of Aln represented the Royal House of Draco, the rival and Sith line of Lucifer, Samana. When the General Dracos of Rigel and Alpha Draconis arrived to investigate the situation, they tried to convince the reptilians that they were not living according to their creed. That they needed to destroy or enslaved the Lyran humans in order to establish the throne of the house of Aln throughout the whole galaxy. Apparently, the humans and the reptilians were already exchanging knowledge with one another, and most importantly, a group of each side from royal bloodlines had already begun interbreeding amongst themselves, creating a whole new cast of what became known as the physical Orion humanoids led by the house of Ananda.

This interbreeding created a whole new royal bloodline providing the grounds for polarity integration. This interbreeding also allowed the fifth-dimensional Lyran etheric humans to inherit the lower chakras, thus rooting them into the lower spheres of matter, in the third, second, and first dimensions. In turn, it also allowed the now hybrid reptilians to inherit the higher chakras setting the grounds for their eventual ascension back into the Adam Caedmon. There is no doubt that this interbreeding provided the grounds for the two species to begin integrating their differences in order to complete the game of polarity integration of merging the higher and lower chakras, the higher and the lower dimensions. Despite the new race of hybrid human-reptilians and their co-existence, it turned out that the general Dracos had finally convinced not only the majority of the Reptoids but also most of the new hybrids which became known as the Orion physical humanoids to launch an attack on the etheric- quasi-physical Lyran/angelic/humans who were mainly inclined towards spiritual growth. These Lyran humanoids wanted nothing to do with technology for they had no interest in the development of the lower chakras as they only sought to be spiritual. Two things fell in favor of the attack; one was that the non/hybrids Lyrans were not embracing the technologically driven mentality of the new hybrids (Orion humanoids) and Reptoids. At the same time, the Lyran-humans had another planet by the name of Avalon in the same solar system that they colonized, and the reptilians brainwashed by their Draco leaders were beginning to think that the Lyran humanoids were eventually planning to not only populate the Lyra constellation but the entire galaxy. This was in direct violation of the Draconian creation myth because according to their myth, it is the Reptoids who were to populate our entire galaxy. So, what started off as a wave of rumors ended up becoming the first galactic war of our galaxy, taking place in the system of the lyre.

According to Anu, the process that led to the very first galactic war in our galaxy between the Lyran celestial humanoids and Dracon reptilians was gradual and swift. The now convinced reptilians under the direction of general Dracos sowed seeds of discord and hatred as they managed to infiltrate the Lyran humanoid colony. First, they infiltrated the royal house of Avon through their new Human halfbreeds who were claiming to be the new royalty. After the interbreeding of draconian royalty with Lyran royalty, there was a split in the spiritual-Lyran-humanoid family.

Now we had two types of galactic humanoids. The original feminine spiritually oriented Lyran humanoids that didn't inherit the lower chakras by not interbreeding with the Reptoids on one hand, and the masculine oriented humanoids that become the offspring of the interbreeding Humanoids who had developed the lower chakras making them more material into the fourth and third dimension.

These humanoids were known as the masculine inclined half breeds who eventually only geared towards technological development at the expense of their spiritual growth under the influence of their Reptilian allies. Then, we are also the fourth branch of humanoids that were also hybrids becoming the house of Ananda, who successfully integrated their lower chakras while maintaining their spirituality and loyalty to our creator. It was this line of Ananda that created a whole new race of spiritual and material beings that later became the liberators in Orion when the Draco enslaved the rest of the Orion humanoid population.

This shows that the tactics of infiltration were first set into motion millions of years ago by the Draco reptilians to overtake the first humanoid colony and hence the galaxy. Apparently, the masculine inclined humanoids and their Reptoid allies had begun to insinuate conflict against the more spiritually oriented humanoids that again were mainly geared towards spiritual development and antitechnology. It wasn't long before a full war broke out. What began as a civil war, between those that wanted to preserve the royal house of Avon and those that wanted to replace it with the house of Aln, turned out into a war that devastated and completely destroyed the original home planet of the Lyran humanoids.

However, if the draconian succeeded in establishing their creed, then Avyon would become an empire. This was in direct opposition to what the house of Avon (The lion) had established. Eventually, the feminine spiritually inclined humanoids under the guidance of the celestial hierarchy in an attempt to preserve their home planet launched a preemptive strike against the reptilians and their new masculine oriented humanoid allies who had apparently join sides in pursuant of the Draconian creed. It's only obvious, that the Draconian were only using their new masculine-oriented humanoid allies to destroy the feminine-inclined spiritual Lyran humanoids. The ultimate and underlying goal for the Dracos of the royal house of Aln, was to destroy all humanoid populations in our Milky Way Galaxy.

The first Lyran humanoids survived the war but their first home planet Avyon was destroyed as neither species came out victorious, as polarity integration failed in what Anu refers to as the first earth grand experiment. According to Jellailla Star of the resorted Nibirian council, the first earth grand experiment is what began the great galactic battle between man and dragon. After this conflict, the feminine (spiritually) incline humanoids resorted back into their etheric vehicles. Of course, the celestial hierarchy decided this, since they always control the outcome of all situations.

However, in the aftermath of the first galactic war, the Lyran humanoids became known as the Etherian Sirians and never got a chance to inherit their lower chakras. They ended up residing as an etheric civilization in what become known as Sirius C, as revealed in the restored Niburian council. According to this revelation, Sirius A along with Sirius C was colonized, as Sirius B became a planetary system that was used as galactic storage for the forces of light. In fact, our earth's scientists have recently confirmed the trinary star systems of Sirius utilizing modern-day technology, as the brightest stars in our galaxy.

On the other hand, the masculine inclined humanoids that completely leaned towards the other extreme had inherited lower chakras and therefore were able to stay connected with the lower dimensions preserving their fourth and third-dimensional physical form, however losing their connection to the light. They became known as the Orion humanoids, which were sent to live in the Orion constellation since Orion was grounded in all dimensions. This outcome enabled them to now live with and co-exists in the fourth and third dimensions in Orion along with the reptilians that apparently had already resided there. It was this transference of the masculine Orion humanoid family that for the first time led to the gradual population of humanoid civilizations in Orion. However, the house of Aln, the Draconian royalty who believe Orion was theirs, didn't wait long before the masculine Orion humanoids were forced into slavery as decreed in their Draconian Protocol. It was then that the physical fourth and third-density Orion humanoids family experienced slavery for the first time in our galaxy.

Fortunately, though, some of the Orion physical humanoids were led and protected by descendants of the house of Ananda, who remain loyal to the spiritual way of life, while integrating the lower chakras. This third group of beings that achieved polarity integration among themselves were able to form a resistant band of galactic spiritual warriors in Orion that become known as the Black league of Orion. This resistance movement eventually provided the grounds for another galactic battle and thus as mentioned earlier the real Star Wars began in Orion between the now physical Orion humanoids and the physical Orion reptilians.

In fact, the power of the Orion angelic/humanoids was characterizing by blue that represented the Blue bright light of Sirius that stems from the Klusian blue ray of Lord Michael, as the leader of the forces of light. As for the Dracos, there's was red which was symbolic to their desire for absolute power as red is also the color of the root chakra, the lowest chakra. Perhaps George Lucas taped into the Akashic records of our galaxy to retrieve a buried galactic past.

Overall, the wars of Orion lasted for millions of years between the Orion humanoids and the Orion Reptilians. Eventually, thanks to the Orion black league, formed by the resistance of the Orion humans, the formation of the Galactic Federation of free worlds in Orion came about approximately 5 million years ago. It was this Federation of light that eventually began restoring the star systems of

Orion, thus bringing peace and freedom to not only the entire Orion region but to other parts of the galaxy that have been controlled by the Draconian Empire.

However, before we attempt to uncover our own planets forbidden history and how the humanoid race came to our planet, we must first understand some events that transpired in the Pleiades star system since our solar system belongs to it

# CHAPTER NINE

## OUR CONNECTION TO THE PLEIADES, A BRIEF HISTORY OF OUR GALAXY PART THREE

According to higher sources, the fourth group of Lyran galactic humanoids that fought bravely in honor of the light by integrating both the higher chakras and the lower chakras inherited the Pleiadian star systems for their permanent home. From the beginning, the Pleiades became the haven for the house of Avon, which was ruled by the direct descendants of Lord Michael.

This information is verifiable in the ancient records of all ancient traditions and when the halls of records open in Egypt underneath the sphinx, all our universal history will be revealed in detail and confirmed. For starters, the higher intelligence has confirmed that Alcyone is the central sun star of the entire Pleiades and since we are part of its system, it is our local central sun in which our solar system revolves around in a revolution of 25, 650 years or so.

Alcyone transmits a universal life force; light and energy from the great central sun of our galaxy and operates like a giant storehouse of galactic records for our sector of the galaxy.

In turn, the Pleiades is also intimately connected to the trinary Sirius star systems and both star systems revolve around our galactic hub together representing the branch of our descending angelic/humanoid family, as our solar system is also and most important part of the Pleiadean/Syrian arm of the galaxy.

Now since all three systems are in different positions in reference to the galactic center, it takes them all slightly different years to make a complete revolution around our galactic hub. Although the average number as calculated by our new science is a 225, million-year cycle, of course, based on the revolution of our solar system around the great central hub of our galaxy.

So, for the record, Sirius, the Pleiades, and our solar system are part of the same swirling arm in our galaxy.

As the story goes, there were seven Pleiadean star systems in the early age of our galaxy, however, after the battle in Lyra, the star system that contained the original Avyon (original planet of the descending angelic/humanoid family) had been thwarted outside of its original circuit (orbit) from Lyra and luckily it was caught by the Pleiades central sun Alcyone.

This was a smart move by the forces of light; otherwise, the reptilians would have captured this planet, long ago.

For the record, our sun as supported by all esoteric literature is known as Helios Envesta and is the eighth missing star system orbiting around Alcyone, in cycles of 25,000 years. Other Pleiadean star systems like Coela, Taygeta, Electra, Maya, Merope and Atlas, orbit around Alcyone in shorter cycles.

It so happens that our solar system is furthest from the central sun of the Pleiades and that is the reason why it experiences longer durations in darkness than in light.

However since our earth is vital to the Pleiades, then what happens on earth reflects on all seven star systems and according to research our solar system has completed fifty-two revolutions of 25, 650-year cycles around Alcyone, it is now ready to be settled in light forever. That is why many Pleiadeans have come from the future to help the earth ascend in these days in order to prevent tyranny and darkness from spreading into the other seven-star systems and eventually the galaxy. These Pleiadean time travelers are known as timeline healers.

Also, on a different note, our planet is the most precious planet in our entire galaxy, for it contains all the seeds of all life forms that no other planet could match. Other inhabited planets recognize this diverse biologic storehouse known as our earth. Other star systems marvel at the great variety of life forms, which exist in our planet. In fact, it was revealed by a PlPleiadianister, by the name of Barbara Hand Clow that our earth contains all the biological life codes that will be seeding our entire galaxy upon her ascension since less than twenty percent of our galaxy has thus far been colonized by intelligent life forms.

The reason less than twenty percent of our galaxy has not been colonized is that in the beginning stage of our galactic war (between the sons of light the angelic Creation of the Adama Kadmon race and the sons of darkness the reptilian race), in an effort to preserve our Milky Way galaxy, the forces of light narrowed the galactic war down to a single planetary affair here in our current world.

Upon the earth's ascension, however, the stage will be set to begin the colonization process of our entire galaxy. This means that our star system, being the last orbiting star system of the Pleiades is about to become restored by the Federation of free worlds. This validates the fact that our planet is about to meet the celestial host of heaven and this corresponds with all ancient traditions regarding the coming of the angels.

At the beginning of the Pleiades expedition, things were moving along peacefully without any interventions or problems from the dark forces, of the Draco Orion Empire. However, the spiritually feminine inclined

angelic/humanoids began once again only inclining towards spiritual ascension without integrating the lower chakras, and since the plan of the universe called for polarity integration something needed to happen, as viewed from a higher perspective.

As a result of this, it was decided by the higher celestial councils, overseers of many galaxies and for the sake of proper spiritual evolution, that it was time for the one-sided galactic humanoids, to once again remember about integrating their lower chakras, which were initially represented by their reptilian counterpart. At that point, orchestrated by the celestial hierarchy operating from the center of our galaxy central sun, it was time for the angelic/humans to once again be faced with the Draco reptilians from lower Orion and the Alpha draconic and Sigma Draconic systems.

According to higher intelligence, this confrontation facilitated another opportunity for polarity integration as our creator at the highest level decreed it. This necessary adjustment meant that the great divine plan calls for the integration of spirit and matter, higher dimensions with lower dimensions.

To further elaborate this concept, this means that the creation of the Adamah (physical organic man) would not have come into fruition in the material spheres, as it is in HEAVEN (spiritual Adamic man). In addition, it is extremely important to understand that the lower chakras are crucial in order to exist in the lower material dimensions of the fifth, fourth and third densities.

Therefore, if it weren't for the arrival of the reptilians, polarity integration would have never been completed, especially as scheduled in our current time wave today, which is what the restored Nibirian council refers to as the third earth grand experiment.

Eventually, this conflict that became known as the second earth grand experiment, ended with the destruction of the second Avyon planet. The seven sisters were secured except for our solar system. This was the third major galactic war since the never-ending battle of Orion.

Another important matter that was revealed by the now restored (NC) Niburian council is that, the Etherian Sirians, (the etherichumanoid light beings who failed at inheriting a lower material vehicle, had scanned the galaxy for another planet to inhabit that was rooted in the lower dimensions of organic physical form.

They found a planet by the name of Tiamat in our current solar system, which is believed to be the re-incarnating Avyon planet before it became our current earth.

As reported by the Nbirian Council, Tiamat/earth was formed from remnant debris that was leftover from the first destruction of Avon/earth in Lyra-Sirius (during the first galactic war) before it was caught by our current solar system.

Since the Etherian Sirians sought to colonize it, as planned by the galactic celestial hierarchy the Etherian Sirians needed to evolve a third-density organic physical vehicle that would allow them to exist in the lower fourth and third dimensions of Tiamat/earth.

So, the plan was set in motion to begin developing a perfect Adamah organic vehicle from the bottom up for the use of the Etherian Sirians of Sirius C. But this requirement meant evolving a vehicle from the ground up, in order to really integrate and develop the lower chakras.

Now according to the Nibirian revelation, the problem with this expedition was, that some Sirians of this particular group, decided it was in their best interest to jumpstart the evolutionary gun to explore the lower dimensions by incarnating in the premature vehicles of the third-density evolving mammals, without waiting for the completion of their upright standing organic Homo Simian 1.1 vehicles.

Apparently, after the Etherian Sirians had incarnated to explore physical life in Tiamat they had forgotten about their true nature and got stuck in the animal/mammal reincarnation cycle and so needed to evolve back into full conscious galactic humans, through a series of vehicle upgrades. There will be more on this subject later when the true history of our planet is revealed.

Also, it is important to understand that all humanoid intelligent life forms in the multiple worlds are either a product of direct seeding by the Galactic Federation under the orders of the celestial councils. Also, by virtue of cosmic rays coming from the center of the galaxy mammalian hominids (simian primitive races) are sprung into existence from the bottom up starting from dimension One. However, in some cases as in the case of the reptoid/droid/insectoid species, planets have also been seeded, but those were a few because the Reptoid's intentions were the domination of already existing species.

Fortunately, the Galactic Federation reached our planet and solar system before the

Draco reptilians and had arranged for this system to be a galactic humanoid home from its beginning. In fact, many researchers believe that our earth is intimately connected to the Sirius star system, providing further proof that Earth was named Tiamat millions of years ago. Apparently, Tiamat/Earth resembled in appearance the original home planet, Avon in Lyra, since it was formed from a chunk of the original planet.

So, it came to pass that Tiamat/earth became colonized by the descending angelic/humanoids from the Pleiades and the etheric nonphysical light beings from Sirius A. This was a perfect colony as beings from different parts of the galaxy that were aligned with light and life also arrived, including some scientists scouting reptilians, who eventually settled there as a result of the rich mineral, animal, and plant life that existed in Tiamat/Earth. Luckily, a co-existence in Tiamat/Earth was made possible because the celestial humanoids that came from the Pleiades with the help of the higher non- incarnated Etherian Sirians collectively created another glorious civilization that become geared towards its spiritual development while integrating the lower chakras.

Apparently, the reptilians that had arrived were scouting patrols, scientists, and explorers who were scanning other star systems for life forms and they found it here in Tiamat/Earth. When this happened, the celestial hierarchy beamed much love and light to them to once again create harmony between the arriving reptilians and the already settled celestial humanoids from the Pleiades, Sirius, Alpha Century, Orion, and various other free star systems.

Little by little the few reptilians that arrived eventually had multiplied to millions and even their offspring lived in harmony with the humanoids from the systems of light, for a few hundred years.

Initially as reported by the NC, the arriving reptilians got along well with the Galactic humanoids introducing their knowledge of superior technology to them. This was another repeated pattern if we recall the first galactic war in the Lyran system. Perhaps, the celestial hierarchy from the higher dimensions also orchestrated this situation to integrate both the spiritually inclined humanoids and the technologically inclined reptilians, thus bringing the galactic wars to an end.

However, the word of this peaceful co-existence traveled fast through throughout the galactic grapevine eventually reaching the homeworld of the Draco reptilians in the Draco star system.

The Reptoids immediately sent out their patrols working for the Draconian Empire to convince the reptilians in Tiamat/Earth that living in harmony with the humanoids went in direct violation of their Draconian protocol.

Eventually, the Dracos managed (through infiltration a process that is reptilian in nature) to gradually convince the reptilian leaders of Tiamat/Earth to secretly plot the destruction of the descending celestial humanoids.

As galactic history repeated itself, the Draco reptilians From the Draco system, had convinced most of the reptilians who managed to live in harmony for the most part, to launch a pre-emptive strike against the Galactic Humans and the cetaceans (Dolphin People) that also co-habited on land in Tiamat.

The celestial hierarchy and the Galactic Federation foresaw this plot. As a result, immediately the galactic humanoids, Cetaceans, and a few reptilians that disagreed with Draco protocol were safely transferred out of Tiamat/Earth by a galactic ship known as the Pegasus to safety to other star systems. Some went back to the Pleiades, while others went to other star systems that had already been settled within the Galactic Federation of Free worlds.

The result of this transfer resulted in the complete destruction of Tiamat/Earth by the Galactic Federations battle planet Nibiru, who was under the command of Anu in those days. Anu revealed that the order to destroy the reptilian civilization in Tiamat came directly from the high Command of Sirius.

According to Anu, Nibiru blew up Tiamat by imploding the power generators at the center of the planet, destroying nearly ninety-eight percent of all reptilian life forms except for the two percent that sided with the humans and cetaceans. In the aftermath of Tiamat's destruction, the upper half of Tiamat became the asteroid belt, also known as the hammered bracelet, as translated in the risen Sumerian clay tablets. The other half eventually evolve back into a planet that became the new and current earth in which we live in. This fact confirms that planets are beings like you and me who also reincarnate, as there is no end to their spirit.

The embodiments of the material universe are obviously reflected throughout all its levels and is a vehicle of growth for the Great Spirit of the cosmos that all indigenous traditions refer to as THE ONE. We are all micro versions of the one macro omnivores-central universe, reflecting its entire splendor within ourselves.

Nonetheless, the opening of the halls of records, which corresponds to the revelation of the Akashic records, our entire galactic and universal history will be revealed. This ends a brief revelation of our forgotten Galactic past, for an entire history in detail would take up a whole third-dimensional library.

# CHAPTER TEN

## THE REAL HISTORY OF EARTH
## IS MORE THAN A FEW THOUSAND YEARS

One of the greatest discoveries in today's restoration is the uncovering of facts that reveal a prehistoric history that perhaps goes back millions of years. With the help of modern-day archeology in tandem with channeled information from the spiritual community, we can now safely postulate the idea that we have been on this planet longer than recorded records.

In fact, we are now rediscovering that our humanity, in general, has been digressing from what appeared to be an advanced ancient civilization that predated Egypt and Summer. Plato, his colleges, and later the underground Gnostic movements who had access to the esoteric (secret) knowledge, have all agreed about the existence of an advanced civilization that now has become popularized as Atlantis, which flourished for thousands of years, before recorded history.

But there is more, it turns out that Atlantis was one of various advance ancient cultures that existed before recorded time. In fact, it has been revealed that Atlantis was a rather newcomer advanced civilization. Other revealed ancient advanced cultures that existed before Atlantis, were Lemuria and the first great advanced culture was the ancient civilization of Mu. In fact, according to forbidden archeology and anthropology, civilizations have existed on this planet for more than two million years.

For millenniums, agents of the dark brotherhood (those that opposed a divine community of sisterhood and brotherhood on earth) did everything they can in the attempt to make us forget our prehistoric advanced societies. They even went as far as modifying calendars in various times that would objectively impose the beginning of the world to only a few thousand years, by eradicating any records pertaining to the last of the advanced societies called Atlantis.

For example, all history records indicate that human civilization supposedly began in 3600B.C. in Mesopotamia. In fact, this was the dark brotherhood's, the first attempt in re-setting history from that point onward. Then later under the direction of the same brotherhood, at different times they revised the calendar further, to make history seem even shorter by imposing the Gregorian calendar. Therefore, during the time of the darkest ages as produced by the dark brotherhood, all traces of an advanced prehistoric society, was almost completely eradicated due to the destruction of the vast storehouse of knowledge, the library of Alexandria.

For hundreds of years thereafter, any notion of an advanced civilization was forbidden knowledge until the late eighteen century when a lady by the name of Prêtova Helena Blavatsky, who founded an esoteric school of thought known as theosophy. This event resurrected this knowledge and little by little over the last two hundred years and with the aid of the age of information in modern times, this knowledge has now become accepted as more than a theory.

Especially with scientific evidence coming from the fields of archeology and anthropology, which are saying something different about, our advanced yet mysterious past.

Of course, the skeptics who were influenced by the temporary dark powers of this world have done their best to disclaim this knowledge as myth, not fact. They have used the theory of this lost prehistoric civilization as entertainment for the masses in creating kid movies like El Dorado, the Little Mermaid, etc. to aid the myth theory of Atlantis.

Despite the attempt to cover it up, by those who have governed the reigns of power, at the same time there is massive evidence in favor surfacing from not only channeled information revealed by divine and celestial sources but also by scientific evidence coming from archeology and anthropology. This new factual evidence also aids the new science as proposed through the new branches of Quantum Physics, Unified field theory, M- Theory.

The question arises, why would the powers that temporarily govern the affairs of this world, not want us to know the truth about our prehistoric advanced society? The answer is in the first few chapters of this book. First and most important, they did not want us to know about our divine heritage and stellar linage.

Second, they didn't want us to know that at one time, perhaps many thousands of years ago, we lived for thousands of years and that we were all connected to the creator source, as the entire planet was vibrating with the higher dimensions.

The bible records this as a time when the celestials (angels) walked with men together as one brotherhood, uniting HEAVEN AND EARTH. It is apparent now that these facts would have ruined the dark brotherhoods game plan of world domination.

After reading about our galactic history, we can now understand that the same drama between the Draco reptilians and the celestial descending humanoids that engaged our galaxy was transferred over to our planet and thus our true ancient history began, millions of years ago earth time. We will continue where we left off in our galactic history, to see how life might have originated in this planet.

After the destruction of Tiamat/Earth, the Galactic Federation and the spiritual hierarchy gave the battle star-planet known as Nibiru new tasks. That task was to deliberately end the Orion wars in favor of the celestial/ humanoids of the royal house of Avon. The second directive as ordered by the Federation was to destroy the Draco home planet (Aln) in Orion.

Lord Michael gave the order to finally cleanse Orion from the Dracos of the Rigel system and the lower Bellatrix systems as well.

The destruction of the reptilian's home planet Aln, by the Galactic Federations battle planet, Nibiru might have ended the galactic wars in Orion, however, the Draconian Empire and the remaining Dracos (Sith's) silently transferred to a new home planet in our current solar system that becomes known as Maldek. Maldek was the eleventh planet in the family of our solar system. Nevertheless, roughly a few million years before the arrival of the remnant Dracos in Maldek, after losing the war in Orion, there was initially flooding of celestial galactic humanoids from various free star systems that populated every planet in our solar system including the jovial planets Neptune, Saturn, Uranus, and Jupiter.

Since the celestial galactic humanoids were multidimensional, they existed from the higher fifth dimension to the lower fourth dimension. At this point, the third dimension that existed in Tiamat, transferred only to the new-formed planet earth, since our earth holds all twelve dimensions. Therefore, the three-dimensional mammals and those Syrian souls that got stuck in mammalian bodies during Tiamat's days returned to the new earth. There is no record indicating, exactly how many years ago the celestial galactic humanoids populated our entire solar system, but according to speculation, it all took place about three to four million years ago earth time. Considering this, once upon a time, our entire solar system had multidimensional life forms living in it.

Everything from the humanoid family to cetaceans (dolphin people), to shapeshifting snakes, to different types of Amphibians and mammals, lived in our solar system and in harmony.

The celestial galactic humanoids came from the free star systems of the Pleiades, Arcturus, upper Orion, Lyra, Vega, Alpha Centauri, Betelgeuse, Mintaka, and Al Nil am in upper Orion, as well as Sirius, and some even migrated from our neighboring galaxy Andromeda who had already ascended prior to the seeding of our galaxy. It was also revealed that in our galaxy, all biological species were genetically engineered by the Felines who were an advanced spiritual race from a different galaxy as reported by the restored Nibirian Council.

So when Tiamat was reborn as our current earth, at the onset of what came to be known as the second seeding and colonization, roughly three or four million years ago, one of the first galactic civilizations emerged on earth that became known as Mu pre-dating both Atlantis and Lemuria. This civilization, however, was considered luminal and not etheric- material like Lemuria. In other words, it existed on the highest frequency or celestial dimension here on our planet a long time ago, when our earth was connected to all twelve-dimensional spheres. Perhaps this was a civilization corresponding with the Sirius C civilization, which is the most evolved civilization (population three galactic star system) in our galaxy.

Whatever the case may be, through a succession of civilizations on earth, it seems that each civilization that succeeded the other, had become denser and denser material, this makes perfect sense since we start off as spiritual luminous beings and through the process of descension, we begin to condense into eventually becoming congealed solid form as revealed earlier. This process is repeated but on a planetary level. For the most part, let's go by the theosophical records of the secret doctrine, which reveals that the first great civilization that came to exist was the land of Mu. Mu according to the secret doctrine was not only galactic but it openly interacted with the civilizations on other planets in our solar system as well with civilizations throughout our entire Galaxy and other galaxies. It was a perfect society composed of some of the most advanced beings from population two stellar and three galactic systems, which lived in harmony. This was known for the first time and it was inhabited by advanced beings operating with bodies of light existing in all nine dimensions.

In this civilization, only purity was exercised and even some converted Fifth-dimensional reptilians co-existed with the advanced celestial humanoids as well as other sentient beings. Among them were the Cetaceans (dolphin people) the Felines (cat people) and even a race of people known as the diniod race. The droid race was a converted race that used to be hostile like their reptilian brothers before coming to Mu.

Apparently, during those days all extraterrestrials coming to our solar system were being screened by the Galactic Federation to see if they had evil intentions. For those that didn't pass the screening for whatever mal-intentions sensed by the Federation were immediately escorted out of our solar system into other parts of the galaxy through a stargate that would open and close by remote control at the hands the Federation. In fact, every planet in our solar star system roughly a few million years was colonized by the support of the Confederations of free worlds of a type two-stellar space-age cultures.

Now according to the higher intelligence, the celestial galactic humanoids occupied all the planets except for Maldek, which eventually become a military outpost for the Draco- reptilians of the Draconian Empire some two and a half million years ago. However, planet earth was the most guarded because it is the most important planet in not only our galaxy but in our entire local universe.

By adopting this theory and as we continue our planetary history, which is connected to our galactic history because if we follow the history of our planet earth, that is if earth came from Tiamat while Tiamat came from Avon in Lyra, Sirius, then what we see is the same drama except it is now in its last stage and ready for completion as confirmed by Anu of the restored Nibirian council. In the end, Mu the first great civilization in our planet lasted for a million and a half years, until the reptilians hailing from what used to be the planet Maldek launched a preemptive strike against all celestial galactic humanoids in our solar system. This war was devastating because it destroyed all the galactic human colonies in our solar system including the civilization known as Mu the first great galactic advanced culture on earth.

This was about two million years ago. The process that led to a full-out galactic war in our solar system was gradual and secretive from the beginning; the planet the Draco-Reptilians (demons) saw fit was obviously Mars since it had an inter-dimensional doorway to Orion.

Perhaps the Federation forgot to close it, or maybe there was a double agent in the Federation who oversaw closing it and accidentally forgot in service to the Draconian. Whatever the reason, this mistake ended causing the Federation the destruction of the first great seeding in our solar system. This meant that the dimensional vortex in Mars would act as a doorway of escape to certain draconian of Orion. And it did, as some Dracos leaked into our solar system, by shapeshifting into human form in order to deceive the galactic humanoids as they transferred into our solar system through Mars. This is likened to how the Sith in "Star Wars" shape-shifted into the Chancellor, in the Revenge of the Sith.

Shortly after the Dracons (demons) managed to infiltrate the Martian colony from within by entering through an inter-dimensional doorway, they quickly began to infiltrate and take over the affairs in Mars.

Bear in mind that inter-dimensional stargates are now a scientific fact, rather than science fiction, as there is one in the Bermuda triangle as well as in the Gulf of Eden and many other places on our planet.

The Dracos knew that this solar system was well guarded by the Confederation of Free worlds, which could detect their ships from miles away. So, the Dracos went about it in a different way. First, they could have infiltrated the Federation because the whole idea of double agents was also practiced then as it is today with modern-day secret societies. The second possibility is that they themselves could have managed to open the dimensional doorway in Mars, from Orion, since they fell under the category of type two space-age civilizations, capable of manipulating stargates.

As to how they did that there is no data yet, however, what is known, is that eventually, the Martian colony that was inhabited by galactic humans fell from being connected to the universal life force of the great central sun when they submitted to the outer technologies given to them by their new visitors, the shape-shifting Draconian.

This was a two-way plan by the Draconian of the royal galactic house of Aln. Now as to how they also managed to totally occupy a planet (Maldek) of their own in our solar system remains a mystery. Perhaps after coming in through the stargate in Mars, they slowly began building their secret colony in Maldek, which was apparently ignored by the human colonies. Nonetheless, this was a secret expedition that was apparently undetected by the Confederation of the guardians of councils. Whatever the reason was, there might have been a force greater than the galactic councils that allowed for this to happen, for everything has a purpose. The planets that were most affected by the attacks from Maldek were the terrestrial planets. As far as the jovial planets, they were secured in higher dimensions than the fifth where the Draconian had no more access, thanks to the cleansing of the higher dimensions conducted by Lord Michael. For at one point in this cosmic drama Lord Michael and his forces of the galactic command had curtailed the dark forces from existing in the higher dimensions beyond fifth and up.

Today it is believed that those civilizations in the higher etheric and celestial spheres on the Jovial planets, have been existing till this day and have been aiding the Federation of Free Worlds, from the council of Saturn in the liberation of our planet. However after this demise that took place in our solar system millions of years ago destroying the human populations of Mars, Venus, and Earth, the Draco-reptilians were prohibited from entering our solar system by the Federation and were now confined to the fourth and third dimension only.

Even though this war in the early history of our solar system, brought the destruction of the first galactic human colonies in our solar system, the planets remain intact in their orbits ready to be seeded once again, by the Federation. Also adding the reason Maldek was able to cause such havoc was because Nibiru, the patrolling planet of the Galactic Federation was too far off in the Sirius system during its elongated orbit.

Apparently, Nibiru was programmed by the Galactic Federation to only come into our solar system every 3600 years, so that it may patrol other systems and worlds during its lone elongated orbit across other parts of our galaxy. By the time Nibiru got to our neck of the woods, all civilizations in our solar system were destroyed.

Nevertheless, Nibiru didn't waste time upon arrival, beaming the planet Maldek into pieces, destroying the Reptoid and Dinoid population in a split second, with only one percent or so who barely survived, because they managed to escape. As a result of Maldeks destruction, the Colbert belt was formed.

In support of this theory, there is now scientific evidence that is being slowly released from NASA indicating that there was life on other planets such as Mars and Venus. For instance, they have found old water canals and dried-up riverbeds on Mars. Not to mention ancient monuments and pyramids have also been discovered on Mars. One example of this would be the face monument located in Mars that could be dated to at least two million of years back. Well according to the Niburian council, this was a monument built by the Galactic Federation in Memory of the great stellar human civilization that existed there, millions of years ago.

Today Mu and the other civilizations that occupied our solar system during those times are slowly becoming a discussable topic since we are living in the fullness of times.

Nonetheless, life on earth continued as the Pleiades and Sirians quickly set about to re-seed our planet for the second time, to create the second great galactic civilization that become known as Lemuria. As for the other planets, Mars and Venus's life perhaps ascended to a higher dimension, no longer existing in the fourth and third densities.

During the times of Lemuria, Light beings had become denser than during the times of Mu. According to the secret doctrine, each civilization that followed becomes denser and denser. Theosophy also revealed that while Mu was considered the first root-race of our planet, Lemuria was considered the second root race.

In fact, Lemuria was considered the second Garden of Eden. From the beginning, Lemuria like Mu had developed as a Syrian- LyranPleiadean society, gearing towards spiritual feminine growth, with no technology.

Some say that Lemuria acted as a model for a true democracy. It was considered a perfect world, with lush green, blue skies, and seas; it was a garden independent of external technologies, a true Garden of Eden.

The inhabitants were etheric material (spiritual matter) and gross physical (organic matter) existing in both dimensions at once. Since there was no external technology and everyone was tuned with universal consciousness. Back then every sentient being humanoid and otherwise was a co-creator of their own reality. However, as in the case of the Pleiades second earth grand experiment, the Lemurians becomes two polarized towards spiritual evolution and were going to lose touch with physical reality lower than the fifth dimension.

In other words, they were going to make our entire planet ascend without fully integrating the lower chakras or in the case of our planet (the lower dimensions). So, the time to continue the game of polarity integration had to be adjusted one more time by the higher-ups, for its success. So by decree of the higher bits of intelligence, higher than the sixth dimension, the Atlantean colony was formed by a group of fifth dimensional Pleiadeans (galactic humanoids) who had adopted the use of technology but in balance with their spirituality, which is the result of polarity integration on both a cultural and spiritual-material level.

At this point, Atlantis would be the solution by the higher-ups, to bridge the lower dimensions with the higher ones, to maybe succeed in polarity integration.

From a higher perspective, all root races were steps in a greater development that would eventually establish an eternal Utopia on our planet.

For instance, according to esoteric (secret) knowledge, Atlantis became the third root-race collectively developing the group mind of the planet. Lemuria was developing the feeling center or emotional body of our planet, while in Mu we were learning to evolve a physical body.

In the fourth root-race, which is our current stage, and after developing our mental body during the times of Atlantis, we were given 13,000 years to learn to balance the mind (technology) and emotions (spiritually) for the next 13, 000 years or so.

So by the time we enter the fifth root-race of the seventh golden age which is now, we can begin to once again develop our light body in a speedy upward evolution to the higher dimensions where we came from while staying grounded in the lower material dimensions. In this case, a correct ascension would finalize the integration of spirit and matter, higher dimensions with lower dimensions.

This makes perfect sense if we invert the descending process of involution from light (spirit), to mind (ether), to feeling (astral) to material (physical). This also corresponds to the four-body system describe in the eastern traditions and all would agree that the whole purpose of the great descent is for us celestial light beings to inherit a perfected physical vehicle that is grounded in all dimensions.

Furthermore, despite Atlantis's original intention to be the integrating point between spirit and matter, the dark forces turned things around in Atlantis for one last round before the age of spiritual evolution begins in 2017-2022 A.D. One last round because according to ancient prophecies the forces of darkness (duality) come to an end at the rise of the fifth Root Race, which is happening in our current times.

Before we continue our true history let's refer to our planetary logos because it is important to understand the lineage of the forces of light a bit more. The history of Lord Sanat Kumara goes back to Sirius, but really to Salvington, the headquarters of our local universe of Nebadon. In fact, Lord Sanat Kumara is dispatching, descending high son of light (Melchizedek) serving in the order of the Ancient of Days of the super universe governments.

He works directly under the guidance of Lord Michael the creator son of our local universe. While lord Michael is also considered our universal logos and head of the cosmic order of Melchizedek for the twelve major creations, the last major universe, Sanat Kumara is his representative on a planetary level and heads the planetary order of Melchizedek or what is known as the planetary spiritual hierarchy for the sixth dimension down to the third, since it is materializing in our times.

So, when the great plan was set up to restore our local universe, various high sons and daughters of light volunteered to aid Lord Michael in the restoration of our local universe. Lord Sanat Kumara was one of them and has been aiding the great divine plan before the foundation of this world or its ancient civilizations. He assisted Lord Michael the moment the fallen angels (celestial) planted their seed in our galaxy, and since Orion was the first constellation in our galaxy that was exploited by the fallen ones, his mission had to begin there.

From the great beginning, it was decided by the cosmic order of Melchizedek in conjunction with the order of the Ancient of days, that the forces of light infiltrate the forces of darkness from the beginning of the split in heaven. Lord Sanat Kumara fulfilling his part in the infiltration process had willingly incarnated in Orion as one of the Dracos but really working for the light. This sounds strange; however, it needed to happen in order to work the dark side from within, so that the forces of light may always be steps ahead of the dark ones. First, Lord Sanut Kumara was the first of the incarnated Melchizedeks to demonstrate Ascension in Orion and amid opposition.

He was born directly into the royal house of Aln, although his mother was from the royal house of Ananda, the line that came to Orion from Sirius A, after the first galactic war, in Lyra. The line of Ananda was the merging lines of both the house of Avyon and the house of Aln, in Avyon Lyra before the first galactic war. As the story goes after enslaving the Orion Humanoids his powerful father, a draconian-reptilian general had a child with a descendant of the pure line of Ananda and so he was born.

His mother was an Orion celestial/humanoid and a direct descendant from the house of Ananda. Sanut Kumara, therefore, was the first being to integrate all chakras, thus given him the capacity of the complete power of the force. This allowed Lord Kumara to achieve ascension by the integration of spirit and matter, thus giving him full access to the power of the great central sun. Since then, all descendants of this line carried in their life SUN, which is the highest vibrating substance in our galaxy.

stream, the power of the universal life force, by integrating higher and lower spheres, they had the choice to either use the full force UNIFIED ENERGY FIELD for either good or bad.

Throughout galactic history, those of this line were considered the most powerful beings in our galaxy and were sought after by both the Dracos and the humanoids of the Galactic Federation of light. In support of this, it is confirmed in the secret doctrine, that after connecting the higher chakras with the lower Chakras, a vertical line of energy force would align along the vertebrae in which the uninterrupted full power of the universal life force kundalini energy rushes upwards through the individual's spine giving him or her full access to THE UNLIMITED POWER OF THE GREAT CENTRAL

However, as confirmed in the secret knowledge that the power derived from activating the kundalini energy could only happen if the higher and lower chakras are fully integrated and properly aligned. For without the integration of the higher and lower chakras, there is no Anta Karana (vertical light cord that aligns all our chakras) integrating both the higher dimensions (heaven) and the lower ones (earth).

By incarnating, this allows the individual to become a clear (channel) of unlimited power for the higher forces. This reservoir of infinite energy power potential is what in science is known as the ZeroPoint-Energy field, which is equivalent to the unified field that resonates at the center of all galactic systems.

So, from the beginning of his early days in Orion, Sanat Kumara rebelled against Draconian protocol, he become an outcaste that was both hated and feared by the supreme Draco leaders, because of his power.

And even though the superior Dracos (sixth) did everything in their power to convert or seduce him to serve the dark lords, he remains loyal to Lord Michael.

Initially, lord kumara was embodied as a fearsome dragon warrior until the time came for the order of Melchizedek, and the descending celestial/humanoids (from Lyra and Sirius) to begin the restoration process in Orion. If we recall, after the hybrid Lyran humanoid's arrival in Orion, they immediately were forced into slavery.

So, after a couple of hundred years of slavery, it was Sanut Kumara that rose as a fearless leader, like Moses in our bible, and helped organized the Orion Black League, creating the rebel resistance in Orion.

That was around the time of his ascension and as a result, he inherited his perfected Adamah Cadman body (celestial humanoid) just in time to establish the confederation of free worlds, in Orion four and a half million years ago earth time.

After his mission was fulfilled in Orion, Sanat Kumara (and for the very reasons that this cosmic drama has its finale here in our planet) was dispatched to Venus to aid our solar logos, Helios Envesta, in bringing the light of the great central sun to our neck of the woods. It is also equally important to understand that in the energy body of our solar being (Helios Envesta), Venus represents the love center or feminine aspect of our solar being, while Mars represents its mind center (masculine). Since the earth is in between, it is supposed to be the synthesis and balance of them both, again displaying polarity integration, for the entire universe.

The plan that led to establishing the planetary spiritual council was brought about when the Galactic Federation and the galactic and solar spiritual hierarchies decided that our earth needed a spiritual guiding council other than Nibiru, who only came into our vicinity every 3600 years. As a result, our planetary spiritual body council was born under the direction of Sanat Kumara who the lord of Venus and representative of Michael for our solar system was.

Apparently, after Venus ascended into the fifth dimension, Sanut kumara and two other Kumaras (those of the Ananda line) were chosen to restore the light of the higher realms back to earth, since the first great colony was known as Mu was destroyed. Since then, these three Kumaras have been heading our planet's spiritual counsel from the higher dimensions.

Another Melchizedek and intimate brother of Sanut Kumara, is Commander Ishtar Antares or Ashtar of the Ashtar Command.

Ishtar Antares came to us from our sister galaxy Andromeda and was instrumental in the organization of the Federation of planets in our galaxy, in response to the Seal of Paladar.

He has served as one of the first commanders ever since and today in our current times, is head commander of the Federation of planets here in our solar system, operating from the council of Saturn.

He also served the cosmic divine plan by helping other local universes and galaxies ascend before our galaxy.

Today he is known as the grand commander of the airborne division of the great white brotherhood/sisterhood and works directly under the orders of Michael aka Lord Jesus the Christ, Sananda.

Overall, it was Sanat Kumara who established and built the great civilization of Lemuria with the support of the confederation of free worlds, one and a half million years ago. Sanut Kumara was head of the Lemurian Colony and Earth and the other planets in our solar system were now free from the reptilian forces during the times of the third seeding. However, this wasn't the end of the conflict. It turns out that when the earth was still Tiamat, the few surviving reptilians that sided with the humans later proved to be untrustworthy.

To make matters worse, one of them happened to be a direct descendent of the house of Aln.

This was the reptilian queen Dramyin, who sided with the humans during the Tiamat/earth conflict.

So in an attempt to establish peace and harmony among the remnant reptilians, Commander Anu of the Nibirian battle star decided that in order to maintain peace on the NEW earth, an alliance needed to take place between the Syrian/Pleiadean descending celestial humanoids of Nibiru and the surviving reptilians that allegedly had a conversion to the light.

The Alliance was crucial because it required a truss between the royal house of Avyon through Anu and the house of Aln, through Dramyin, a direct descendant of the Draco house of Aln.

Anu to integrate both groups came with a solution, which was to marry Dramyin in order to maintain peace on Nibiru as well as on the NEW earth that was beginning to blossom again.

Meanwhile back on earth, a few Plaiedian beings had already begun the third wave of re-colonization. This was the period of about one million years ago.

We had had not only Lemuria which become the motherland of the new earth development, thanks to Lord Sanut Kumara our planetary logos who worked in unison and in balance with the great mother goddess represented by the womb of the earth, Gaea.

During the second seeding, other colonies were also established by the descending celestial/humanoids in different parts of the globe.

We had the YU colony in Asia, the land of Rama in the India region, the Mayan colony in the Yucatan area, which was seeded by the Pleiade's second star system known as Maya.

The developing Atlantis was glooming thanks to Atlas, a Pleiadean grandson of Anu, in the middle of the Atlantic Ocean.

With the rise of these advanced prehistoric cultures, our earth and its solar system were once again galactic in nature, being a full-fledged member of the confederation of free worlds and maintaining a harmonious stellar civilization on our planet for the next 500,000 thousand years.

As in Mu and Lemuria, Starships would come and go to and from the planet as the earth was beginning to once again become an exchange zone for galactic commerce, as planned by the higher-ups, as some would term, the original founders of our local galaxy.

At this point everything was running smoothly; the marriage of Anu to Dramyin gave the Nibirians Enki, who in our mythology, was known as the earth builder EA. He was half Pleiadean descending celestial/humanoid and half draconian reptilian. Some believe he was another attempt to synthesis both groups. But overall, as we shall see, Enki as well as his half-brother Enlil became extremely influential in the course that our planet took thereon, as they usurped absolute control of our planet from the galactic federation and the rest of our cosmos.

As the story goes, these two brothers quarrel for control of the planet. After a while of bitter tension between the two half-brothers, and since Commander Anu assumed absolute responsibility for the earth, divided the earth into sections.

Enki was given Africa, the absu region as well as the Atlantean ocean region corresponding to the ancient Greek god Poseidon who ruled Atlantis according to Plato.

Enlil was given the Mesopotamia region, including Europe, corresponding to the ancient God EL of early Israel. Eventually, the rest of the planet became divided up by the Nibirians and their offspring as the story of the ancient gods (celestial humanoids) unfold.

According to Zachariah Zitchin, a cultural-linguistic scholar and primary translator of the Sumerian clay tablets revealed that Enlil was against the spiritual development of the evolving Homo erectus ascending animal/human/mammals in restoring them back into full conscious celestial/humanoids. On the contrary, Enki was allegedly their benefactor and one who worked for their restoration, as translated from the Sumerian tablets. Now according to the restored Nibirian council, the story begins to sound slightly different, as the Sumerians tablets could have been tampered with. The restored Niburian council confirmed that Enlil was never opposed to his bothers plans of helping evolve the Homo erectus into homo sapien-sapiens that he himself biogenically engineered by admixing DNA from themselves (celestials) and the evolving Homo erectus (terrestrials) that were a product of natural progressive and intelligently directed organic biologic evolution.

Truth is, Enlil believed in a gradual evolution, while Enki preferred a rather quicker one, which was one of many reasons these brothers clashed. The restored (Nibiruan Council) is more reliable since the ancient Sumerian tablets were edited by the high priest of Marduk in Babylon and as we will come to know Marduk became the chief fallen celestial draconian angel leader of the forces of darkness, in our world. At this point let me remind us that we are spiritual beings encased in an organic vehicle, made from the natural clay of the earth.

Therefore, the missing link from Homo erectus to Homo sapiens only provided a vehicle for us spirit beings descending celestial to begin the incarnational process of whole light beings in third dimensional upright physical bodies, to finalized polarity integration of spirit and matter.

This tells us that the ancient astronaut theory as well as the risen knowledge in the Sumerian records is correct uniting both sides of the spectrum, however in favor of creation by intelligent design, and not evolution by random change.

Also, it is important to understand that our bible was a consolidation of all this ancient knowledge, in condensed symbolic form in the first five books known as the Torah.

For example, in its not symbolic form, all records attest to the fact that Enki becomes instrumental in the dissemination of the higher Knowledge, or as some would say the knowledge of the Nibirians (gods).

Many scholars are beginning to believe that this was metaphorically camouflaged as the apple incident in our bible.

From a higher perspective, Enlil saw that offering this type of advanced knowledge to beings of low intelligence, that were not ready for advanced technological evolution, was like trying to offer a dynamite stick and a lighter to a five-year-old child to play with.

As a result of this, Enlil believed that the evolving Homo sapiens were to take a gradual growth for their spirituality to mature before discovering advanced technologies regarding the use of powerful energies.

Enlil believed that the Homo-Sapien-sapiens (that were biogenetically engineered from the Homo erectus with not enough spiritual growth or evolution would destroy themselves with advanced technical knowledge, which proved to be correct in the later days of Atlantis as we shall see.

In fact, based on these early galactic family feuds, we could now trace all our current world problems to the never-ending battle that took place hundreds of thousands of years ago by these two half brothers and their descendants.

For the record, these beings were our ancestors and biologic uplifters that bridged the gap between descending celestial intelligence and ascending physical organic intelligence.

These gods were the ancient celestial/humanoids with twelve strands of DNA that came mainly from the Pleiades, Orion, Lyra-Sirius, and Alpha Centuras and some carried the line of the Draco lineage, which was the line of Aln/Lucifer.

According to the Urantia material, these celestial/humanoids (not gods) are the descending sons and daughters of light that originated in the central universe of eternal spheres Havona.

Urantia refers to them as citizens of the Jerusalem system of a population two statues that dispatched the descending super men and superwomen of the Caligastia one hundred corporeal staff. For the record, other than the descending celestial intelligence that from heaven to earth came, we also had the evolving Homosapien-sapiens who were the Etherian Sirians and the not so evolving Homo primitives who seize to exist about 30,000 years ago, according to the fossil record, as only the strain of Homo sapien-sapiens continued.

Again, this group known as Homo sapien- sapiens was the ascending primates, which were evolving the small percentage of Sirians souls that got trapped in the mammal reincarnation cycle during the days of Tiamat three million years ago. It was this strain of ascending spirit beings that became the evolving line of primates that later suddenly overnight become Cro-Magnon man and as the Nibirians continued to add their superior DNA, eventually CroMagnon man evolved into the mankind of today, homo sapiens sapiens.

This truth provides evidence of the sudden leaps or missing links in our incomplete theory of evolution, indicating that mankind today is the final product of something bigger than just evolution from the bottom up, but rather a middle point was involution (descent of spirit into matter) from the top-down meets intelligently engineered evolution from the bottom up, thus providing further proof of creation by Intelligent Design.

It appears that the gods (celestial humanoids) of ancient times were important key players in the completion of the grand divine masterpiece known as modern-day mankind. According to all records, Enki become the one-two bring this process into fulfillment, Although eventually Enlil also began to contribute his life plasma as he also become a benevolent protector of the evolving ascending Homo Sapien-sapiens, especially those that came from his strain, carrying a heavy concentration of fifth-dimensional Plaiedian, Syrian and Lyran life plasma.

However, according to the Urantia material, the Life plasma of the violet race, (the descending fifth dimensional Pleiadeans) failed to spread to all of evolving ascending man causing the fall of advanced civilization and culture in our planet, as evolving mankind was mostly dominated by their lower animal self.

According to all records, the Nibirians came for our planet's gold supply. The question is why was Nibiru in need of such large quantities of gold from the earth. Again, the answer lies in our suppressed galactic history.

As confirmed by the Nibirian Council; and as revealed earlier Nibiru was losing its atmosphere upon arrival about 450,000 years ago, due to the destruction of the planet Maldek.

As recalled, this was the planet the Dracos inhabited in our solar system before they launched their attack on Mu the first stellar human colony during the first seeding. This piece of information about the cause and tare in Nibiru' s atmosphere has not yet been confirmed by Sitchin, but since it comes from a higher source (Anu) then it is more reliable than the Sumerian tablets. As the real story goes, the battle star-planet Nibiru had become damaged with radiation the moment they blew up the planet Maldek.

It turns out that Maldek was a planet full of nuclear weapons and in blowing the planet up, it emitted dangerous radiation that eventually reached Nibiru atmosphere and damaged it, causing a leak. Without repair, and after almost one and a half million years later, eventually the inhabitants of Nibiru would decrease in life span. So, a plan was created by the Nibirians to find the element that they needed in order to save their planet. That element was gold and the hot source for it was our planet earth. The information regarding the coming of the Anunaki to our world for gold is well understood by our world scholars now and it has been confirmed to be true by the translated Sumerian records. At this point, it is important to understand that the Anunaki of Nibiru were the same beings that our bible refers to as the watchers as revealed in the Book of Enoch and another biblical term used was the Elohim as revealed in the book of Genesis.

In our bible, particularly in the left out books of Enoch, Jubilee, and others and as confirmed in Genesis, the Nibirians were recorded as the sons of God (Elohim) plural for the many celestial beings who descended upon the earth in those days for many reasons. First of course, as confirmed by the Sumerian records, was to extract the gold they needed to save their planet. Second and perhaps most importantly, as we shall see later, they came to also mate with the daughters of evolving (ascending) men in order to upgrade the genetics of the indigenous evolving earth race in preparation for spiritual evolution in order to integrate heaven and earth, spirit and matter.

In truth, these Anunakis, Elohim or watchers whatever you would like to call them, who appeared humanoid in all ancient accounts, were our ancient original angelic elder brothers and sisters and apparently our parent race, since we were made in their image and inherited there (life plasma) genetics, as revealed in the book of Genesis. "Let US go down and make man in OUR image".

More references to the existing immortal humans are also confirmed in the Egyptian translations describing the same beings that came from Nibiru (heaven) to earth. Also, in India, according to their ancient manuscripts known as the Rig Vedas; there is a reference to an ancient group or race of superhumans that intermingled with the early primitive evolving humans of our world.

China had its versions as well, in their ancient text. In ancient times, the Chinese taught their people that a god, half man, and half fish brought them civilization from the sea. For the sake of no confusion, let's call these ancient celestial beings Nibirians.

Now, the plan to genetically modify a group of beings (us) higher than the hominids (primate) and lower than the descending celestial/humanoids (gods) came about as a two-way resolution, as we shall see. As mentioned, the first reasons were that the Nibirians nevertheless, needed to extract gold from the interior of our earth in order to save their planet's atmosphere as revealed by both Anu and Sitchin.

According to all accounts, Anu sends Enki and his best astronauts to mine the gold in Africa. As the story goes, these ancient astronauts eventually couldn't take the heat inside the earth, so they mutinied and when Enlil arrived, they held him hostage until Enki arrived to release him. Enlil enraged, demanded that his brother Enki received punishment, believing that it was Enki who conspired to have him captured.

This very incident is what caused a sudden change or jump in the natural evolutionary ascend of evolving primates. This is the first and primary missing link that Darwin himself could not figure out. Not to mention, this was the beginning of the defining point that demarcated the end of nature but yet intelligently directed evolution between the old evolving hominid primates that evolved out of a mammalian strain, of five hundred thousand years ago and the humans that exist today, who were a product of divine intervention and genetic upgrade manipulation that came into the picture roughly around 30,000 years ago.

According to natural evolution, what took place overnight in the jump of hominid (primitive) man to homo sapien-sapiens -(thinking) man has scientist heads spinning. From a higher perspective, this biogenetic upgrade of evolving hominids was a two-way plan that would help in the restoration of the Nibirian atmosphere, as the descending celestial/humanoids needed a worker group of semi-intelligent people to mine the hot interiors of our earth. If we recall, the Anunaki astronauts, were a group of fifth and fourth-density stellar humanoids of a population two of space-age cicivilizationshat that hated to toil and work like any other being would.

Most importantly, this upgrade would also provide a series of progressive vehicles for the gradual restoration of the stuck Sirians who needed to evolve back into full functioning celestial humanoids. Again, bear in mind that everything happens for a reason.

Therefore, this plan was erected and approved by both the celestial hierarchy and the Galactic Federation of free worlds in conjunction with the Niburian command. The idea of creating a worker race of primitive beings was brought forth by Enki to the Nibirian Council as a solution to both dilemmas, and it was approved.

Not to mention this would allow for the eventual incarnation of the descending celestial/humanoids (STAR PEOPLE OF THE VIOLET DNA) into third-dimensional vehicles so that polarity integration would finally be a success in this final third earth grand experiment, as planned by the founders of our galaxy, who have been overseeing the whole process from a population three galactic system civilization existing at the center of our galaxy.

According to all records, it was Enki and his half-sister Ninhursal (Nimah) the medical officer of the Niburian command, who became in charge of the Homo erectus upgrades.

Both ancient Sumerian translations and restored Nibiruan records reveal that Enki was a master geneticist and maverick scientist, and his half-sister Nimah was proficient in all the medical arts. In fact, it appears that they were both tutored by her mother a greater sixth-dimensional being, and Feline from Sirius A.

So, from the highest levels, it was obviously necessary to jump-start the evolution of the mammalian primates so that they may evolve back into full functioning celestial/humanoids, by the end of what is known as the great cycle, 2017-23 AD.

The first two upgrades were conducted at Shurapuk, the medical center of the Nibirians which was one of their various earth settlements, next to Nippur, Bad Tibarra, and Eridu, all located in the region we know as Mesopotamia.

At first, and as revealed by all accounts, the Nibirians biogenetically engineered the new species in their laboratory, using test tubes.

Then as the time when on they were upgraded to reproduce by themselves and finally the third missing link upgrade came about when the Anunaki themselves came down from Nibiru to mate with the more advance of the evolving earth humans, which were those that carried the highest percentage of Nibirian Life plasma. The interbreeding between the sons of God (Nibirians) and daughters of men (earth) produce the heroes of old as revealed in the biblical book of Genesis and as confirmed in the excavated ancient Sumerian tablets.

In mythology, they were known as the demi-gods, or as we would now refer to as fourth-dimensional conscious humans in third-dimensional vehicles. These heroes of old existed during the times of Atlantis as recorded in all ancient accounts.

According to the secret doctrine, the Elohim or the supposed ancient mythological gods were full conscious humanoids or descending spirit beings, while those passing as the daughters of men were the upgraded evolving earth humans who were evolving a vehicle for the descending spirit beings, the Pleiadean Nibirians, to finally incarnate into third-dimensional vehicles, to complete the long descending process of involution, which is the descent of spirit into organic matter to then transform the organic matter into the spiritual matter.

Also, the difference between the upgraded earth-based primitives, which later evolve into homo sapien-sapiens and the rest of the primates was that after about the third vehicle upgrade, the new evolving homo sapien- sapiens were now capable of downloading their light body, in becoming like their descending celestial/humanoid parents, however, they were programmed to only use ten percent or less of their light body capacity, which is equivalent to today's ninety percent of our untapped genetic material. And that is why the homo sapien-sapiens sapiens-sapiens of today are sleeping giants only functioning at less than ten percent of their full divine celestial capacity, explaining the so-called junk DNA our scientists have discovered.

Nevertheless, after the upgrades, things were originally peaceful for all the inhabitants of all colonies about 300,000 thousand years ago. The descending celestial/humanoids (our ancestors) appeared to live forever since they were in full use of their light body, complete DNA material. As for the evolving homo sapien-sapiens, their life span was about a few hundred years since they were only using less than ten percent of their light body-DNA. For the record, in our advanced past, after the extinction of the entire hominid primitive strains, there existed three types of races. The evolving Cro-Magnon, who were the ascending earth humans and the Nibirians descending celestial humanoids. And out of this intermixing a third human was produced known as the demi-god, half earth human, half descending Niburian Pleiadean.

This was a co-existence of fifth, fourth, and third-dimensional humanoids. This apparently, had to do with the connection of the third, fourth and fifth dimensions through the functioning cosmic current that was produced by the operating grid system or as the Urantia material refers to as the life circuits, which connected the higher realms of heaven with earth. However, the cosmic current was later shut off as the earth's grid system became deactivated when Atlantis collapsed.

In fact, our biblical Noah who happened to be one of Enlil's biological sons, not Enkis was a demi-god who lived for almost a thousand years, as apparently did Gilgagesh. Now according to our bible, about ten percent of all humans today come from the line of Noah/Zissudra/Anapushtim. That tells us that all humans that descendants of a Demigod (Noah) are those of an Rh-negative blood type.

Those that are RH positive blood type could be the descendants of the evolving earth Cro- Magnon, that came from the primitive earth stock.

For it is written in all ancient accounts, that the superior celestial humanoids fathered various children that were born to the evolving female humans. In all due respect, this was supposed to happen in order to continue the vehicle upgrades of those Syrian souls that were trapped in the lower animal bodies during the times of Tiamat/Earth. It also becomes evident that Enlil and Enki weren't the only descending celestial/humanoids that mated with the evolving earth humans.

These gods or rather these celestial/humanoids had not only other relatives involved in the project but other extraterrestrial factions that were not in alignment with the Galactic Federation and the office of the Christ of the great blue lodge of Sirius (the Seal Of Paladar) and therefore began conducting their own genetic experiments.

Some records have revealed that a small group of AnunakiNibirians was not only biogenetically altering the evolving race's DNA but in the process created some half-beast, half-human species that were not part of the original divine plan. This type of tampering with advanced genetic altercations involving earth-based human DNA was conducted by these other ET factions (fallen angels), who contributed strongly to the eventual decline and disintegration of the Atlantean golden age. In fact, right before the fall of Atlantis, the evolving humans and those heroes of old (demi-gods) half god and half human that gave us Hercules become famous for their battles against the different types of monsters that emerged as a result of the uncontrolled genetic tampering. For the most part, Atlantis was supposed to be a marvelous civilization

that was meant to integrate spirit and matter, spirituality and technology, Venus and Mars; however, they polarized toward the technological side at the expense of spirituality, when the Dracons of the.

# CHAPTER ELEVEN

## THE FALL OF ATLANTIS WAS THE FALL OF MAN

During the days of Atlantis, our planet had two types of existing civilizations. These are perhaps the civilizations that our new science refers to as, a population one planetary system and population two-star stellar system space-age cultures.

For instance, back then, not only was our planet a full-fledged active member of the Galactic Federation of free worlds but had developed a levitation-based transportation system that allowed citizens of Atlantis to travel to different parts of the world, in minutes.

This only implies that back then; we had mastered inter-dimensional travel and electromagnetic hydraulic technology which is the equivalent of a population of two space-age stellar civilizations.

According to restored records, Atlantis was truly a golden age for the most part. Well at least its original intent and phase. Apparently, some fallen (Anunakis) angels that were not in alignment with Enki and Ninhursag could have been secretly in favor of the Draconian who were once again attempting to infiltrate the new earth colonies from within as Atlantis became their new Mars. All was fine until again the Draconian agenda leaked in. The place of this draconian infiltration was in Atlantis during its second golden age, by what some my term renegade E. T.'s. These Renegade ET's became the fallen angels that apparently change sides to serve the Draconian agenda to not only further corrupt the pure bloodline of Lord Michael but to impose the Draconian empire in our world.

Originally and from its inception Atlantis was in line with Lemuria who was the mother continent in administrating things according to the celestial order of Melchizedek, which is the order of light. Therefore, all sister colonies favored Lemuria as the motherland since Lemuria was a galactic Lyran-Sirius feminine

community-based culture. The Lemurian's ideas were based on freedom, harmony, and spiritual community. Also, it is important to understand that the original founders of Atlantis ruled in favor of the Lemurian mother colony. That is, they practiced and lived under a perfect commonwealth as did the Lemurians and the other sister continents. These co-existing cultures venerated the divine feminine in balance with the divine masculine.

Although Atlantis started off as a spiritually oriented community, it gradually began shifting towards a scientific-technological technocratic empire, as more and more beings from different star systems came to explore it. Eventually, as the balance was tilted towards technological development, the Atlanteans become like the Martian colony and so began evolving one-sided. As mentioned, Atlantis was originally an idea and manifestation of the forces of light; and since Atlantis was an active population two stellar system civilization, there were stargates and dimensional portals that were active in those days, but secured by the Federation of councils, so that the Dracons could not enter our solar system anymore. So, what happened was that Marduk, one of Enki's sons, managed to seduce some of the Pleiadean descending celestial humanoids within the lower ranks of the Federation, into joining sides with him. It was these few renegade beings (fallen angels) aligned with Marduk that became the key players in the infiltration and demise of Atlantis. Marduk was the son of Enki by another reptilian princess, who believed that the descendants of the house of Alan should rule this planet. It is now obvious that Marduk was in favor of the Draconian Orion empire and as the son of Enki was connected to the Niburian council, while secretly favoring and working for his mother's line serving the galactic Draconian empire. In the attempt to take over Atlantis, Marduk and his renegade allies first infiltrated the Atlantean ruling body. They applied the same reptilian tactics implemented earlier in Lyra, when the reptilians infiltrated its ruling body. It was precisely this same tactic of infiltration that gave rise to the Draconian agenda which became executed by the renegade Pleiadeans who were in line with the few Dracon reptilians who controlled the re-organized dark brotherhood with Marduk as their leader. This took place fifty thousand years ago in Atlantis.

Eventually, after the infiltrators managed to separate the original ruling body, Atlantis fell under the control of the renegades under the leadership of Marduk and everything in Atlantis changed. The ruling class was divided by those the majority who now wanted to change Atlantis into a totalitarian system of absolute control under the direction of Marduk, and the minority who remained loyal to the Spiritual way of life. The priest-scientist that favored Marduk had converted to the dark side in pursuance of the new path of technology mixed with the corrupted spiritual knowledge that later developed into black magic and sorcery.

This new and dangerous system was inspired by the technologically polarized faction who wanted to develop a technology of death in which they would use to establish absolute world domination. The bait Marduk used to achieve control was supreme nationalism. Marduk convinced a great number of Atlanteans that Atlantis would be a much better motherland than Lemuria if they allow for the new system (party) to take control. As bait, he introduced advanced reptilian technology that was given to him by his fourth-dimensional reptilian uncles on his mother's side. Bear in mind that this was the beginning of the dark brotherhood in our ancient world that has, for the most part, ruled our world since then, as described in our bible and other ancient accounts.

The celestial/humanoids who remain loyal to a democratic and spiritual form of government sought refuge and safety by going into the underground, creating a rebel resistance, that would secretly oppose the new regime. These loyal stewards of democracy believed in the concept of the one God and understood that everything in the universe was connected as one living body.

This was the underlying foundation that encompassed a perfect utopian commonwealth as the Ancient Order of Melchizedek protected it.

The new dark powers denounced the order of Melchizedek and develop their own priesthoods, based on the arts and practices of Black Magic. Some say that this new band of Sorcerers and magicians is what ended up controlling the new Atlantis as Marduk's henchman. So, in the aftermath that the forces of Marduk took total control, everything began to decline for Atlantis. They put a stop on all education including science; only the servers and soldiers of Marduk were eligible for any sort of education and training. Only a small percentage of Atlanteans that willingly submitted to the new Atlantean Empire could live in a communistic system, while those that resisted were killed and forced into slavery. At this point, Atlantis had ushered in the Dark Ages, and they were now getting in a position to execute their plans for global domination on the rest of the planet. But first, they needed a powerful weapon to do so, as they were endeavoring to rule with an iron fist.

So, under the direction of Marduk, the elite sorcerers managed to develop a Crystal technology that they used to harness a power so strong that it was able to move neighboring space objects close into the vicinity of our Planet. Only a civilization of a type two statues is capable of such things. Apparently, Marduks Draconian uncles (demons) managed to transmit the information for the creation of this technology of death into the mind of the elite Sorcerers.

At that time our earth had two moons and what the Atlanteans did in an attempt to force their new power over everyone else on the planet is used a tractor beam, generated by the Crystal power source, to move our other moon into proximity of earth, in order to threaten first the colony of Lemuria, who was the mother continent.

Unfortunately, with our any warning, the Atlanteans imploded the moon right over the Lemurian region and destroyed the entire continent in a terrible cataclysm.

For the most part, a great number of beings perished as some of the Lemurians fled into the underground, and others to other star systems escaping the destruction, especially those that had operational light bodies.

This took place roughly about 25, 000 years ago, according to the Akashic records as Lemuria had become an example to the other continents that Atlantis meant business.

Eventually, the other continents were next, as the Atlanteans were now getting ready to use this advanced tractor beam technology to destroy the other civilizations like the Yu colony in today's Asia region, the Rama colony in today's India region, and the Mayan Colony in the Yucatan Meso American region.

The other advanced colonies were unmatchable against the New Atlanteans because they didn't possess the advanced draconian technology of death as the Atlanteans did.

In fact, there were several attempts made by the other colonies to convince the Atlanteans, in a diplomatic way, to change back into the Lemurian form of Government (a commonwealth) but it was useless. The Atlanteans demanded world domination, so the other colonies either had to summit or be destroyed like Lemuria. Despite any diplomatic compromise the Atlanteans attempted to destroy the Yu colony next. Using their Draconian technology of death, they harness a colossal size asteroid this time and brought it into the vicinity of earth however just in the nick of time, Nibiru had arrived from its (thirty-six hundred year orbit) and counteracted the attack, causing the colossal size asteroids to fall on Atlantis instead resulting in its own demise.

According to all esoteric records, this took place roughly about 12, 000 years ago. It has been revealed by the akashic records and the restored Nibirian council that the plan for world domination by Atlantis was bigger than just taking control of our planet.

The Atlanteans first wanted to regain absolute control of our planet so that in turn, they may control our solar system and eventually seize control of the entire Pleiadean system to eventually and finally regain control of the entire galaxy again. It was a matter of step by step for Marduk to begin the process of executing control of our entire galaxy for the Draconian Empire however that wasn't the case, for the forces of Marduk were stopped by the arrival of Nibiru, our biblical watcher.

Now according to another version known as mythology, Atlantis was originally established as a democracy whose rule was given to Poseidon, who according to the Greeks was the brother of Zeus.

Again, this could be paralleling the story of the Anunaki. Poseidon in turn had five pairs of sons who eventually divided up Atlantis into ten districts. When the ten kings set their aims toward world domination, they began by attacking the city-states of independent Greece. According to Plato, Zeus and the council of gods intervene and stopped this madness by destroying their continent and thus saving the rest of the world. This, of course, is a condensed version.

For the record, let it be understood that Atlantis was intended to represent a perfect balance of polarity integration in fulfillment of the great cosmic divine plan. The idea was to maintain a spiritual lifestyle while creating a technologically advanced utopia. This unification would provide the grounds for polarity integration (the integration of the higher chakras and the lower chakras) thus ending the duality of light and dark, by uniting spirit and matter in a process call Ascension and this concept is the authentic meaning of HEAVEN

ON EARTH, the merging of all dimensions as one again. In the end, the Atlanteans become seduced by Marduk and his forces and eventually failed, as the saying goes; the pride comes before the fall.

# CHAPTER TWELVE

## EARTH HISTORY FROM THE FALL OF ATLANTIS
## TO THE RISE OF A NEW ERA, 12,000 BC-6,000 BC

After the fall of Atlantis, several remnants of the celestial descending humanoid spirit beings survived. One was what became known as the Osirian group. The fore-bearers of this group were revealed to be the rebel resistance (the white brotherhood/sisterhood) consisting of benevolent celestial/ humanoids who went against Marduk' s plans. These benevolent celestial heroes maintained their twelve strands of DNA in full function by escaping the cataclysm of Atlantis. They were led by their leader Osiris who some say was later known as the ancient Egyptian god of light and son of Ra who parallels the one god, El or Aton of the later Hebrew people. On the other hand, some believed that he was also one of Enki's sons, perhaps displaying the light aspect of Enki, while Marduk displayed the dark. As for the strands of DNA in full function by escaping the cataclysm of Atlantis. They were led by their leader Osiris who some say was later known as the ancient Egyptian god of light and son of Ra who parallels the one god, El or Aton of the later Hebrew people. On the other hand, some believed that he was also one of Enki's sons, perhaps displaying the light aspect of Enki, while Marduk displayed the dark. As for the dark faction that was led by Marduk (another of Enki's son), they also survived in their spaceships and returned to the earth as well. Something to understand is that since Enki was both Dracon reptilian and Pleiadean celestial/humanoid his offspring became the backbone for the new battle between good and evil, since the fall of Atlantis. Through his son Marduk or Set in Egypt, the draconian agenda continued and through Osiris, Isis, and Horus, the great work of light continued.

Other survivors as in the case of Lemuria sought refuge by creating their own underground civilizations today commonly known as the Agartha and Shamballa networks. Most of these survivors remain loyal to the light and were given a chance to continue the original Lemurian form of government but in the inner earth. They establish what is known today as the Agartha network that connects various

underground cities throughout the world, including Mt. Shasta in northern California and Shamballa an etheric city in the mountains of Tibet. Some believe that these underground cities exist in the higher fourth and fifth dimensions and could only be accessed by a chosen few.

This inner earth Lemurians also maintained a twelve-strand DNA function by escaping the cataclysm beforehand and have been living till today waiting for the great day of planetary ascension to resurface and reunite with us. As for the evolving humans that were at the level of Homo-sapiens sapiens-sapiens, also survived but only a strain, as later in the times of Noah.

Again, it is important to understand that the descending children of light or the fifth and fourth dimensional Pleiadeans (the angels talked about in the bible) were not able to incarnate into a third-dimensional organic vehicle until the evolving hominids reached the level of thinking and reasoning, which was right after the level of Cro-Magnon.

This was possible only after so many vehicle upgrades that were made possible by those that came from HEAVEN TO EARTH.

Again, this remarkable event demarcated the distinction between the old evolving hominid, and modern-day Homo Sapien-sapiens, who are the descendants of the celestial/humanoids then known as the descending sons and daughters of light.

According to Urantia, Adam and Eve became the first of its kind descending material son and daughter of light, which gave birth to the violet race of man, which is the revolutionary and evolutionary completion of whole spirit beings descending into the densest vehicles integrating spirit and matter.

Therefore, based on these higher restored concepts, we can now conclude that Adam and Eve were the first descending celestial spirit beings to incarnate into a third-dimensional body-ready vehicle approximately 30,000 years ago. Even our new science confirms the coming of modern men 30,000 years ago with the ending of Neanderthal men, 30,000 years ago as well.

Of course, a dualist would believe that this meant the spirit entrapment of light beings, but an adept, mystic and saint, would see this as the integration of spirit and matter, HEAVEN AND EARTH, light body and material body, where the descension meets the ascension.

In addition, let it be revealed that roughly about 12,000 to 30,000 years ago human beings, as we now know as homo sapien-sapiens sapiens- sapiens were using about five additional strands of DNA, than what we have used for the last 12,000 years. These explain the amazing lifespan of our old biblical patriarchs.

With the incarnation of higher beings (Pleiadeans) into third-dimensional organic human bodies, (us back then), homo sapiens- sapiens lived for almost a thousand years.

However, not quite like their Pleiadean Parents who lived for hundreds of thousands of years.

As mentioned, it was around 30,000 years ago, that celestial beings have been incarnating into homosapiens vehicles, as supported by science now. Also, the descending of celestial beings into third-dimensional organic physical form goes for both the descending celestial/humanoids (angels) and the descending Draconian reptilians (demons). In the case of the reptilians, they had established themselves through their own hybrid homo sapiens bloodline that manifested later in the personages of Cain, Ham, Cush/Cish, and Nimrod. This bloodline is what our bible refers to as the Abomination of Desolation.

For the forces of light, it was about maintaining a pure genetic line, allowing for the eventual incarnation of even higher dimensional light beings.

Eventually this unique linage of divine celestial life stock in third-dimensional form, later become established as the sacred bloodline that gave us, Horus, Noah, Moses, Abraham, Judah, Zarathustra, David, and Jesus to name a few of the incarnating celestials.

These Heroic personages have been considered in esoteric circles the direct descendants of the reincarnating sons and daughters of light of both the west and east, for we also had the incarnated sons and daughters of light in the east, like Krishna and Buddha.

In galactic terms, this was the re-establishment of the royal house of Aln, through Nimrod and his descendants, and the re-establishment of the royal house of Avon the lion through Abraham and his descendants. However, unfortunately, our world has, for the most part, been under the control of the reptilian human hybrids of the Nimrod line who have for millenniums been the powerful families that have dominated our world for thousands of years. The final earthly representatives of the draconian house of Aln. However, their reign has ended, as we enter the new millennium Heaven on Earth.

As the story continues, from what has emerged in today's restoration, after the fall of Atlantis, the old order of the Commonwealth that followed the Osiris-Isis group went to build what became known as the ancient civilization of Egypt. This was built upon the previous land that was then known as Hypatia/Lybia, as revealed in the Yanihian Script. This early Egyptian civilization Hyptia Lybia was destroyed during the Atlantean cataclysm. According to the Yanihian revelation, Hypatia-Egypt was a sister branch of Atlantis that developed and maintained their society as a free world following the original feminine Lemurian (Sirius-Lyran) blueprint.

According to Ancient Egyptian records, these were the times of the Egyptian rule by the Neteru. (a group of benevolent gods, the angels). The pantheon consists of the mighty council of twelve in which Osiris acted as the leader representing the son of the invincible but yet all radiant one god Ra, which sees all things and was later translated by the Hebrews as El Elyon or simply Aton, the one GOD.

160

According to the secret knowledge, even the early Egyptian gods believed and honored the one creator and had set up their council in similar fashioned with the higher-ups known as the universal council of twelve who are the original adepts of the twelve living universes, as revealed in the "Yanihian Script".

In fact, it was Osiris and his halfsister Isis that came to represent the perfect balance of the divine masculine and the divine famine as did Jesus and Mary Magdalene in later times. This balance is what gave rise to an Egyptian golden age that lasted for about -two thousand years.

It is important to understand that the concept of the council of twelve has always been a model representing the higher orders of light. Even the pantheon of celestial/humanoid Greek gods, recognize the one God as their creator source from which everything comes. That meant they were originally adopting the blueprint of the order of Melchizedek by establishing their council of twelve in ancient Greece as well. This is the divine order of sonship ruling the affairs of the sons and daughters of light, for it is the symbolic representation of the living twelve universes and the twelve living energies that run through all celestial/Adamic/humanoid races as the twelve chakra energy systems.

Furthermore, in the representation of the higher orders of light, King Arthur had the round table of twelve as well as king David of Israel who was recorded to be the most righteous monarch that ever reigns.

Of course, they came from the same bloodline, as direct descendants of the royal house of Avon which is also known as the royal house of Lord Michael.

Nonetheless, during the fall of Atlantis, it was believed that the Osirian group established themselves right before the time the commonwealth of Atlantis was usurped by the new tyrannical form of government. So, when the forces of Marduk took over, those that remained loyal to the original plan of manifesting HEAVEN ON EARTH, escaped into the underground in the region we identify today as Europe.

This explains the mysterious schools that later manifested as the order of the Celts and Druids which were originally established by the followers of Osiris. This also explains the Monolithic monuments like Easter Island and Stonehenge, that these groups created with their advanced knowledge. They also secured not only the sacred celestial divine knowledge from total elimination, but also preserved that same knowledge (threw mystery) schools that is now coming forward in our times, in preparation for the Ascension of our planet at the closing of the great cycle and as we end the age of Pieces.

For the record, let it be known that the elimination of knowledge (by the dark brotherhood) was first implemented in Atlantis, about 26,000 years ago and later during the rise of Babylon around 3400 B. C. and then recently about 1,700 hundred years ago by the Holy Roman development.

Another parallel to the days of Atlantis is the story of, "Lord of the Rings", which some belief was a memory record of Atlantis as it parallels the story of the ten ruling kings who were the sons of Poseidon/Enki. In either case, Atlantis fell as later its successor Babylonia did in 2400B.C. as we shall see. All because this world was never meant to be under a totalitarian system of absolute power and control. Nevertheless, when Atlantis fell, a New Golden age began in Egypt, with the rebuilding of a New Era.

In the NEW Egyptian golden age, the benevolent celestial/humanoids in Egypt had established the mystery schools to re-educate the surviving ascending evolving humans.

Apparently, most of the evolving humans had regressed, due to the cataclysm. They had lost their telepathic abilities and their right brain (creative aspect) lay dormant only operating from their left brain, bringing them back to the level of the Old Stone Age Cro-Magnon.

As a result of this downgrade, the benevolent gods (celestial/humanoids) knew that not every evolving ascending human was immediately ready to learn the knowledge of the higher celestial evolution. So, they set up the first initiatory pathways by establishing the mystery schools of the higher mysteries and the lower mysteries. The lower mysteries were for the mass number of people who had to first take baby steps in the spiritual re-education process. The higher mysteries were taught to those that showed signs of readiness and spiritual maturity, as they were ready to understand the knowledge of the celestials.

It appears that these benevolent celestial rulers of Egypt did not want to repeat the same mistake as in Atlantis, in offering advanced knowledge to all surviving evolving man, who had regressed to a primitive level again. As reminded, the problem that led to the fall of Atlantis was that advanced knowledge was given to many earth-based evolving Homosapien-sapiens who were not spiritually mature yet. This could have been the lower strains of evolving humans that were not inheriting much of the violet celestial DNA, for they were still displaying barbaric behavior.

With the establishment of the mystery schools, the descending celestial humanoids were able to give such knowledge only to those that were worthy. So evolving mankind was carefully selected to learn about the higher celestial cosmic evolution, and this became the beginning of the Oral tradition. This happened because not enough spiritual evolution was achieved by much of the regressed Homo sapien-sapiens. In other words, spiritual evolution must come first and then technological progress, so in Egypt, the plan was to first evolve spiritually, in order to prevent what happened in Atlantis.

Only those evolving Homo sapien-sapiens that stemmed from the direct line of Adam (first celestial being humanoid to incarnate) 35,000 BCE were allowed for more use of their genetic potential. This line was kept intact until the final upgrade that took place two thousand years ago, which made this bloodline available to the thousands of the now incarnating descending humanoids in our current time.

Overall, in the aftermath of Atlantis, the higher divine celestial knowledge was only to continue with certain people, known as the prophets, seers, and sages.

This also happens to be the time in which our planet was isolated or quarantined from the rest of our galaxy, as we digressed from an advanced stellar space-age culture to a primitive isolated world. Our planet's isolation from the rest of our galaxy's free star systems was done by the forces of light in order to prevent the newfound dark forces that destroyed Atlantis, from spreading to other star systems in our galaxy. So the system circuits that connected the higher spheres (fifth dimension and up) with the lower spheres (third dimension) allowing celestials/angels/gods and man to co-exist was disconnected after the fall of Atlantis and the biblical veil set in, separating the higher celestial evolution from our developing primitive world.

On the other hand, those humans from the direct seed of Adam had learned to not only value the divine knowledge but also use it wisely. As a result, some of the direct descendants of Adam had ascended back into their full potential becoming full functioning conscious beings integrating spirit and matter as was in their DNA prior to their incarnation.

These ascended evolved humans lived for many hundred years; and now they have gone to become the ancient ascended spiritual masters of old or heroes of old as recorded in our bible and are still alive in the fifth dimension, serving the great divine plan. It has been prophesied that these ascended beings' direct descendants of Adam, were to return at the end of time to help in the re-establishment of the office of the Christ.

One descendant of the Adamic line that helped in the restoration of the higher divine knowledge after Atlantis was the biblical Enoch, who was of the direct line of Adam through his son Seth. Enoch was recorded in the bible to have walked with God and ascended into heaven without tasting death. One thing to understand about ascension is that when one ascends back into their original higher spirit self (full conscious bring), one could either continue to higher levels (dimensions) or one could remain and help the rest of humanity achieve the same goal. Enoch was one that stayed and become known as the messenger of the gods in mythology. To the Greeks, he was Hermes Trismegistus, the god of wisdom.

Well, initially he was an ascended human who transformed his evolving organic body and reactivated his light body, becoming like a human celestial angel who helped in the establishment of the ancient mystery schools in Egypt, as well as in ancient Greece in order to keep the higher knowledge of the celestial evolution on earth.

Due to this recovery by the forces of light, the Egyptian golden age established by Osiris and Isis lasted for about two thousand years as it coincides with what later will be explained to be the procession of the equinoxes. As the story goes, the forces of Set who were really the forces of Marduk were endeavoring to overthrow the council of Osiris and Isis who ruled righteously in line with the brotherhood/sisterhood of light of the order of Melchizedek, the order of Michael and the order of Enoch. This attempt by the god Set (Marduk of Babylon) to overthrow his rival half-brother Osiris was unfortunately executed. This was the time period, two thousand years following the demise of Atlantis. So, it was approximately 8,000 BCE when this occurred. According to legend, Set/Marduk seceded in killing his half-brother Osiris and as a result overtook Egypt for a while. This takeover ended the first Golden Age of Egypt since the fall of Atlantis. The plan again as in Atlantis, was to rule righteously in line with the brotherhood/sisterhood of light of the order of Melchizedek, the order of Michael, and the order of Enoch. This attempt by the god Set (Marduk of Babylon) to overthrow his rival half-brother Osiris was unfortunately executed. This was the time period, two thousand years following the demise of Atlantis. So, it was approximately 8,000 BCE when this occurred. According to legend, Set/Marduk seceded in killing his half-brother Osiris and as a result overtook Egypt for a while. This takeover ended the first Golden Age of Egypt since the fall of Atlantis. The plan again as in Atlantis, was to bring the entire world under a totalitarian system of absolute power and control, under the rule of Set-Marduk, who later became identified as Satan in our bible.

However, right after the usurpation of the Egyptian golden age, representatives were sent from the underground networks of Shamballa, (the underground city of the survivors of the Yu and Rama civilizations) in a diplomatic attempt to prevent Set-Marduk from taking over the planet on the surface. Apparently, these underground networks were aiding the Osirian group in dedication to the great divine plan (the great work of all ages). It was their support in providing Horus; the son of Isis all the help he needed in order to defeat his uncle Set- Marduk, collectively knowing that if the dark forces took over, the great divine plan would end there.

It is important to understand here, that the brotherhood of light, the order of Melchizedek- Michael-Enoch operates on various levels, as it has always been the case. For it encompasses beings from multiple dimensions, all the way from the highest celestial levels down to the terrestrial planetary levels. Meaning that not only was the Isis-Osiris group of ancient masters an outpost of the brotherhood of light in ancient earth but were also assisted by the underground networks of Shambala and Agartha that exists as great etheric cities of light in the fourth and fifth-density levels of the inner earth. In other words, in the underground networks of the brotherhood of light, there exist full functioning celestial humans that are working with our planet's spiritual council as well as with the Galactic Federation (sky angels) for the restoration of our beloved planet.

Now, since Set realized he was outnumbered against the forces of the underground network of Shamballa who were then operating on the surface in China, Tibet, and India and also hearing that his nephew Horus had been groomed to overthrow him, he went about destroying the thousand-mile firmament in our atmosphere that provided a protective fence from the sun's harmful radiations. This purely selfish act not only caused his demise but the demise of all the land civilizations, including Egypt. His rule ended and apparently so did all the other civilizations when the tons of waters from the firmament came crashing down causing what our bible refers to as the great flood. According to restored knowledge, Set/ Marduk/ Baal/ Satan accomplished this by imploding one of the underground pyramids that supported the sky firmament in place. It was this deluge that destroyed ancient Summer, Egypt, India and the resurfaced Yu/China civilizations that were again rebuilt after Atlantis.

This war lasted for approximately two thousand years and that is the reason why the flood story has been echoed through all ancient records including the Sumerian tablets that predate our bible. In mythology, it was known as the wars of the olden gods, the children of Anu, however, this was just the beginning of another battle that would last for another eight thousand years. The celestial beings, (gods/angels/E.T.s) were only part of it for another three thousand years as we will see, as their war was transferred over to the evolving organic humans when the gods/angels/E.T.s decided to live the scene.

The only beings that survived the deluge were the celestial beings who fled in the nick of time in their ships (flying boats) and of course the celestial beings that went back into the underground of Agartha and Shambala. As for the evolving ascending Homo sapien- sapiens sapiens-sapiens, they were all destroyed because they were being used as war ponds and had been totally corrupt with the exception of one evolving ascending human family that survived the deluge and that was Zissudra/Utnapishtim, commonly known as our biblical Noah. This line would continue the ascending Adamic organic vehicle for the eventual incarnation of more celestial beings into third-dimensional organic mortal bodies to once again bring the great divine plan to the earth of integrating spirit and matter.

Noah/Zissudra/Utnapishtim, whatever you want to call him depending on which ancient manuscript you read, was a direct descendant of Enoch, who again carried in his direct bloodline the highest concentration of the twelve living energies. In the Sumerian text, he was known as Utnapishtim. In Vedic lore, he was Zissudra and to the western world, he was known as Noah.

Collectively gathered from all accounts, we know that the deluge transpired approximately six thousand years ago. Noah as a direct descendant of Enoch was chosen to preserve the evolving human linage as it was mandatory, or we would not be ready for completion today in the fullness of time. As the story goes, and in the aftermath of the deluge, Horus defeated his uncle Set-Marduk-Baal-Satan and restored the commonwealth of righteousness in Egypt modeled after the principles of the order of Melchizedek.

So, the benevolent celestials/gods/angels/E. Ts continued their rule in Egypt under the guise of the Neteru. Horus and his mother Isis watched over-educated and protected the evolving human family who was once again populating through the line of Noah/Anapushtim/Zissudra. The attempt to restore HEAVEN ON EARTH was once again being carried out by Egypt under the rule of the children of the one God of light that later translated as RA or Aton-El Lyon, the God of the early Hebrews.

This peaceful ERA of course lasted about a thousand years. In the time being, however, of which the evolving humans through the line of Shem and Japheth were evolving according to the knowledge and spiritual ways of Lemuria and Lyra.

As a result of their righteous living, the descending celestial beings of Nibiru were now ready to bestow upon evolving mankind their own right to rule. So, for the first time in our earth's history the Anunakis-Nephilim, Watchers-Neteru-angelic celestial beings, whatever you would like to call them, decided to lower the right of rulership of the earth to the evolving humans.

Of course, we also must remember that even our Pleiadean/Nibirian parents who initially took matters into their own hands regarding the affairs of our world, eventually began to operate under the orders of the confederation of Councils and the planetary spiritual hierarchy.

So we may also say that the time of Nibiru's direct influence on us had come to a close when the Nibirians finally lowered kinship to third-dimensional organic man as a directive given to them, by the higher beings of the Galactic council, who have been and still are till this day overseeing the entire earth expedition.

For the record, let it be known that the earth up until the fourth century BC was ruled by the (celestial humanoids/gods) Niburian celestial beings until around the time of 3700 BC.

There are a few accounts that confirm this to be accurate. Among the accounts is the restored Nibirian council, as well as Zachariah's astonishing work on the earth chronicles series, both agreeing that mankind was given control of the planet by those that came from HEAVEN TO EARTH, the Bnai Elohim or sons of God.

According to the restored Niburian council, the first human ruler was recorded to be Allium, who was also reported to be the grandfather of Tarah, the father of Abram, or Abraham our biblical patriarch. Whoever he was, he had to be of the direct lineage of Noah/Utnapishtim/Zissudra, perhaps through the line of Shem, Noah's most righteous son.

Whatever the case may be, this was the beginning of a NEW ERA once again for the evolving ascending human race. They were now ready to govern themselves, of course with the help of the celestial beings (gods/angels) who even though we're not around anymore, we're still assisting evolving man from the unseen higher dimensions.

Since Allium of UR was the first human king, according to restored records and since our biblical Abraham was from his direct line, then that explains why Abram or Abraham, was chosen to be our evolving ascending human patriarch for the God most high. This tells us, that Abraham was of the direct bloodline of the galactic royal house of Avon, the seed of lord Michael who through his lineage, the divine seed of descending celestial sons and daughters of light may continue to incarnate, especially Jesus and Mary Magdalene who we know was of this direct line as well.

In our world, Abraham's lineage become the highest carriers of celestial genetics at least the highest concentration of it, which meant that they carried the highest interaction of the twelve living energies, out of the rest of our human family. Although it was evident that after the flood, all evolving humans were carriers of the twelve energies centers to a degree with the exception of the linage of the abomination that resorted to the infusion of restoring reptilian DNA, as established through the seed of our biblical Ham.

For the record, today it has been discovered that all humans have twelve chakras and twelve strands of DNA, indicating that we all have inherited the twelve energy centers of our descending celestial parents. According to the esoteric tradition, the five chakras outside our bodies, plus our seven chakras inside our body, allows for the full flow of kundalini energy making one capable of using more than four percent of their total mental and DNA capacity.

As mentioned those that carried the highest concentrations of these twelve energies established the bloodline that gave us the ancient house of Israel.

The seed of Israel was given the divine right to rule only as they established a type of convent with the higher evolution (angelic celestial kingdom) who wanted overall to see their fellow evolving ascending humans reach celestial statues again. This pact was established as Program Israel which later became the sacred covenant or program Zion between mankind and God the highest through lord Melchizedek and Abraham.

This divine/human contract was established for the sole purpose of uniting HEAVEN AND EARTH and bringing to pass the immortality of all evolving mankind.

Melchizedek was no other than the first incarnating Ancient of days known in the east as Sanat Kumara, the lord of the world and head of the planetary spiritual council who operates from the fifth dimension and up, and he could have also overshadowed the ascended master Shem, the son of Noah, who was Abraham great grandfather.

In fact, the entire spiritual hierarchy of descending celestial humanoids and Ascended earthlings that operate and influenced our world from the higher dimensional densities have been known to overshadow all the prophets and spiritual teachers throughout all history. In this case, the ascended master Shem could have been overshadowed by the descending Lord Kumara/Melchizedek.

Overall, it is important to understand the level of influence that the higher dimensions have on the lower dimensions. As mentioned earlier, everything that happens in the higher levels of existence eventually manifests in the lower levels as well. "As above so below".

So it is obvious that even though the Anunaki "those who came from heaven to earth", were manipulating events on earth, their power was limited and to a degree influenced by the beings in the higher fifth, sixth seventh, and eighth dimensions who are higher-level celestials/angels, then the celestials who came on Nibiru.

In fact, to our astounding discovery, both brotherhoods dark and light are influenced and controlled by the beings of the higher fifth, sixth and seventh dimensions, by virtue of administrating the seven rays into the lower dimensions down to the third.

It is from the fifth, sixth, and seven dimensions were the masters of Shamballa (spiritual planetary council) administer events on earth on behalf of the Great Blue lodge known as the Syrian high council, the outpost of the great white brotherhood/sisterhood in our galaxy, who serves the great central sun of our galaxy, Kolob/Ophiuchus/tzolkin the center and throne of our galactic council.

So in truth, both factions good and evil, whether it is fifth, fourth-density humanoids (gods) or ascending organic man on the third-density earth plane, are being ethereally manipulated by the higher authorities or the space commands of the higher evolution all serving under the direction of Lord Michael.

This perhaps explains why light is always going to prevail since all reality is orchestrated and influenced by the higher dimensions. Evil is only an illusion that manifests on the lower dimensions to provide greater growth in the higher dimensions. When the ascension process occurs, this duality then becomes complementary and polarized even in the lower dimensions, thus manifesting the only true reality known as the singularity, the true meaning of monotheism, for we are all one.

# CHAPTER THIRTEEN

## WHEN KINGSHIP WAS
## LOWERED FROM (HEAVEN) NIBIRU TO EARTH.

Considering the new evidence, we now know that for millions of years until about 5000 years ago, our planet was being governed by beings from other worlds. According to all restored records, may we say the rulership was lowered from Nibiru (HEAVEN) to evolving mankind, roughly five thousand years ago. This also marked the beginning of earth's time as we know it.

For instance, around 3600, BC the first calendar was issued in Mesopotamia. The beginning of our calendar at around 3,600 BC is confirmed by both the translated Sumerian tablets and the restored Nibirian council. And if we believe that our world began 6000, years ago, then our own Judeo-Christian calendar began right around the same time.

Now let it be known that even though mankind could govern themselves, they were still being influenced by the descending angels/celestials in an indirect way, from the fourth dimension. It appeared that after the Nibirians left the scene, great temples were built for sacrifices as the evolving human family constantly petition their gods for goods. In Egypt, during their golden age, the evolving humans worshipped and lived under the influence of the one God RA. By decree of the divine right of rule, the early Pharaohs were direct descendants of Horus, Osiris, and Isis.

In the lands of Summer and Akkadian, they were descendants of Ninurta and Sin/Nannar the sons of Enlil/Jehovah /Zeus. Under the guidance of these benevolent descending human angels, the evolving ascending human kingdoms were prosperous, during the rule of Allium of UR in the land of Shinar and in Egypt during the first dynasty of Egyptian Pharaohs. Not to mention, the establishment of the righteous kings of the east in China and Japan who were descendants of Japheth (second son of Noah-Zissudra-Utnapishtim) and by divine intervention in India by the descendants of Krishna, who is recorded to be one of the incarnated Kumaras-Melchizedeks.

Initially, when the Pleiadean Nibirians lowered their kingship to evolving mankind, peace did reign on the earth for a couple of hundred years, until the sons of darkness Beliel (Marduk/Satan) as recorded in the secret knowledge began infiltrating Mesopotamia in a region today known as Babylonia.

The key players here were Marduk the fourth-dimensional aspect of Satan and leader of the dark forces on earth and his son Nabu. The plan for them was first to seize control of Egypt and then the world.

The reason being is that Egypt was home to some of the most advanced monuments, the Pyramids for example that were used as powerful generators of energy, not to mentioned they housed vast amounts of knowledge not only pertaining to our planet but the entire universe. This vast record of knowledge is known, as the halls of records, and according to Edgar Casey, and another spiritualist such as Madam Blavaski, these records lay underneath one of the paws of the Lion sphinx.

In addition, in the conquest of Egypt, the plans then later became directed towards the land we identify today as Israel and the Cedar Mountains right above, which is modern-day Lebanon. The reason is that the Cedar Mountains contained a spaceport that was used during the times of Atlantis and according to the secret knowledge, there existed also a vast energy vortex (stargate) underneath those mountains which was used as passages into other parts of our galaxy, and Marduk was after everything. Also, part of the agenda for Marduk and his son Nabu was to re-take the area known as Mount Moriah, in Israel, for the same reason as the previous two, this area also contained an old functioning spaceport and star-gate that was used during the times of Atlantis.

The initial intent by Marduk was made to usurp the throne in Egypt, this was, of course, a war brought on by the Babylonian god of war, Marduk, as this also became known as the second pyramidal war in pre-history. According to the restored knowledge, Marduk and his son Nabu accomplished this by deposing Thoth- Hermes-Enoch and in the process ended up killing Dumuzi, the husband of the goddess Inanna, the granddaughter of Enlil/Zeus/Jehovah.

While succeeding in overthrowing Thoth and for killing Dumuzi, Marduk was later imprisoned by a decision made by the council of the gods (Nibirians). As for Thoth, it was revealed that he went to America, to reestablished what later become known as the greatest civilization ever, the Mayan Culture, which flourished peacefully for about five hundred years in the regions we know today as southern Mexico and Central America.

Back in Egypt after being imprisoned for a while, Marduk eventually was freed and returned to Babylonia to continue his dark agenda, as his time to rule was coming soon, based on his astrological sign of Aries.

Therefore, let it be understood that Marduk was considered to be the fourth-dimensional aspect of Satan who managed to establish among the evolving humans, his own wicked bloodline that would go on in becoming the rival of the righteous bloodline of divine benevolent Priest-kings.

This Mardukian corrupt bloodline of tyrannical kings that originated with Marduk was a hybrid between an evolving human woman and his son Nabu, who was also considered a Dracon- reptilian carrying a higher concentration than Marduk. This hybrid mixture is what once again activated the reptilian brain or what is commonly known as the R-complex in science, after the flood, becoming another attempt by the dark side to contaminate the pure celestial bloodline of Enlil/Zeus/Jehovah that would eventually give us Jesus. This explains why the early Israelites were prohibited from mixing with any other descendants especially the Canaanites who were heavy carriers of reptilian genetics.

As we know Marduk was seventy percent reptilian and his son Nabu was a hundred percent because his mother Damkina was also a descendant of the royal house of Aln, the reptilian royal seed that originated in the Rigel star system of Orion as described earlier in our galactic history.

The human carrier of this reptilian gene became known as Cish or Cush, the firstborn of this abomination, who went on in becoming the grandfather of Babylonia's Nimrod who even carried a higher concentration of it. For the record, Cish came from the line of Ham, the sorcerer and third son of Noah, who went astray as described in our bible. As the real story goes, Ham in endeavoring to rule over his righteous brothers, Shem and Japheth, conjured up Nabu to impregnate an evolving human female thus giving birth to a reptilian /human hybrid.

This act contaminated our world with the serpent gene once again through the seed of Ham-Cish-Nimrod. The time period was around 3400BC and their diabolical project was the Tower of Babel. This expedition was originally conceived in the mind of Ham, continuing with Cish and culminating with his grandson Nimrod. Babylonia had become now the new cradle of power for the dark brotherhood that was being controlled by the fourth-density extra-terrestrial demonic Marduk, except to the Babylonians he was known as the god Belial or Baal, to whom they erected temples to and worshiped.

Contrary to the dark activities of the Babylonians, by 3400 BCE well within the era of the rise of the new dynasties, the kings of Egypt, Summer, Akkadia, and Assyria were led and guided by Ninurta, Adad/Sin, Nannar, and Ashur, all sons of the righteous descending celestial Enlil/Zeus Javova. Though Egypt's line of righteousness came from Enki and Ninhursag through their descendants Osiris and his sister Isis. Both lines ruled righteously attempting to establish a commonwealth gearing towards spiritual evolution, following in the ways of the ONE creator, MONOTHEISM.

At this point, it is important to consider the many correlations between the Sumerian god Enlil and the Old Testament tribal god Jehovah/Yahweh also known as EL/ Elyon, El Shaddai, and Zeus to the ancient Greeks. After all it was revealed by the Nibirian council that Enlil was a full Lyran/Syrian/Pleiadean celestial/humanoid transferring a pure genetic divine line through his sons and

175

daughters.

Therefore, the sons of Enlil were of the pure line of the descending Lyran-SyrianPleiadean celestial/humanoid seed, which translated as the early Hebrew CLAN.

This would make perfect sense, since according to scripture; the early Israelites were not allowed to intermix with the other surrounding clans, such as the Canaanites. This was done in order to preserve as much of their divine stock that was being threatened by the spread of reptilian genetics in Babylon, through the Canaanites, Amosite, and other - ites.

In the bible, it was concealed under the idea that the other clans had blemishes and were unclean, but with more actual knowledge of things, we may conclude that Marduk/Satan has always attempted to contaminate the bloodline that led to Jesus. The kings that were of the line of Enlil/Jehovah/Yahweh were taught the mysteries by Enlil sons as they were led by righteousness. Something to notice is that it was around this time Enlil/Jehovah/Zeus began sharing the higher divine celestial knowledge with his chosen people, (early Hebrews). First through the oral tradition than through the Kabala which was composed by Moses, because due to the contamination of the serpent seed in Babylon, the higher knowledge or what is called today, the esoteric secret tradition was preserved and taught to the line of what become known as the succession of righteous Priest-kings. These were the kings that came from the line of Allium and Horus. However, the lesser mysteries, or what they called the exoteric interpretation of knowledge was taught to the masses, which were then spiritually immature due to the influence of the false idolatrous religious systems of Babylonia.

Before, the influence of Babylon, the righteous communities who were educated by the mystery schools were flourishing and expanding in the arts, science, astrology, mathematics, architecture, metallurgy, and meditation. This higher education caused people to awake to their higher potential and everyone in those communities would therefore contribute their individual skill toward the greater whole of humanity. In fact, the entire community under these righteous benevolent rulers rested firmly on the belief in the ONE God, in the sense that the universe, or may we say the multi-verse is one. This was and is the original program Israel that became established with Abraham and his descendants. During this time period, the righteous Priest-kings had twelve advisors setting up their councils like their benevolent watchers establishing the council of twelve in our world. This is the same tradition that was later continued with King David, Solomon, and later through the Druids and King Arthur of the courts of Wessex.

As a result of such justice, love, knowledge, and righteousness, the evolving human race had almost reached full celestial statues; they were slowly becoming like their descending celestial progenitors. It was reported, by the higher intelligence that from the time period of Alulim's reign to about almost three hundred years, there was peace on earth and because of the success in implementing the right knowledge and higher values, the evolving humans activated other strands of DNA and were becoming telepathic as they once were during the times of Atlantis. This meant that the people during those days were obviously using more than ten percent of their entire genetic potential. Telepathy is a spiritual universal language of communication from mind to mind without the barriers of words or sounds.

These were the days prior to the tower of Babel, where people from all over the world were united under one understanding. In biblical terms, these were the times right before the languages were confused, and the division of the earth's people. Unfortunately, this peaceful era came to an end, with the rise of our history's first Babylonian Empire.

The Babylonian empire came about through the reptilian/human hybrids led by Marduk setting themselves up in Babylon to continue what Marduk couldn't accomplish in Atlantis and later in Egypt. Something to note here is that every war that has been fought since the days of Atlantis, has been wars fought by the dark brotherhood to justify the ends they couldn't accomplish in Atlantis.

Fortunately, however, because this world is completely under our creator's care, the forces of light have never given up and have always fought the dark brotherhood of Marduk/Baal/Satan. They have been the resistance waging a war against the forces of darkness. And as we know now this righteous movement originated in Atlantis with the Osirian Groups as well as through the children of Enlil/Jehovah/Zeus and also with the establishment of the networks of Shamballa, Agartha, and Telos, the inner earth movements that remain loyal to the ancient order of Melchizedek.

In fact, these inner earth groups, survivors of ancient civilizations have always been connected to the networks of the orders of light on the surface, through benevolent secret societies. In turn, the entire brotherhood of light on the surface is also connected to the galactic command (space brotherhood/ sisterhood) through the Ashtar command, our solar systems airborne division of the great white brotherhood/sisterhood and higher celestial forces, which are all overseen by and work under the direction of Lord Michael.

As for the forces of darkness, their influence remains prevalent only on the surface, since they were curtailed from the higher dimensions, and in some cases, some were also confined to the inner earth. Some even believe that within the underground networks of Agartha, there could have been some negative extraterrestrials (demons) that might have also been pulling strings.

Nonetheless, we have witness periods and moments, that were sponsored by the forces of light, that is to say, moments of peace, sisterhood/brotherhood, and prosperity which only lasted, until the cloak of the Illuminati was put on by Nimrod, around 3400BC. A few things occurred; one was that the Babylonians under Marduk/Baal, had developed a high level of technological capacity at the expense of spirituality, as in the case of Atlantis before its decline. Secondly, since Nimrod carried the highest concentration of reptilian genetics as a descendant of Cish, he had been given special education into the arts of Black magic and sorcery by the brotherhood of his forbearers.

He was considered a son of Marduk and Nabu or as in mythology, a son of Belial (Baal) who the Babylonians worshiped as their supreme god. As the suppressed story goes, Marduk through his earthly son Nimrod had convinced the Babylonians that their God was superior to the other gods of the pantheon. To prove this, Nimrod had to become his mediator and since Nimrod exceeded all his forefathers before him, in the arts of Necromancy, was therefore given advanced technology by the Dracon E. T's of the fourth dimension.

Apparently, Marduk saw in Nimrod the potential to fulfill his mother's plans (Dramin, the serpent queen) of secretly establishing world domination.

Since Marduk was a fourth-dimensional being, an Anunaki of almost pure draconian descent, he used his established earthly third-dimensional bloodline to operate his diabolical plans thereby using his grandson and human hybrid Nimrod as his tool on the third dimension. Nimrod was taught some of the deepest secrets including the fact that we were not alone in the universe.

However, Nimrod had become a mighty man when he implemented the advanced science and techniques of activating his light body as revealed to him by Marduk/Baal.

By doing so, Nimrod's kundalini energy fired up causing him to become a fully functional superhuman possessing the same capabilities as the descending celestial watchers. This made him a mighty man among man as recorded in all ancient accounts.

Consequently, this super-genius developed a launched pad, (spaceport) which was camouflaged (symbolized) in the bible as a vertical tower. He created a Shem for his people as he discovered the ability to develop flight UFO tech. (5000 years ago) so that they may reach the home of the celestial/humans (Nibiru) and make a name for themselves. Therefore, by establishing his own spaceport launching pad in Babylon (tower of Babel), he was setting himself up as ruler of the entire third-dimensional world. His plan was to bring this technology (spaceships) and many others to the rest of the ascending evolving humans, so that, they may incline towards technological development rather than spiritual growth, as in the case of Atlantis.

However, the stipulation was that after everyone become introduced to such advanced technologies, Nimrod would be crowned King of the four corners. This would be a victory for Marduk and his forces, making Marduk the supreme god of the fourth-dimensional pantheon, overthrowing the rule of his uncle Enlil/Jehovah/Zeus, who ruled on behalf of his father, Commander Anu head of the Nibirian council, the battle star planet of the Pleiadean Federation Star League operating within the Syrian high council.

Apparently, this would have been a two-way victory by the dark forces, if the Babylonians would have accomplished their spaceport. (Tower of Babel). The good news is that they failed because as in the case of Atlantis, this world was never meant to be under a totalitarian system of tyranny. Second, because if the (ascending) evolving human race, had leaned towards superior technological development, before reaching spiritual maturity, then they would have repeated what had happened in Atlantis and program IS-RA- El, which means, to bring heaven to earth would have been aborted again.

However, that wasn't the case, because Enlil/Jehovah/Zeus as supreme chief of the earth Anunaki council (the Pantheon of the celestial/humans) decided to thwart the plan as he did in Atlantis. As explained in the bible, the lord Jehovah (Enlil/Zeus) struck the tower down, by divine intervention. Enlil/Jehovah decided also to confuse man's language, so that they may not understand each other. Well considering today's restored knowledge, this makes perfect sense.

Enlil/Jehovah/Zeus realized that by confusing mankind's (evolving humans) ability to communicate with one another, it would be impossible for them to learn about the advanced technology that was being introduced by the Babylonians.

According to the higher intelligence, it was decided by the Nibirian council led by Enlil- Jehovah to disconnect some of the developing strands of DNA, so that the ascending humans may lose their ability to communicate telepathically. In the biblical book of Genesis, it is explained in the words, "Let us go down and confuse their language".

This happened when the Pleiadean/Nibirians disconnected all strands with the exception of two, downgrading the evolving humans to the use of only their left brain again which compelled them to develop their own language with actual words and sounds making them incapable of understanding each other telepathically.

In other words, the right brain and pineal gland are only fully functional, when more than two strands of DNA are operating. Apparently, it is obvious that the more genetic material we use, we become more spiritually divine which is multi-dimensional. This information has been confirmed by the higher intelligence. The importance of such an act could be understood when one considers the fact that overall, no matter what happens, there is a reason for everything that happens.

Many scholars in the esoteric realm, believe that according to the astrological sign of the bull, it was the time of Enlil/Jehovah/Zeus to rule during 3,400 BC, not Marduk. Nevertheless, Marduk didn't give up, for now, he had an established bloodline, the abomination of the earth. According to the astrological signs of the heavens, Marduk's times to rule would begin at the age of the Ram or Aries in 2024BC. So from about 3100BC to about 2100B.C., peace did reign on earth again, and even though the evolving (ascending) humans were not as spiritually developed as they were before the tower incident, they all for the most part, lived in harmony with one another starting from scratch again without any technology.

Eventually, great exchanges and commerce become established again in the regions of Mesopotamia, the Indus valley, India, and China. So, from about 3100BCE to about 2100BCE everything was running smooth regardless of the differences. This alluded to the fact that the age of the bull was ruled by the descendants of the benevolent celestial/humanoids of the Osirian line in Egypt and the Enlil/Jehovah/Zeus line in Mesopotamia. Then as the age of the Bull (Enlil/Jehovah/Zeus) came to an end in 2024BC, tension began to set in between the different regions, as the time of Aries/war Marduk was coming.

As mentioned, even though the rule was given over to ascending evolving man since around 3600BC, the descending fourth-dimensional watchers in which the humans built their sacred temples to, were still influencing events from the higher fourth dimension of the earth plane and through their secret societies.

In India, it was the children of the descending celestial/human guardian Indra. In Ur of Mesopotamia, it was the children of Enlil/Jehovah/Zeus. In Egypt, it was the children of Osiris. In the region we know today as Ireland and England, the descending celestial/humanoid Odin ruled his council of twelve. Each region was ruled and overseen by a descending celestial/humanoid guardian that ruled in favor of the One Unseen God of Melchizedek and of the order of Michael, of the royal House of Avon. This was the establishment of the great council of twelve, that produced the best commonwealths, since the days of Isis and Osiris, following the fall of Atlantis. It was this concept of righteousness and just administration that inspired Plato to later write "The Republic" to inspire future generations of governments.

For the record, the ancient mythological Deities were not a myth, nor were they gods including Marduk. They were descending sons, daughters, and grandchildren of the Great Nibirian celestial/ humanoid Overlord and commander of the Nibirian council who inserted the rule of the council of twelve for his children to follow Unfortunately, this prosperous age of the bull ended with the rise of the age of the Ram (Aries). The year was 2024BCE, Marduk knew his time had come; however, it came with a price.

The plan for the dark forces under the direction of fourth-dimensional Marduk-Baal/Satan (the Babylonian deity), was to seize control of the space sports and stargates, beginning with the one located in the Cedar Mountains, and another near the region we identified in the bible as Sodom and Gomorra. This is also the time that the biblical Abraham came into the picture as he become the most important figure for the forces of light in the events that shaped the history of the world since then.

As the story goes, Enlil's sons, Ninurta, Nannar, and Adad/Sin and along with one of Enki's sons Nergal, all had knowledge about the plot that Nabu and Marduk were hatching in an attempt to usurp the Nibirian title of the "fifty" that is of supreme earth lord held by Enlil/Zeus, Elyon, Jehovah during those days. They all knew that Marduk was going to try to usurp that title so that he may declare himself the supreme god of the world. However as revealed by the restored (Niburian Council), Marduk and his forces had other plans in mind and that was to gain full control of our planet to then eventually seize full control of the Pleiades and hence retake control of the entire galaxy from the Federation of celestial/humanoids. This was a multiprocess step on behalf of Marduk and his dark forces.

But first, they needed to gain control of the space sports and of course, the stargates which are certain major electromagnetic grid points on the planet that access other realms in our galaxy, and since our planet had been quarantined by the Federation after the fall of Atlantis, this portals and spaceports had been hiding by the forces of light since the fall of Atlantis.

If Marduk had gain control over these vortexes and spaceports, he would have gone to other parts of the galaxy. Also in order to secure the possibility of spreading tyranny to the rest of the galaxy, Ninurta and Nergal and Nannar all celestial descending sons (the three angels in the bible) worked in secret and in tandem with the ascending earthling Abraham to destroy the space sports and stargates in the Sinai Peninsula and the Cedar mountain region.

They did it by using what earth scientists today, would consider a Plutonian bomb. This weapon of mass destruction, equivalent to a few atom bombs, was apparently hidden very well from the negative E.T. fallen celestial forces. This bomb apparently, had the power of spreading enough radioactive decay that was needed in order to destroy the stargates. It was Nannar, Ninurta, and Nergal who were considered the three biblical angels involved in the warning of Lot and his family.

Now since the mighty weapon was hidden, Abraham was the chosen one to carry out the assignment since he was a descendant of the royal bloodline of the Priest-kings of Ur.

Abraham therefore with the aid of the three celestial beings (Nannar, Ninurta, Nergal,) placed the Plutonian explosives in the regions of the space sports and stargates to detonate them. By destroying the space sports first, Marduk and his forces would be stopped by gaining control of the space facilities and stargates that would otherwise allow him to gain access to other parts of the galaxy.

The space sports were destroyed, as well as the nearby cities of Sodom and Gomorra, which all went up in a big mushroom-like flame, as explained, in not only the biblical account but in the ancient Sumerian text. This was a smart move by the celestial forces, descending sons of God, Bnai Or Elohim whatever you would like to call them.

In either case, this explosive event also marked the end of the age of the Bull and the beginning of the age of the Ram. As soon as the age of the Ram sat in, Marduk did reign supreme on the earth, as the age of his uncle Enlil-Jehovah ended. This was technical, the actual time that the dark brotherhood really began to take control of the affairs of our world, since the days of Atlantis and the beginning of the dark ages, ensued again.

The age of the Ram became the age of the wars of evolving ascending men, as the dark forces usurp control of our planet, mainly through their Dracon reptilian

183

human hybrids. This Dark Age was the beginning of the dominance of the Ham-Cish-Nimrod bloodline which issued the era of the empires. Also, it has been revealed by the restored Nibirian council that Marduk and his forces had not only to gain control of the earth in 2024BC but also control of Nibiru, the twelve planets of the Nibirian/celestial/humanoids. It was revealed that Marduk secretly brewed an army of clones in the deserted planet Mars, knowing that his time to rule was coming.

When his time came, knowing that the cosmic clock landed on his sign, Marduk went about to dispose of his grandfather, Commander Anu from Nibiru, by force. This gave Marduk absolute control of our planet as did Enlil- Jehovah during the age of the Bull. As a result of directly taking control of our world, Marduk and his forces went about changing everything around as they did in Atlantis. All records were changed to suit his agenda of world domination, making himself the supreme god of our earth. The first thing he did was eliminate the veneration of the sacred divine feminine which for millenniums under the councils of light was held in balance with the masculine energies of the creator source. With Marduk reigning supreme on Nibiru, women become inferior and the rise of the masculine totalitarian patriarchal world ensued.

Now it is important to know, as confirmed by all prophetic traditions, that his age would come to an end and that an age of light (HEAVEN ON EARTH) would come again. Therefore, Marduk (a fourth-dimensional aspect of Satan) and his forces were given temporary control of our earth, as revealed in the bible, although his power was limited.

So, from 2024BC to 1800BC, the region of Mesopotamia had become a warfare battle zone between the different regions, as the war of the kings began. Of course, the wars were primarily initiated by the ascending evolving hybrid reptilian-human bloodline of the HamCush-Nimrod seed who were endeavoring to impose their totalitarianism as their age permitted.

During this era the dark forces which under the direction of its secret master sorcerers, were endeavoring to restore the second Babylonian empire which was aborted with the fall of the Tower of Babel, thanks to Enlil- Jehovah-Zeus.

In the succession of Nimrod through his genealogy, the human reptilian-hybrid that led the quest for world domination operating under the direction of the fourth-dimensional Dracon Marduk/Satan was our historical Hammurabi.

By 1760BCE Hammurabi had declared himself king of the four corners of the world. Unlike Nimrod his predecessor, Hammurabi was not as powerful, as he wasn't a demi-god, but obviously carried in his DNA the urge for power.

However, thanks to the forces of light who opposed the empire with the help of their benevolent watchers who never left the scene, the earth allies, ascending human descendants, and followers of EnlilJehovah and Horus remain behind for three primary reasons.

The first and most important was to oppose the rise of the Babylonian Brotherhood. Second, they also acted as protectors and custodians of the higher spiritual knowledge, the ageless wisdom preserved by the Osirian groups that later resurfaced in classical Greece, through Pythagoras, Socrates, and Plato and finally to continue the preservation of the righteous bloodline of Priest-Kings, also known as the Holy Grail lineage.

Overall, these benevolent descending beings (the celestials) and their brotherhoods of light preserved the higher knowledge initially through their hereditary lineage in which the celestials would continue a relationship with members of the evolving human race particularly those from the Enlil and Horus bloodline, which became known as our biblical prophets. For example, in the west, this covenant was established as the God-men partnership.

As we know, this special pact was made between Lord Melchizedek and Man through Abraham of UR who carried the highest concentration of the twelve energies (twelve chakras) which indicated that he was from the direct line of the priest-king lineage of benevolent descending celestial/ humanoids of the pure line of Michael. Some believe Abraham could have been both a descendant of Enlil-Jehovah and Horus through the Osirian Enki lineage, uniting both dynasties as the Ananda line here on earth. Nevertheless, our biblical Abraham became a central figure in the history of our world, as he perhaps was chosen to integrate both the lines of Enlil and Enki, through Ishmael and Isaac.

By divine decree, during the rise of the age of the Ram, the program ISIS-RA-Elyon established through the Melchizedek-Abraham covenant was kept intact even after Marduk took power.

It was this program (Israel) that preserves the secret knowledge (kabala) through a hereditary initiatory succession of Priest-kings. Historically this was known as the Oral Tradition. In fact, the Oral Tradition was the basis for the existence of the most secretive of spiritual knowledge, which was kept from falling into the hands of the wicked.

Since then benevolent secret societies and mystery schools had been established on behalf of the lightworkers so that when the time was right for the restoration of the planet, this higher knowledge would resurface again to usher in the promised seventh Golden age that would last for all life and all eternity.

Throughout all history, these benevolent secret societies were collectively known as the ancient and modern brotherhood of the Quest. And the quest was to establish the kingdom of light on earth as it is in Heaven.

This was initially the case regarding the brotherhood of light which always operated and functioned under the direction of the ancient Egyptian and Mesopotamian order of Melchizedek.

In fact, their quest to establish a Utopian world is a vague memory of what ancient Lemuria and the original Atlantis were to the members and operatives of this order, known as the priesthood/priestess of Melchizedek.

The war of the kings became the war of the bloodlines. From the beginning of the age of Aries, the dark brotherhood sought the destruction of their rival bloodline of the benevolent Priest-king line of messianic descent.

These dark ones had always sought to kill any trace of the descendants of Enlil-Jehovah-Zeus and Horus which according to the secret knowledge was the rightful bloodline of benevolent priest-kings.

This explains why throughout history certain male babies had to be hidden, like Horus of Egypt, which parallel the story of Moses and Jesus of Nazareth, not to mention those that were left off the record that also becomes unknown historical heroes, like Mithras from Iran, Dionysius of Greece, Krishna of India.

Since the beginning of their reign, the dark brotherhood understood that according to the ancient oracle (prophesies), their reign would end at the coming of a Messiah that would deliver mankind from all evil.

Nonetheless, the attempt to restore the old Babylonian empire in !760BC, by Emperor Hammurabi, failed thanks to the banding of the rebel groups known then as the Nation-States democracies who were influenced by the networks of the secret brotherhood of light, of the Order of Melchizedek.

The Nation-States democracies were those surrounding groups like the Greeks, Assyrians, Hittites, Spartans, and other freedom fighters who believed in the commonwealth, democratic form of government.

Nevertheless, the reign of Marduk and his Babylonian allies brought about an overt endless attempt at imposing totalitarianism since 2024BC.

For instance, when the dark brotherhood failed in 1760BC through Hammurabi, they disseminated into the land of Egypt in order to infiltrate it from within to continue their plan there once again.

So, after Babylon, the networks of the dark brotherhood transferred over to the land region of Egypt, which has always been the main target for them, because of the power and mysteries associated with the great pyramids.

To usurp the Egyptian throne from the descendants of the Osiris-Horus bloodline, the Babylonian brotherhood slowly began to influence circumstances that eventually led to the rise of what history calls the Thothmosis dynasty.

This was the imposter bloodline of the Babylonian secret human reptilian hybrids, which later gave us the biblical Ramses that brought about the corruption of Egypt.

Many secret records show the correlations between the Moses exile that took place after Thothmosis the third took power. Apparently, Moses came from both Enlil/Abrahamic and Horus lineages, therefore, making him the proper ruler of

Egypt.

As a result of the Babylonian infiltration of Egypt, a massive attempt was made by the dark brotherhood, to once again put an end to the original bloodline of benevolent kingship. Since Akhenaton (Moses) the son of Amenhotep the IV was of the rightful benevolent bloodline, he had to be taken away into hiding by his mother. The plan was to save Moses (Akhenaton) from being slain by the new corrupt political party of the new dark pharaoh, who believe that by ending Moses' life, the Messianic line of righteous Priest-kings would end. During the time of Egypt's turn over, in the aftermath of the Babylonian infiltration, which gradually took over the affairs in Egypt, the order of Melchizedek disseminated into refuge establishing a settlement known as El Amarna, which was led by the surviving Moses, outside the Egyptian region. From that settlement, under the guidance of Moses, who believed in the concept of the one God, began influencing and building armies of freedom fighters who later worked in tandem with Moses as the outside groups.

These were the nation-states of Elam, Anshan, and Martini, among others which were areas outside of the Egyptian region. And as true history recalls, these nation-states brought down the dark brotherhoods' second attempt to establishing world domination in Egypt.

According to higher sources, these were the Israelites that lived outside of Egypt; however as biblical documents reveal, that the Israelites that lived within the Egyptian boundaries have slaved. This sounds like the galactic scenario that took place when the Orion physical Humanoids were enslaved by the Orion Draconian in the aftermath of our galaxy's first galactic battle.

Now regarding the suppressed history of the forces of light, let's refer to the twelve tribes of Israel that stem from Jacobs's children and the direct descendants of Ishmael. First of all, let it be known that Abraham and his half-sister Sarah our biblical patriarch and matriarch, had the highest concentration of the twelve energies that represent the twelve living universes of all humanoid races in which we are a part of and therefore became the genetic progenitor of the Program Israel. On a deeper and more spiritual level, the Program Israel had really to do with awakening unto our divinity (celestial statues) and remembering that we are light beings, exploring the lower dimensions of the material spheres.

Nonetheless, according to higher sources, Sarah's and Abraham's lineage came directly from Lord Michael. They carried all twelve chakras making them eligible for ascension and capable of downloading their light body, Merkabah. During those days, most of the other humans had only developed seven chakras. They needed to anchor and integrate the five higher chakras outside of their physical vehicle, in order to connect with the higher Spheres of light.

After all, considering the restored spiritual knowledge, it has been confirmed, that we have seven major chakras aligned within the physical body and five outer chakras outside our physical body that connects us to the great central sun. This meant that project ISRAEL (contend with light) which leads to program Zion (free world) would be the only system of government that would establish a true HEAVEN ON EARTH, as symbolized by the star of David. Therefore, the promised restoration of ZION in 2000 BC, at the peak of the war of the kings and during the rise of the empires, was left in the hands of Abraham and his descendants in the west.

That meant that through his genealogy, all offspring would carry the highest concentration (spin) of the twelve energy centers (Chakras) that would one day allow his descendants, especially those that carried the highest celestial DNA count as in the case of the Messianic lineage of King David, to become fully conscious again of their divine nature.

Secondly, because the descendants of Abraham also carried the lowest, if not any count of reptilian DNA, which in those days had contaminated most of the other evolving humans.

As mentioned and according to the bible, the word blemish is a metaphor describing a high count of Reptilian DNA in the old near east such as in the case of the Canaanites. The fact of the matter is that all humans in our planet today are descendants of the PleiadeanNibirians through the family of Anu, whether we came from Enlil, Enki, or any of their many children Anu, therefore, could have been considered the sixth-dimensional aspect of god the father, our human progenitor through either of his two rivaling sons Enki- SamuelPoseidon and Enlil-Jehovah-

Zeus who's celestial DNA we all have. And in case we have forgotten, it is important to remember that all celestial beings, including the Nibirians, had their stellar roots in Lyra as sixth and fifth-dimensional beings and then continued into the Pleiades which at some point earlier in our galactic history became a promised land for the migrating celestial descending humanoids of Lyra.

And since all of existence is cyclical then Abraham and his descendants who carried within their DNA, the entire original celestial human genetic code, have also been given a Promise land as well, Zion, the free world.

Considering this today, we may say that America was the brotherhood of light's most recent attempt for Zion.

It is precisely this promised land of milk and honey that our world would experience if the earthly representatives of the celestial/humanoid house of Avyon which stems from the Abrahamic bloodline would have taken over the affairs of our world.

Unfortunately, the dark brotherhood through the earthly reptilian representatives set up by Marduk and his reptilian forces through Nimrod have been the powers that be and the reason why our world has only experience suffering and hard living conditions, as the wrong DNA program came to power. Again, this entire conflict that echoes in our world today is nothing more than the ancient galactic battle that has been taking place between the descending celestial humanoids (children of light) and their rival and fallen angels, the Dracon reptilians (children of darkness). With this have said, we can now begin to see clearly how a handful of families, the oligarchy have been manipulating the masses in an effort to impose a total fascist system not only in the times of Atlantis, but as early as the times that the bible considers the war in heaven, or the wars of ORION.

Except at one point, it involved many star systems in our galaxy as the various star systems took sides, but now this ancient celestial galactic conflict has been reduced to our little planet which is the most significant world in our entire local universe in which we are a part off. In other words, the earth is not only the last battleground for light and dark but also as it becomes a HEAVEN ON EARTH; will mark the beginning of a new creation, one that has been in divine design since before the foundation of our local universe.

Nonetheless, in the ancient world, the Babylonian Brotherhood of darkness continued their agenda in secret even after they lost power in Egypt thanks to Moses.

Moses, the greatest Old Testament prophet, not only saved the children of Israel (those that contend with light, life, and freedom) but managed to establish the grounds for a few hundred years of peace and harmony, in the midst of the age of AriesRam. In the process, the Israelites were led to the Promised Land, as they received protection by their descending celestial allies, the Nibirian/Pleiadean (the angels of the bible), who apparently continued to influence things, for the restoration of light, from the invincible fifth dimension and up.

This momentum culminated with the once again, rise of the Messianic earthly representatives of the House of Avyon, in an effort, to establish the kingdom of Zion, These coincided with the emergence of King David who was the son of Jesse who was the son of Perez who was the grandson of Judah who was the son of Jacob and carried the highest concentration of the twelve energies as direct descendants of Sarah-Abraham. Therefore, the kingdom of King David was considered a true commonwealth in the occidental world of the Middle East, and through his son Solomon they were going to bring freedom to the rest of the planet, however, their time was not yet in season, for we were well into the age of Aries/Ram, which according to astrology is ruled by the god of war, hence Marduk.

Unfortunately, this temporary triumph of the brotherhood of light was interrupted by the death of Solomon. As a result, this rightful bloodline of priest-kings had to go into the underground to seek refuge from the outer world, once again. This seclusion was brought about by the dark brotherhood's rise to power, with the Neo Assyrian conquest which was maneuvered by the secretive Babylonian brotherhood, under a new name and new region, Assyria. This move by Marduk's forces placed Tiglath Pilasser the second in power who was a direct descendant of Nimrod. Pilaster become Emperor and conqueror in 960BC as the temporary kingdom of Zion (light) fell. Pilasser's s reign continued with his son and successor Shuripal and later through his grandson Shalmaneser the third and his great-grandson Shalmaneser the fourth.

191

By 729BC and after Shalmaneser the fourths reign his son, Tiglath Pilasser the third reclaimed and revived the restoration of the third Babylonian empire which evolved out of the Neo-Assyrian conquest. Here is the connection to the Babylonian networks.

Pilasser' s the thirds; reign was followed by Nabupolasser who was of Babylonian origin since Nabu was the son of Marduk. The reign of Nabupolasser was then followed by his son Nabunasser who by 626BC had Babylon merge sovereign over Assyria. Therefore, the rise of Tiglath Pilasser was obviously a vehicle and steppingstone for the resurrection and rise of the third Babylonian empire. With this in place, now we had a full resurrection of the Babylonian Empire as Nabunasser's reign was followed by our biblical Nebuchadnezzar.

According to biblical scripture, it was this kingdom the prophet Daniel described as the head of Gold, and system of the beast, (Draco reptilian).

In the biblical account, the Prophet Daniel warned King Nebuchadnezzar that his kingdom represented the head of gold and used the allegory of the four beasts, describing the rise and fall of the succeeding empires that would follow his reign in the last days of the age of the ram. For the record, the reign of Nebuchadnezzar was considered the third resurrection of the Babylonian Empire, which again was the expedition of the Reptilian human hybrid bloodline of the dark Brotherhood that stemmed from the Ham- Cush-Nimrod lineage. At this point around 625 B.C. and as prophesied by the Prophet Daniel of the white brotherhood, there was a succession of attempts to overtly establish the Empire under the direction of the dark forces. As for the brotherhood of light, the ongoing order of Melchizedek, had to resort to the underground and remain hidden after the reign of Solomon, but would still guide the ancient Israelites through their prophets.

However, the brotherhoods of light were not inactive. During their refuge in secret, the brotherhood of light established a network of benevolent secret societies known as the Order of the left and right eye of Horus. This was a continuation of the spiritual teachings of the ancient Mystery Schools that began in Egypt and that were later refined by Moses in the composition of the Kabala. The whole purpose of this Mystical school revival was to train spiritually enlighten people especially those of the Davidic bloodline that descended from the ancient bloodline of Horus and Enlil/Jehovah/Zeus, to become even purer than they already were in order to facilitate a higher vibration in their bloodline in preparation for the coming of the most radiant one, Jesus the Christ.

The mental discipline and spiritual exercises practiced by the Horus mystical schools are designed to raise the vibrations of the celestial bloodline through meditation, prayer, and spiritual devotion, etc. Of course, the brotherhood of Melchizedek, knew that the most radiant one would come from the priest-king line of King David.

This disciplined began with the descendants of King David and culminated later with Mary and Joseph who were also high initiates in the mysteries of the Order of Melchizedek, as direct descendants of the celestial bloodline. When the time was right after the close of the age of Aries-Ram, Mary who carried the highest concentration of Mitochondria (indicative of celestial DNA) was impregnated by our creator in order to give birth to the highest vibrational human being that ever walked the earth, Jesus the Christ. In Christian traditions, he was known as the lion of Judah. It was his coming that shifted the entire planetary frequency because he carried such a high level of light Quotient, purity that totally transformed the energy field of the entire planet, shifting its direction into the age of Pieces.

Now, regarding the activities of the dark brotherhood, we know from both biblical revelations and historical events, that Babylon has always been considered the abomination of the world. In fact, in our biblical text, Babylonia is known as the whore of the earth, the abomination of God, the desolation of desecration etc., and in the words of Jesus Christ himself, the brotherhood of Satan or the hidden hand. In short, the timeline of world domination exercised by the dark brotherhood and their bloodlines became the source of world oppression through all of history.

According to the book of Daniel, the system of the beast was first Babylon, which reemerged sovereign with the conquest, led by Pilasser the third. Then later to be replaced with Nabupolasser was succeeded by Nabunasser who in turn was succeeded by Nebuchadnezzar by the year 625BC. Then as the book of Daniel describes, and as indicated by astrology, the Babylonian empire was quickly replaced by the rise of the Medo- Persian Empire who was controlled by the same Babylonian bloodlines through Cyrus the Great, as Conqueror. This Empire was replaced by the Macedonian Empire of Alexander the Great, who according to Zachariah Zitchin was documented to be a descendant of the Babylonian Nabu-Nimrod line.

And finally, the Macedonian Empire was replaced by the Roman Empire, the last of the beast (Dracon) systems that were to overtly impose a system of absolute control and power. This succession of Empires was executed by the dark brotherhood of Marduk (a fourth-dimensional aspect of Satan) because they knew that their Age (Aries) was soon ending. Luckily the brotherhood of light has always banded together, to bring down every attempt at establishing the Empire.

As in the case of the Sovereign-Nation-states of Elam, Anshan, and Martini during times of the Expanding Egyptian Empire, to the rebel states of the Greeks, Spartans during the rise of the Medo-Persian Empire as demonstrated in the great Hollywood film "The 300 Club".

And finally, the rebel states that collapsed Rome to its knees, historically known as the ten unknown barbaric tribes that worked in tandem to collectively bring down what history considered the most powerful empire ever.

As mentioned, after the reign of Solomon, the brotherhood of light went into the deep refuge, and later culminated as the benevolent secret society of the Qumran community, who was connected with the spiritual orders of Egypt, India, Tibet, Spain, Gaul, and England Ireland.

Another thing to understand here is that King Herod, the Roman governor of Judea was from an imposter bloodline design to fool the powers of Rome-Babylon. The networks of light, not only carefully guarded the celestial bloodline of Messianic descent but also preserved the kabala and esoteric knowledge which was the higher Divine knowledge that culminated with the community of Qumran, the Essence and other mystical orders, during the times of Jesus.

The existence of the benevolent secret society of the Essence is now coming to light thanks to the risen records of the Dead Sea scrolls of Nag Hamadi. According to these scrolls and other sources including restored ancient holy books and channeled information, the Essence set themselves apart from the rest of society, in order to continue the great divine plan in secret. It was this secret brotherhood/sisterhood of illumined souls (saints) that provided a haven for the coming Messiah. They understood universal laws and divine knowledge and applied all they knew daily. In fact, most biblical characters, like John the Baptist, during the time of Jesus were members of this secret society of Priest and Priestess who became practitioners of the ancient Egyptian mysteries of Thoth-Hermes-Enoch.

This benevolent secret society become well-crafted in all the esoteric sciences from Alchemy to Masonry and therefore the bible describes Joseph, the father of Jesus as a carpenter who in its original Hebrew term meant an alchemist. Not to mention that Joseph was also the reincarnated ascended master of light, Saint Germaine who was chosen by the order of Melchizedek to act as the primary protector of the Messiah. Again, this is the same line of Divine sonship that stems back to ancient Egypt through the lineage of Horus/Enlil and their direct descendants, which as revealed earlier could be traced back to Nibiru. It is no doubt that the early Israelites were from the direct line of the royal house of Avyon.

Now in connections to the continued celestial line of righteous pries-kings, here is another revelation; history had us believe that Rome was collapsed by ten barbaric tribes. Well, the truth of the matter is that those supposedly ten barbaric tribes were no other than the lost ten tribes of Israel that fled Mesopotamia during the diaspora of the early Israelites. They became the early European nation-states of the Franks of early Gaul-France, the Celts of ancient England and Ireland, the Visigoths of Spain, the Ostrogoths of Portugal, the Vandals of the middle east, the Burgundians of Italy, the Lombardi's of Sicily, and lower Italy, as well as the Saxons, Normans, and Nordics of northern Europe.

These were the sovereign nation-states and spiritual lands of the lost ten tribes of Israel, before the rise of modern European culture. Therefore, these pre- European spiritual cultures co-existed during the times of the Roman Empire, without being detected by Rome-Babylon, for they were the lost ten tribes of the program Israel. After all, the ancient practices of the Druids of pre-European settlements were all influenced by the secret brotherhood of light as the Essence of the community of Quorum operating in secret from the caves of Nag Hamadi in Judea.

Now following the collapse of the Roman Empire, the dark brotherhood once again took control of the new affairs as the "Jedi bloodline" of the Messianic descent of the Essen Secret Society once again disseminated into the refuge. After settling for a couple of hundred years in India, the brotherhood of light transferred the holy bloodline to its new location in the south of France.

After Rome, the dark brotherhood reorganized as the "Whore of the Earth", as revealed in our bible, Rev. 17. This was the immediate solution to consolidate the power of the church and state so that the dark brotherhood may spiritually control the new monarchies of early Europe with the result being the resurrection of the Holy Roman Empire. This move by the dark brotherhood plunged our world into the darkest ages, as a last desperate resort to resurrect the empire under the façade of religion which was launch by the last of the Roman Emperors, Constantine, who was also a heavy carrier of the reptilian gene. Considering today's knowledge, the Holy Roman Empire become the source of all corruption and vehicle for the dark brotherhood, from that time on till the present day. This institution was the reemergence of the old Babylonian religion of idolatry and dogma, once again placing the emphasis on God as something outside ourselves

This Holy Roman Empire placed itself as the only mediator between the heavens and earth and was sponsored by the followers of Marduk. In the bible the prophets warn, you shall know them by their fruits and beware of false prophets that will deceive many. If the results were the darkest ages ever experienced at the influence of this institution, then it was of darkness. The Holy Roman Empire's real agenda has always been world domination (Babylon) not spiritual liberation.

# CHAPTER FOURTEEN

## THE INHERITORS AND SUCCESSORS OF THE ORDER OF THE ESSENE, FROM ABOUT 900 AD TO THE PRESENT

A few hundred years into the dark ages, the forces of light began reorganizing in secret and began planning their reemergence once gain. These were the remnant seed of those independent nations, Celts, original Britons, Franks, and Visigoths, etc.

The original Essen members had reorganized as the Order of the Grail and now needed an outer vehicle to protect it. This vehicle came about when nine French men decided it was their obligation to protect what history would consider the Priori of Zion, (the guardians and keepers of the holy grail).

The truth can now be revealed regarding the real name of the benevolent secret society that was protected by the Knights Templars, known as the Order of the Grail. This new mystical western spiritual order was connected to all the spiritual centers, in Egypt, Tibet, Agartha, and most important to the order of the unseen masters, known as the ascended masters of light, that guide humanity from the higher fifth dimension in Shambala.

Due to our multi-dimensional reality, the networks of light have always had the advantage because they are being assisted from what our new science calls the unseen dimensions. On the same token, the dark brotherhood has been only operating from the lower fourth dimension and third dimension as they have been curtailed from the higher dimensions. With that said, letslet'sntify the meaning of the priority of Zion, which was the allegiance and oath of the legendary Knights of the Temple. The priority of Zion reverts to the program Israel that was established with Abraham and archangel Melchisedek. Again, Zion in its original context means the promised land of freedom and prosperity, as the system of the commonwealth and free world, the true meaning of the program Israel.

It was this ancient Abrahamic concept that became the millennial project resurrected by the Templars in 900 A. D. as sealed in 2000BC by the pact that Abraham established through his holiness archangel Melchizedek, when Marduk overtly took control of our worlds system. In modern times today, we could conclude, that America was the latest established Zion of the millennial project, for it became the land of opportunity, prosperity, and liberty. Overall, the seeds of the free world and spiritual enlightenment have been an idea carried out and protected by all existent benevolent secret societies.

Let's do the math. The Nights of the old temple of Solomon become the Templar's at the beginning of the tenth century A. D. This happened to be the exact time that the Holy Roman Empire development had reached a heighten peak, as they controlled all the new European developed kingdoms, thanks to Otto the Great, the first regent crowned Holy Roman Emperor. As in all prior times in history, this threat of imperial European absolutism, at the end of the tenth century compelled the scattered remnants of the brotherhood of light to resurface and once again thwart the imperial dynasty, as they did back in Rome. There needed to be a counter affective plan as a solution to the dark ages.

This plan came about when the brotherhood of light in medieval times, known as the Order of the Grail, began infiltrating the Roman Church from within, through a heroic figure by the name Bernard De Clairvaux, who 'quickly rose to a high position within the ranks of the church's hierarchy. The first thing Clairvox did was establish several monastic branches for the church among them the order of the Cartesians, among others.

At the end of his ascend in the Roman church, he was chosen to be the Pope's primary advisor, which was planned by the order of light, to work the church from within. Bernard was an important key figure, a marvelous actor of his time working secretly as a member of the white brotherhood of the Grail. With his position within the hierarchy of the Holy Roman institution, the secret order of the Grail was once again ready to reemerge and most importantly once again to secretly plot the emergence out of the dark ages, that had been coerced by the development of the Holy Roman Empire, the new Babylon.

The plan was simple. Since fundamentalist Islamic invaders were not only attempting to seize control of the holy land in those days but also planning the eventual takeover of Europe, something needed to be done. It was exactly this event, that provided the means and perfect opportunity that worked in favor of the newly organized knights of the Temple.

According to all suppressed records, the rise of Bernard the Clairvox enabled the papacy to condone and charter a military Christian order of Knights that would become the Christian military protectors of the holy land and of course, Europe, from the risen Islamic invaders.

This would not have been possible if Bernard De Clairvaux of the brotherhood of light would have not become the primary advisor of the Pontiff Vicar during those days. By his request, the knights were chartered by the Roman Church, and so this military order who was the first design to protect, the old holy land became in essence, the secret protectors and guardians of both the ancient knowledge of Solomon and the concepts of the free world, that the Holy Roman Empire was attempting to destroy.

Therefore, the order of the Knights of Templars becomes the outer and protecting vehicle for the inner group that in turn protected the ancient bloodline of the king-priest linage of celestial messianic descent.

According to various scholars within the fields of Templarism and Freemasonry, the families that were direct descendants of the grail which means holy divine blood was known as the Desposiny. It was revealed that these families later rose to power in southern France, through the Carolingian dynasty as well as in Scotland through the Stuart dynasty during even later times.

In truth, they are the descendants of the nation-states that ransacked the Roman Empire to its knees, corresponding to the old nation-states of the past that opposed every risen empire. It is history repeating itself but in different times.

As mentioned, throughout all of history the existing nation's state democracies were the lost scattered tribes of ancient Israel.

Considering this biblical connection to the historic unknown tribes of Israel, it is obvious that they were intelligent organized independent states co-existing peacefully in the early region of Europe as descendants of the nation-states of Jacob-Israel. Of course, the nation-states have been degraded to barbaric tribes in our history books, during the revision of history by the Jesuit order (modern-day dark brotherhood). Apparently, they were thrown under the bus as the bad guys implying loyalty to Rome, the system of the Beast, who is ruled by the (Anti-Christ) descendants of the Mardukian-Nabu-Nimrod-Esau Draco-reptilian bloodline.

The Knights Templars were the rightful inheritors of Solomon's Knowledge and treasure, as King Arthur was the rightful one for the Excalibur sword. It was, therefore, destined for the brotherhood of light to retrieve the esoteric higher knowledge and treasures that had been buried in the old temple of Solomon, before the Vicars (old Caesars) of the Holy Roman Empire. The brotherhood of light knew that the sacred lost divine knowledge that the dark brotherhood sought, to absolutely control the world was included in those records.

In other words, if the Holy Roman Empire got to those records before the Templars, the reformation and the renaissance would have never happened, and America-Zion would have never been established.

After all, the dark brotherhood under the auspices of the Roman Church destroyed and eliminated every library in existence during those days.

In the end, this lost arcane knowledge was the great gift that the Templar's gradually restored to the earth. Therefore, it was divine destiny that they inherited this lost treasure instead of the dark brotherhood.

In a situation like this, one can only imagine that the Templar's discovery was not only the unearthing of Solomon's knowledge, but it was part of the divine contract that extends back to Abraham. After all, it is well understood that the archangelic and angelic realms have been working closely with members of these benevolent secret societies.

For instance, some of these valuable accounts of information that were unearthed were the blueprint and concept of the great Republic, the government of righteousness, as it reflected the Lyran-Pleiadean Lemurian system. Other important records revealed the truth regarding our spherical planet and its solar system, and that explains why Galileo of the white brotherhood like his contemporary before him Copernicus, both associated with the white brotherhood, revealed this information when the time was right. The fact of the matter was that the concept of astronomy as known by Solomon, was known by the inner circle of the order of the temple, (Templars) for 389 years before they revealed it to the masses through figures like Nicola Copernicus, and Galileo Galilei. As a result of inheriting the ancient knowledge of Solomon, by the turn of the first millennium, the Templar's knew that our planet was spherical and not flat and strongly believed that landmarked by a star name La-America, was chosen to be the great Zion in the restoration of the program Israel. In fact, they were sailing the seas hundreds of years before the great Columbus.

According to esoteric records, the templars came to the Americas in the late twelve hundred A.D. and had established a pact with the Iroquois Indians that had marked and blessed this land for the eventual establishment of the New Jerusalem/America.

Overall, the establishment and accomplishments of the order of the Temple and their activities in medieval Europe was the western world's solution to end the medieval dark ages. All historical events, like the reformation and renaissance that got our world out of the dark ages, were the work of the Templars. Despite what history has mentioned about them, they were knights that stood for chivalry, truth, justice, and brotherhood/sisterhood among other benevolent things.

Most importantly, they were able to restore the lost ancient arcane spiritual knowledge that would return our worlds back into a golden age. The highest masters of this order were healers that developed a network based on the principles of brotherhood and freedom that extended to other mystical groups like the Sufis who were direct descendants of Ishmael, the other son of Abraham.

The templar brotherhood also included a group of stonemason workers who were initiated by Templarism to become the builders of the cathedrals in modern Europe. It was only through these networks of early European freemasonry that brotherhood and liberty existed among man in those days.

As a result of these networks of light, the re- emergences of the esoteric knowledge, the system of initiation that existed during the times of Egypt, throughout the old world and implemented in secret by the Essen's in Jerusalem had once again become a beacon of light in Europe. Of course, the Templars only initiated people who were ready to once again understand the ancient divine knowledge of the descending celestial beings.

It was precisely, this esoteric knowledge that illuminated Christian Rosenkranz into establishing another white brotherhood organization known as the order of the Rosicrucian's, which had its roots in Egypt as a branch of the order of Melchizedek. It is this secret knowledge that enables humans to reconnect with the other realms/dimensions, as revealed by our cutting-edge science.

Along with the restoration of the ancient mysteries and its initiation process, it was only logical to attempt to implement the Commonwealth system and so their first attempt was in southern France. It took them a couple of hundred years, though eventually, they managed to create a wonderful utopian community of good people who historically became known as the Cathars of France, almost resembling the Essen community of Quorum. The Cathars existed approximately in the eleven century A.D. Although deleted from our mainstream history, this spiritual-peaceful and educated society was a democratically advanced spiritual community that was wiped out in one of the many inquisitions conducted by the Holy Roman institution, to consolidate power.

This holocaust was known as the Albigensian crusade. However, this holocaust stems to 756 years earlier reflecting the day the Roman inquisition destroyed, the Celts, Druids, Gnostics, Franks, and the other spiritual communities during the fourth century A.D. Despite the destruction of what became the most advanced spiritual culture in France, the knowledge restored by the Templar's influenced great scholars that later along with the Templar's began to associate themselves as the brotherhood of the quest. And the Quest was the re-establishment of the great Zion. In political terms this would be the commonwealth republic, that would be based on an aristocracy of knowledge and education as opposed to one of money and power as was the case for the Roman litigate.

Despite their oppression, we did witness a gradual revival of knowledge that originated with the knight's Templar, which a couple of centuries later developed into the greatest event that brought our world out of the dark ages, the Renaissance. However, before their purpose was fulfilled in getting our world out of the darkest ages known to man, it wasn't an essay victory for the Knights.

As records showed, about sixty years later after the massacre of the Cathars of France, the Holy Roman Institution turned against the Templars in 1307. This coup de at was instigated by an imposter king, Philip de Bell, who managed to get his stooge into the highest rank of the papacy as Pope Clement the fifth and so the inquisition that has Friday the thirteen marked till today, was the day the knights were charged or may we say, falsely accused and thus condemned by the holy inquisition, of 1307. Not to mention that Friday the thirteen was also the date on which Atlantis sunk into the ocean.

Many of the knights were burned at the stake including, the last of the Grandmaster, Jacques De Moley. However, some managed to escape by orders from De Moley to reorganize themselves into different orders of knighthood, so that the quest of the brotherhood of light, which was the reestablishment of Zion, (the free world) would not end.

We may now safely say that all those men and women who contributed to the reformation and renaissance were either members or associates of this brotherhood and sisterhood of the Quest, or heavily influenced by them. For example, Joan of Arc, Copernicus, Galileo Galilee, Leonardo de Vinci, Michael Angelo, Giordano Bruno, Cosimo De Medici, Cardinal Nicolas De Cusa, Rene De Anjou, Philipo Brunellessi, and many others, were all heroic, in a sense that they risk and sacrificed their life's for a better world. In fact, most of them were martyred and others arrested for lifelike Galileo.

In conclusion, these heroes paved the way for a better world first by initiating the reformation, then the renaissance, which led to the scientific revolution and then ultimately to the fulfillment of the Quest and that is the establishment of the free world, The United States of America, according to its original constitution, the NEW JERUSALEM. Of course, this was the millennia project of the Holy Order of The Grail and the Templars. The first and foremost step was that of the reformation which sprung from being able to read the bible for the first time in defiance of the sinister law of Indulgence imposed by the Holy See.

This luxury of reading the bible is what caused the split, from the absolute tyranny of the Holy Roman Empire. This was historically known, as the fifteen-century reformation, but there was more. This originally started off as a reformation in religion than as a result of giving the commoner a chance to read the bible it then gradually shifted its direction into one of re-establishing education as it said in the bible, and with that came the renaissance, for the love and resurrection of art, science, music, medicine and so on.

So after about twelve hundred years of darkness and no literacy, art, math, science, and history began flourishing once again thanks to the fifteen-century reformation. Again, and for the record, all this would have never been possible without the existence and operations of the Knights Templars and their associated benevolent orders of light. Now let it be clear, that most of the inner circle and heroic members like those mentioned above were all considered descendants of the original Israelites or known as the Rex Dux families. For instance, Leonardo De Vinci was from the direct bloodline of King David and therefore of the messianic seed that our Lord Jesus Christ was also born into. For those reasons, the dark brotherhood of the NimrodEssua bloodline that was secretly controlling the Holy Roman Empire during the dark ages was always in the persecution of those that called themselves Jews.

The idea as always for the dark powers and their bloodline was to do away with their rival bloodline as it has always been the case, for two reasons. First to end the seed of the Messianic linage that could be traceable back to Horus and Enlil/Jehovah/Zeus. It was obvious that this bloodline of righteous king-priest stood in the dark brotherhoods way of arriving at world absolutism. Second, after ending the rightful bloodline of priest-kings, the plot was to establish the kingdom of Lucifer which is the Draconian EMPIRE. And as we recall this would have entailed victory for the fallen angels (demons) the ancient Dracon race of the royal galactic house of Aln. If this were the case, then the battle between light and dark would have been won by the dark side and this world would have never made it this far into the fullness of time as we approach the ascension of A NEW HEAVEN ON EARTH today.

It is clear now that our planet is under divine guidance as it was in its conception and as it will be after its restoration. In the closing of this chapter, we may conclude that the plans of the brotherhood of light to re-establish. Zion, the free world was part of the process that would lead to the full spiritual restoration of the planet and its people.

After their persecution, the Knights Templar's reorganized as the Freemasons in Scotland where they sought refuge and protection from King Robert the Bruce, who was in opposition to the Jesuits and their Holy Roman institution. This was around the late sixteen hundred.

Thereafter, the surviving templars had reorganized as the speculative and political Freemasons, along with their seafaring branch known as the brotherhood of the coast, the Pirates, who were Templarians that camouflage themselves as pirates in order to fool the agents of the corrupt European powers.

With this in motion, the brotherhood of light of the order of the Quest perpetuated the plans for Zion, which later culminated in the establishment of the United States of America. This was the promised land of milk and honey that was promised to Abraham, Isaac, and Jacob, Israel as long as they lived in righteousness and in harmony with all cultures.

America also became the land in which all the people of the world could finally be re-united since our division during the tower of Babel. Our world was divided in Babylon it was reunited in America.

For the record, in our modern world, the battle between the brotherhoods, become the battle of the Jesuits and Illuminati serving the Babylonian cause of the system of the beast (the anti-Christ) and the Freemasons and Rosicrucians who become instrumental and served as branches of the Templar's and inner Grail masters of the white lodge of Melchizedek. This branch of the light brotherhood has remained as guardians of what is left of the constitution, till today. As a result of the shift in human consciousness known as the renaissance, the spiritual masters that operate in the higher dimensional octaves known as the fifth dimension interfered during the late eighteen hundreds, as the level of awareness was raised thanks to the restoration of knowledge, three hundred years earlier.

Equally important to understand is the level of influence the ascended masters (earth angels) have over both sides. For they oversee all world affairs and are always guiding our evolution from behind the scenes. The ascended masters work very closely with and through the grail masters of the third dimension, to provide guidance and protection as earth angels as mentioned earlier.

One last thing to consider is that people who are spiritually enlightened know that there is no such thing as death. After one has accomplished his duties in third-dimensional physical form, he or she seizes to incarnate into third-dimensional form and ascends back into the fourth and fifth dimension with a perfected immortal refine metamaterial body. For instance, Abraham like other ascended masters from various cultures, India, China, Tibet, Europe, Africa, etc. never died as we were told, but rather reached a higher level of consciousness, and so we're able to integrate their bodies with their light body in a process called Ascension. In most cases, it takes place at the moment of physical death and others as in the case, of our biblical Enoch; there is no death but a translation of dimensions (from mortal to immortal) that takes place since we are energy-light beings.

Overall, when an aspirant on the spiritual path, reaches a level of consciousness where he or she no longer is blinded by the circumstances of this third-dimensional world, but in control of them, he or she ascends to higher levels of awareness while keeping his their physical form.

At that point, they could either choose to continue ascending to finer realities of light or stay behind in a higher octave on the earth plane in order to help guide and direct the spiritual evolution of the rest of humanity.

Ultimately it is these earth angels' ascended beings, whatever you would like to call them, that have great influence on our world from behind the scenes and work in tandem with the archangelic and angelic realms from even higher dimensions for the restoration of our planet. In truth, we are all part of a greater circuit or field of intelligence, and our science is now beginning to see that. It is my honor to say that all the prophecies about the return to our exalted state of life is now coming to pass. We have witnessed a long journey from the highest point of existence where we had our common origin, from the great central sun of all that is, as whole light beings. We have explored the great descent that took for what appears to be ever, and now we are ready to return as we begin to explore our collective ascent into a higher level (dimension) of existence. What is perhaps the most astounding revelation is that our Plaiedian parents arranged for a time, for our restoration back into full conscious earth beings, as it is encoded in our genetics.

# SECTION THREE

## CHAPTER FIFTEEN

## THE RISE OF
## HOMONAUTICUS THE ANGELS AMONG US

Since everything is been orchestrated from the higher dimensions as revealed, light is always on the winning side. Therefore, the existence of the dark brotherhood is coming to an end, for their time is up. And as mentioned, the world is not going to end, as the dark brotherhood would want us to believe. In truth, our world is being purified as it ascends back into the higher dimensions, as prophesied A NEW HEAVEN ON EARTH or may we say, program Israel, which is the seventh golden age in the east, is finally coming into fruition.

The signs are here, and this is what to expect in preparation for the coming of a NEW WORLD AGE, the millennium. It has been revealed by the creator of all universes that HEAVEN ON EARTH will be established for all eternity on this planet upon the rise of the seventh golden age which will be inhabited, by the rise of superior humans, who will be likened to physical angels upon the earth. In fact, these higher breeds of angelic humans are now living among us, as they are the forerunners, of the next root race that is now beginning to bloom, as a result of using more than just six percent of their entire genetic capacity. Apparently, the time has arrived for the reactivation of more than just six percent of our genetic material that scientists call junk DNA.

However, as we begin to use more than ten percent. Let it be understood that not everyone will be using 100 percent, for various reasons.

The first and most important reason is that the greatest number of people are still not spiritually mature enough to utilize 100 percent of their total potential, allowing them to materialize anything they want into reality by just thinking it. This great power and responsibility of manipulating reality at will, by accessing the realm of pure energy will only be given to a chosen few or what the bible calls the elect.

Out of eight billion people with only about fifty-one percent making the shift of ages into the fourth and fifth-density, only a few will be exalted to such a level of using 100 percent of their total brainpower. As a result of being able to access full use of their light body

unlimited power potential, the elect will be rising to become the governing planetary group known as the new guardians of the earth. They will be transformed into physical angels here on earth and will be operating with a twelve chakra system which is now beginning to form for the rest of humanity, who will eventually evolve to that point, millions of years from now when our planet becomes a population three galactic system space-age culture.

For the remaining of humanity except for a few thousand, they will assemble the third, fourth, and fifth strands of DNA only allowing their body to live for hundreds of years without aging. As a result of using the third, fourth, and fifth strands of DNA, their telepathic channels will begin to open, and their psychic abilities will begin to function but at a very mild level once again. The Elect will be exalted to utilize fifty percent of their full capacity, enhancing their psychic abilities by reassembling strands six through nine, they will appear to be superhuman with amazing supernatural abilities.. It is this group of a few million that will serve the 144, 000 chosen ones in the restored spiritual council of planetary guardianship.

The evidence of utilizing more of our current potential is also currently being discovered by science, through the fields of neuroscience, and a combination of cutting-edge quantum genetic research. The genetic code, has been deciphered and scientist our now starting to believe that the other potential DNA that is currently not functioning, is anytime now ready to be turned on, almost as if our non-coded strands are waiting to be switched on by something, and it is.

In light of the new evidence and based on pass sudden jumps of spontaneous evolution, scientist are predicting the rise of Homo Galactis or what they call Homo Nauticus, which is the next stage in our evolutionary journey of course, from the bottom up, for they have not yet understood the concept of involution (the great descent into matter from the top down, as revealed in this book.

Also, the idea of spontaneous evolution is related to the fact that the energy emitting from the central sun is what is causing a sudden change in the biology of all species and matter in our solar system as we know it.

Afterall, there is scientific proof that all living things on planet earth are going through some sort of genetic mutation; they just don't want to talk about it.

Since DNA behaves like a programmed computer then we may say that our non-coded strands our apparently fallowing a program in a way that is responding to and operating to an inner hard drive (blueprint) that has been set to eventually begin functioning when conditions seem fit.

It appears that the switch that is triggering our Genetic upgrade in the ascension process is scientifically and metaphysically known as the photon belt, in which our earth has been emerging into more so then ever. This provides more evidence that spontaneous evolution is happening as a result of responding to the energy that is being emitted from the central sun, therefore validating the central sun theory and the theory of centrifugal force even more so.

So in an attempt to unite the ancient prophesies with modern scientific discoveries, regarding the return of celestial beings in human form, we are on the verge of witnessing the rise of a whole new breed of humans that would be in comparison to our existing humanity, considered super human as revealed in some of the suppressed scientific evidence.

As mentioned earlier, this new evidence correlates with the risen knowledge of ancient records and unearthed ancient physical evidence that modern-day humans today, are the descendants not of primates, but of the celestial visitors that came from what the ancient Sumerian text and the bible refer to as from heaven (Nibiru) whom to earth came.

The proof of our true celestial heritage has arrived, for there is scientific evidence from all fields of science, which clearly reveals that if we humans on earth today were to use our total DNA potential, we would all be like the ancient mythological characters we wrongly classified as gods. In fact, we may say that our current human race is a degenerate mutant race currently not using its full potential.

However, according to insiders within the secret space program, our humanity on earth today carries the highest potential of evolving divine powers by far surpassing the gods of ancient times.

In truth, as revealed through the spiritual wisdom of all ages humans on earth today are sleeping gods and goddesses with a lower case g, for there is only ONE CREATOR universal spirit force called GOD supreme who deserves that title and that is the universal living life force (light) that works and exist within everything, that is living, from cosmos to elementals. As revealed in this material, we are merely on the brink of becoming fully conscious humans as planned by our celestial Lyran/Pleiadean parents and the entire spiritual and galactic councils, who are overseeing the entire ascension process from what our new science refers to as unseen dimensions. It is also evident, that in our supposed primitive past, we have used more than two strands of DNA, how else would we explain the hundreds of years lived by our biblical figures?

After all, since new records show, that Noah was a demi-god (half celestial/Nibirian, half evolving human) and if we came from his line, then we are all sleeping giants capable of living hundreds of years. It is no mystery anymore, that humans beings today are or have been a downgraded or genetic down steeped version of the visitors that came to our world from what our new science considers a population two space-age civilization that originally began in Lyra, which is millions of years ahead of our current civilization.

This idea that we humans today are light beings expressing ourselves through a human experience validates the current theory of spontaneous evolution, the Ancient Astronaut theory, theory of Creation by Intelligent Design, the theory of convergent evolutions, which clearly states that mankind shares a common celestial ancestry throughout the universe of universes, all of which falls under the grand theory of cosmic ancestry, which solidifies the truth that our origin was and will always be in the always existing spheres of the existing spiritual central universe.

Evidence for the argument of such theories comes from the new fields of quantum and genetic research. The second piece of evidence comes from both anthropology and archeology, which have arrived at the idea that we were once a technologically advanced civilization in pre-diluvial times. How else would we explain the ancient monolithic monuments that are scattered throughout our world, like Stonehenge, Avebury, Easter Island, and those colossal Egyptian pyramids? Not to mention the Nazca lines in Peru and Macha Picchu in South America.

Therefore, in collaboration with archeologists and according to the fossil record, not only has human civilization existed for about hundreds of thousands of years on this planet, but also there is solid evidence providing a clear genetic and origin distinction between today's modern homo sapien sapiens to those prehistoric hominids and Neanderthal, who was a product of natural evolution, that by the way was intelligently designed. The genetic difference lies in the number of chromosomes that differ in the DNA of each type, do the research.

In fact, according to new scientific evidence, the old evolving primates of the past, seized to exist at a certain point, while the more superior strain called, Cro-Magnon evolve into us today as CroMagnon also seized to exist at the dawning of modern man, Homo Sapiens Sapiens. The demarcation line is clearly seen now; the missing link has arrived to satisfy both factions of our confused academia, both with incomplete data up until this point.

A theory of everything for evolutionists and creationists would be complementary to both sides as Quantum Gravity Theory is for both the world of relativity and the world of the quantum. This is the theory of creation by intelligent design. Under this theory, like Quantum Gravity theory, M-theory, and Unified Field theory who fall as different branches of the overall Theory of Everything, we have other branches that fall under the theory of creation by intelligent design. They are the theory of spontaneous evolution, the Ancient astronaut theory, the theory of cosmic ancestry, not to mention the theory of many worlds and multiple dimensions. If we follow them in order, and after being acquainted with the information in this book, we may see them as more than just theories.

Let's begin by validating the theory of cosmic ancestry which states that, we are all eternal beings of light with a cosmic spiritual origin, rather than a physical one. As revealed earlier, we have always existed in spirit form as different rays of light in the grand central universe, before descending to denser material realms. And by adopting the scientific evidence regarding our real nature as energy beings living in a world of energy that is neither created nor destroyed, but only changing form, then maybe by virtue of this new understanding, we are also infinite intelligence that has always existed, prior to coming to this planet, since our real essence is light and light is the eternal source.

The next theory that comes to mind, also under the family of the theory of creation by intelligent design, is the Panspermia theory, which clearly states that all planetary terrestrial life forms come from outer space in the form of living bacteria and viruses that apparently impregnated our oceans when they arrive in an earlier time when the waters were still heated.

In addition to this theory, and according to the Urantia papers, the manipulation of evolution itself was conducted by a celestial group of personalities call the life carriers, who were in charge of implanting the biologic seed in all the terrestrial planets with the living life plasma, while guiding its formation and evolution from an etheric level.

Therefore without discrediting natural evolution, we may say that even natural evolution is a by-product of universal intelligence and spiritual consciousness that has been in operation since before the event known as the big bang, and has been guiding every condition down to the t, for there are no accidents, only divine purpose in everything.

For the record and from the beginning of biologic life inception, there was a guiding and directing spirit in all things that caused living organisms, in the right conditions, to mutate according to the next phase of a carefully planned and orchestrated evolution.

This kind of unfolding also applies to the formation of galaxies and solar systems, as they are also following a cosmic blueprint that allows for the proper conditions that sustain life to unfold. The new evidence is now mathematically suggesting that there are no such things as accidents and that everything has a purpose in the universe, excuse me the META-VERSE, and most important that there is intelligence out there, weaving everything together into a beautiful cosmic eternal tapestry.

The next theory that falls under the theory of creation by intelligent design is the Ancient Astronaut theory. This is the theory that proposes the idea that in our very ancient misty past, an advanced space-age humanoid group of beings from another planet (Nibiru) settled in our planet. They descended to earth approximately 450,000 thousand years ago in their spacecraft, to not only colonize our world but to extract gold from our planet to save their own.

Most importantly they contributed their life plasma for the biologic upgrade of some of the evolving primates, to eventually evolve a vehicle for descending celestial beings to embody in solid physical form. In truth, the ancient astronaut theory helps to explain the sudden leaps in evolution or missing links that began in Mesopotamia about 300,000 thousand years ago. It integrates both the theory of evolution and the theory of creation but in favor of creation by intelligent design.

According to the restored ancient records, after our vehicle was suitable for the incarnation of the descending sons and daughters of light, only Homo sapiens-sapient (superior thinking man) existed side by side with the non- incarnated fourth and fifth-density galactic celestial humanoids or those that came to earth from heaven, as revealed in the biblical book of Genesis. If we accept the idea that we are spiritual beings experiencing the lower dimensions, then we may now conclude that the evolving primates only provided a vehicle for the incarnating descending celestial humanoids, who began incarnating as earth humans (homo-sapiens-sapiens) sometime during the peak of the Atlantean golden age, some 30,000 years ago as revealed through the fossil record.

In esoteric studies, the evolving primates represent the upward evolution of the physical shelf, while the descending celestial/ humanoids (gods) represent the downward involution of the spirit self. It is when the two meet, that the integration point of spirit and matter became fulfilled, part of the great cosmic divine plan in completing polarity integration, uniting heaven and earth, celestial and material. The idea that the evolving primates were upgraded by mixing with the DNA of the celestial visitors is also supported by the Urantia Papers, as well.

In the Urantia papers, it is reported that those from Jerusalem came with a group of about 100 super humanoids immortals who descended upon the earth about exactly the same time the Sumerian clay tablets reveal, the arrival of the Anunaki who came from heaven to earth.

However, in the Urantia Papers, the Annunaki of the risen Sumerian tablets were known as the Caligastia one hundred and it was their mating with the evolving Sangik races, (six branches of evolving primates) that later gave rise to the arrival of the descending material son Adam from Jerusem, whose life plasma contributed to the emergence of the violet race of man, the seventh earthly race, which was the final stage giving us the more superior humans called the Endites, whose descendants we are today. According to this material, Adam was a Morontia (semi-etheric) human being who came to our planet via a seraphic vehicle of transportation. These seraphic vehicles of transportation correlate with the spaceships of Nibiru and of the Galactic Federation. In regard to the reported sankrik races, our science through anthropology has revealed a set of six different primates that sprung from a common group known as the Australopithecus, which correlates with the Urantia group known as the Andorites, who broke off into six different Sangik primitive races. Therefore, the Ancient Astronaut theory is a fact like the other mentioned theories all falling under the grand cosmic theory of creation by intelligent design and theory of cosmic ancestry.

Therefore, we humans today are the descending daughters and sons of the celestial visitors known as the Nibirian Pleiadeans since we were made in their image, as revealed in the book of Genesis. All these theories offer the solution to the Darwinian missing links while satisfying the religious view that, we earth humans were created in the image of our creators, Elohim, as revealed in Genesis, "Let us make men in our image" They are both correct, but yet incomplete in describing our entire cosmic origin and great descent (involution), from light heaven into matter earth.

Also, it is important to understand that in our bible, the many messengers or what we call the angels were a further condensation of the original Bnai Or Elohim plural describing the many celestial beings that walked with man in pre-diluvial times. Mythology referred to them as gods, in the bible we know them as angels and in today's scientific world we have discovered their presence in our skies as the benevolent humanlike extraterrestrials serving within the galactic guardian of councils.

The fact that there are other humanlike beings out there validates the fact that humans on earth share a common ancestry throughout the cosmos, which proposes another theory known as the theory of convergent evolutions. So if the theory of convergent evolutions is correct then the theory of many worlds is also correct, then it is only logical to assume that this theory suggest that all of mankind that exist throughout the multi-verse share a common ancestry as we were all made in the image of the one creator, of the central universe.

This evidence again is being confirmed not only through the fields of science but through restored records given to us by celestial intelligence and from the esoteric secret knowledge that has been preserved in the records of the great white brotherhood, all confirming the un denying truth without a doubt, that we humans today are powerful light beings utilizing less than ten percent of our full capacity and should no more be compared to the species of the evolving animal kingdom.

To further validate the new scientific evidence, we will now examine new restored information coming from a benevolent group of E. T's.

Known as the Sirians, who are the angelic guardians of our galaxy. As revealed, the Sirians are one of the most evolve civilization in our galaxy and is a galactic epicenter for the cosmic order of Melchizedek (ancient of days) and the Order of Lord Michael (Union of days).

Perhaps the Sirians are what our new science considers a Population three galactic star system civilization, since the Sirians do harness the power of our galaxies central sun, protecting the great Tzolkin/Ophyocus the seat of divinity in our galaxy. As mentioned, from the center of our galaxy, the office of Christ has been guiding all spiritual councils in our galaxy, beginning with Sirius and Lyra.

From the seat of the great central sun, the Sirians have been given the responsibility to act as the cosmic directors of the Federation of light for our physical universe and that is why they have now come forward to reveal, that the current humans on the planet are transforming or genetically mutating back into fully conscious beings capable of operating in multiple dimensions. According to this revelation, today marks the end of a long evolutionary journey, as earth humans are getting ready to complete the final phase of their development.

As revealed by all extraterrestrial/angelic sources, we are becoming upgraded genetically, as our Carbon based DNA is transforming into a Crystalline based DNA, since we have inherited Syrian DNA, which is the purest of all lines in our galaxy, altering our atomic and molecular structures into a higher density vibration. Of course, this genetic change is happening as a result of our world's emergence into the photon belt. These changes have been taking place at the etheric level, affecting both the cellular and molecular structure of our bodies. It is being triggered from the great central sun of our galaxy, which controls the life circuits that generate all electromagnetic fields within its periphery which in turn controls the rate of all atomic vibrations that hold together a reality.

These central sun emanations that are causing all the funny anomalies in our solar system are the scalar waves that have been detected by our earth scientists. To further back this up, according to the restored (Niburian Council), when our Nibirian parents, disconnected ten strands of our DNA during the times of the tower of Babel, they did it by placing implants in our astral/emotional bodies.

These implants prevented the other non-coded strands from reactivating. This shut out our endocrine system, and so our pineal gland stopped working as well as our pituitary gland.

As a result, about 96 percent of our brain organs stop functioning and are atrophied because they had stopped producing the chemical hormone known as beta-carbolines and pemoline.

According to scientific research, these are the chemical substances that activate the pineal and pituitary glands, thus allowing for increased ability in clairvoyance, clairaudience, and clairsentience.

According to the arcane secret teachings, this hormone is what feeds our pituitary and pineal gland, which in turn triggers an upward rise of kundalini energy opening up our energy body (chakras systems) connecting our entire endocrine system and nervous system to the higher life circuits (higher dimensions) allowing for more access to our light body.

The restored (NC) also backed this up, by revealing that the time for the removal of our astral implants in our emotional body has come, as we are being groomed into becoming multi-dimensional beings, like the rest of the angelic/humans that are spread out throughout our galaxy and other galaxies and other universes.

By virtue of the removal of the implants in our emotional body, our non-coded strands will reactivate again, allowing us to raise our consciousness, so that we may plugin into other currently unseen realities (frequencies). Perhaps upon fully emerging in the photon belt, our astral implants automatically dissolve and that is the trigger that will re-activate our non-coded genetic material as suspected by our top geneticist.

In biblical traditions, this is known as the lifting of the veil, allowing a mass perception of what science calls the unseen realities. Now the trigger for this has been scientifically identified as the photon belt, which is a band of highly charge photons (light) that emanates from the central axis of our galaxy.

The photon band phenomenon has been discovered by our science and its now being further examined by all cosmologists, astrophysicists, and even physicists. Many spiritual scholars believe that our non-coded DNA will be triggered into activity the moment we fully emerge in the photon belt, due to its tremendous rate of higher photon energy vibration.

# CHAPTER SIXTEEN

## THE RETURN OF THE HOST OF HEAVEN AND
## THE ESTABLISHMENT OF THE OFFICE OF THE CHRIST

The idea of a returning messiah confused the people that lived in the Middle East 2,143 years ago, who were expecting a superhuman from the sky to supernaturally, overthrow the Roman Empire and save our world. Some even called Jesus an accidental Messiah; however, as a reminder, there are no accidents, for he indeed was the Messiah that changed the direction not only for our world but for the entire universe.

What Jesus did two thousand years ago here on our planet affected the outcome of the entire universe. Apparently out of all the incarnating avatars, celestial beings, that have ever walked our planet, no one compared to the level of Jesus for according to the higher knowledge, he was the creator son of our local universe. The bible, therefore, was correct, Jesus was the incarnating father who made flesh. That is why he said, the father and I are one.

The Urantia material reveals that Jesus the Christ was the incarnating creator son of Nebadon, who by choosing to incarnate in our world, completed his final bestowal mission and became the master son of his local universe domain. The Urantia papers reveal, that prior to his seventh and final bestowal, he was known as a vicegerent son of God, who co-ruled his universe, by virtue of his father, from the isle of the paradise of the central universe of Havona.

It is believed that following the Luciferian insurrection, our Creator son had a chance to put an immediate end to the rebellion from the beginning, with the help of the Ancient of days, but he didn't because he understood that he had a final bestowal or test that was going to make him the supreme master son of His created domain. The test came about when he came to us as Jesus of Nazareth and after being offered control over our world by Satan (Marduk) who tempted him in the desert, his reply was get behind me Satan turning him down. So, considering this, his sacrifice (atonement) for the exaltation of our planet was not only to change the direction of our world but the final test and completion of his seventh bestowal mission making him the absolute sovereign master son of his creation.

According to Urantia, every creator son of every local universe must undergo the same seven levels or tests to become the master son of a local universe.

This meant that all power in heaven (our universe) and on earth became vested in him as it is in his father of the grand central universe. It was revealed, that right before his crucifixion, the entire host of heaven wanted to descend on the Roman armies and wipe them out, but Christ forbade them as he knew what he was doing.

His coming two thousand years ago as a man in the flesh indeed fulfilled the prophecies of old and not only change the course of history and the fate of our world but many worlds. For it is precisely at the point of his ascension back into heaven as he took absolute control of the situation and began the final house cleansing in the heavens while promising to return to us in about two thousand years earth time with the entire armies of heaven and this time in his full power and glory for his final victory. For this time, he will not come as he did two thousand years ago, to be put to death, but with a double-edge sword to do away with all his enemies, Babylon. The time of a returned messiah with the entire armies of heaven is right about now, for the signs of his coming have been known.

Now considering the restored knowledge, we may say that his coming is a two-way process. First, we must understand that Jesus embodied the highest field of consciousness referred to as the cosmic consciousness.

Cosmic consciousness is a field of energy that is now available to everyone, because of the restoration of Heaven on earth. It is a sense of realizing that all in creation is one and attempting to merge our individualized unit of consciousness with the universal mind of everything in existence. It appears that the Christ (all) mind which is a vibration of pure light is becoming realized and activated already on earth. At the great shift of energy and ages, all of humanity remaining will embody the Christ universal mind field.

Therefore, the Christ mind will be realized by those that embody it while the grand event of the return of the host (starships) of heaven will also occur as a result of that.

Clearly now thanks to all the new data, we may conclude, that Christ is returning with the armies of heaven and all their ships (clouds). In our bible, it describes Christ's return, in reference to the clouds. The term cloud was camouflage to conceal the starships that are associated with the return of the host of Heaven.

In the biblical book of Ezekiel, the starships are described as wheels within wheels that descend from heaven. Elijah another Old Testament prophet mentioned chariots of fire. In the book of exodus, the Israelites were led by a moving cloud (ship) during the day and by a moving star at night into the Promised Land.

Now that we have science, we understand that a star in the sky does not move and that a cloud does not navigate or lead anyone into a destination. Therefore, it is evident that the term cloud in our bible literally meant starships. In fact, all ancient traditions talk about the return of a Messiah with a host of superhumans (angels) that are to overthrow the entire corrupt world system and establish the NEW JERUSALEM OF HEAVEN ON EARTH FOREVER.

This coming event, which is to usher in the millennium, as well as the seventh golden age of the esoteric tradition, is now validated and accepted as truth, by most spiritual people, who have eyes to see and an inner sense of knowing. After all, it is clearly stated by John the revelator that the New Jerusalem will descend from above unto the earth.

It appears that considering all evidence today, the New Jerusalem of the west is scheduled to descent on our planet in these wonderful prophetic times. Our world is entering a higher order of spiritual evolution, so if higher evolve beings exist in the fifth, sixth, and seventh densities and our earth is moving into this higher density, therefore, our time to reunite with our celestial family who exists in this higher density, is at hand.

However, in a scientific way of putting it, it has been revealed that our planet is being prepared to make the first contact with the Galactic Federation of free worlds who have been monitoring our planet for thousands of years, under the command of Michael, our creator son. The Galactic Federation of light, (the angels) have already infiltrated our earth's governments and have placed our entire solar system in an emergency rescue bubble since the 1900 hundreds and it was recently removed in 2001 as we prepare to ascend into higher densities.

As of 1987, it was reported by the higher celestial intelligence, that our world has been under Syrian Jurisdiction and that the liberation of the galactic command has been hailing from Sirius since the establishment of the Galactic Federation of light millions of years ago. Overall, in these days to come, as we ascend, the second coming of the entire host is scheduled to happen as a prophetic event expected and observed by many in our universe and other universes.

We are living in unprecedented times and can conclude that our planet and those of us who choose love and oneness over ego and separation are about to enter into the higher densities and as a result, we will experience a mass landing of Galactic Federation starships, (the angels of the bible). From a scientific perspective, we are during a great planetary shift that will restore our world back into a type two intermediate stellar space-age civilization capable of space travel overnight. With that, the idea of other unseen worlds will also become a scientific fact.

According to the keys of Enoch "The Book of Knowledge", the world will be transforming into a HEAVEN ON EARTH and the brotherhoods of man will walk again with the higher intelligence (the Luminaries) as they did in ancient times, prior to the fall of Atlantis and the flood.

Now regarding Nibiru, it has been restored when Marduk abdicated as its last commander in 1999. According to Jellaila Star, the spokesperson for the restored

(NC), Marduk, the fourth-dimensional aspect of Satan, leader of the dark brotherhood of our world, abdicated and has been on the run from his own people (the Jesuit-Illuminati) for betraying them. Apparently, Marduk lost his superior godly abilities and was downgraded to only using less than ten percent of his total capacity becoming a mutant being why else would he be running from the ascending mortals within our world's dark networks.

Without given any details, my inner sources confirmed, that Nibiru since then has been fully recuperated by the Federation and is now under the control once again by the commanders of the Pleiadean Star League and the Syrian high council.

Again, let it be understood that the second coming of Christ marks a two-way event. That is in order to even witness the coming of the host of heaven our awareness must be raised to the higher density's levels of consciousness at least to the fifth-density. As mentioned, this will happen as a result of fully emerging into the photon belt that will in turn trigger what is known as massive Christ consciousness in all humanity, thus catapulting our perception into higher dimensions.

This exaltation of human consciousness and DNA as mentioned earlier will allow us, to witness the coming of higher dimensional light beings, whose light is so strong that it would decimate anyone unable to raise their consciousness to the higher density fields. This explains the destruction of the beast (reptilian/antichrist) system and the wicked upon the shift and coming of the host. It is believed that people who are not compassionate and loving are going to have a hard time raising their personal energy field in order to transition into the NEW HEAVEN ON EARTH, that will exist on the fifth-density field.

This spiritual event also correlates with the harvest of souls as there is also a scientific explanation for this. The idea that we live and are multi-dimensional beings, allows us to understand that we have been in a fallen state or just plugged into a low-frequency range of our entire light spectrum of the greater reality.

Again, not everyone will be ready to make that shift into a higher density and for those that do, they will seem to disappear from the third-dimensional range from those that didn't make the shift in densities, hence the harvest of souls.

In assisting the people of earth in the ascension process, let it be known that our skies are filled with starships, mother ships, and small scouting ships from the GALACTIC Federation who are the same beings known as the angels in the bible. These starships were sent from the creator to help bring about the kingdom of heaven upon our earth plane.

In fact, many of the star beings (angels) are coming forward to a selective few and are working with them in order to prepare the masses for what is known as the first contact. Therefore, earth's acceptance into a galactic community is once again being offered by the Galactic Federation, since the fall of Atlantis.

After all, the Federation has been known to our world governments since the Eisenhower days of Alien visitation. According to William Copper an ex-naval officer, there were several ultra- secret meetings that took place in the late fifties between Eisenhower and two types of

E.T. s. The first meeting reported was with a negative Group of ET's classified as the Greys, who negotiated a deal with a secret government group known as the majestic twelve. The other top-secret meeting is one that is not talked about because it involved a representative of a higher group of humanoid beings representing the Federation.

The name of this being was no other than Commander Sharon Ashtera of the Ashtar Command, who arranged an emergency meeting with Eisenhower to warn him about the destructive use of atomic and hydrogen bombs. Commander Ashtar made it clear to him, that if we continue the use or development of hydrogen or Plutonian explosives, that the Federation would execute an emergency intervention because of the dire effects it will have not only in our world but on other planets in our solar system as well. Ever since then most of our governments have been aware of the Federation of Benevolent

E.T.s (angels) and their involvement with our planet. The Galactic Federation has also offered our government a chance to be part of a greater galactic community, but the United States government under the control of the Jesuit-Illuminati secret world government refused, because the stipulation was for our government and all other governments of our world, to end their war machine and disarm from all weapons. Most importantly, the Federation demanded that the Illuminati one-world government gang give up their power structure of control over our world, and in the event that our governments complied, the Federation was to share their space-age technology with us, which would improve our living conditions overnight...

That meant offering alternative natural and healthier ways of using energy-efficient resources by harnessing the power of our local sun or extracting unlimited power from the zero-point field. The Federation also offered the use of technologies that would heal not only our ecosystem from all pollutions but all illnesses known to man. All of this offer went against the draconian protocol of the Jesuit=Illuminati one-world government who depend on their petrochemical hazardous resources, and their pharmaceutical markets and that's the reason why all evidence of our benevolent ET (the angels of the bible) is being held from the public. Nations that are fully aware of the presence of the Galactic Federation are the United States, China, Russia, the European Union, Japan, Brazil, Argentina, Mexico, Peru, Bolivia, Canada, and the Middle East nations. Overall, there is a massive UFO cover-up campaign being imposed by our world governments because of the control that the dark brotherhood has exerted over our world's political and economic systems.

However, The Federation is in contact with various people like Dr. Steven Greer and other light warriors who are leading the way to end this cover-up and as the veil lifts as we approach the great shift, everyone will witness firsthand encounters that we are not alone.

Everyone should remember that creator created everything visible and invisible as stated at the beginning of the bible.

Nonetheless, it has been reported by the guardians themselves, that all negative ET's are currently being removed from our solar system, the universe, and all universes within the first outer space level of the mother universe.

The housecleaning conducted by archangel Michael has reached our world and they are just waiting for the great shift of the ages.

Here is a revelation of major key players in the restoration process. As mentioned, they are, galactic Federation Commander Ashtar of the Ashtar Command who oversees the Federation fleets of the airborne division of the great white brotherhood/sisterhood in our solar system, hailing from the council of Saturn.

Their headquarters is our local planet Saturn who directs the Federation Council for our solar system on behalf of the Syrian high council, which oversees all federation councils in our galaxy. The Second commander involved in our restoration is commander Georges Ceres Halton, leader of the Pleiadean Federation Fleets and now in charge of Nibiru. Working closely with him is commander Soltec, who is head of the NEW earth geophysics department and has been reported to constantly be sending out scouting ships that monitor the effects of our ascending earth.

Commander Soltec is also in charge of the rescue eco-plan system designed to clean up some of the major hazardous waste that might be too harmful to our planet. There is also, Commander Kortec head of the communication's interplanetary networks, who oversees making sure that the proper Galactic Federation messages come through from the seventh dimension and into the third dimension.

Not to mention, our brethren from Telos, Shambala, and Agartha the inner earth-dwellers who escaped the cataclysm 12, 000 years ago are also going to reunite with us upon the ascension. Our great cosmic reunion is what to be expected. Overall, the facts are obvious; we have reported sources coming from the guardians of councils, the Pleiadeans, Sirians, the Arcturians, the Andromedins,

Alpha Centurions, to name a few, are all under the command of Archangel Michael.

In closing, and for everyone's information, the host of heaven is here in their starships by the masses, due to the greatest transition that our galaxy and the local universe is about to experience. The imminent restoration of our local universe signifies that we have a whole array of visitors from not only our galaxy but other galaxies and universes who are here to witness a cosmic event that only takes place every 206, 000 million years.

In closing our world is being prepared and aided by the Federation of free worlds so that we may experience a healthy ascension.

Remember they are helping us from what science calls the unseen dimensions and as the great shift occurs, we will be reunited with them, as we became initiated into a greater galactic community as we were in previous forgotten times.

It has been revealed that our planet earth is shifting directly into a population two interplanetary stellar system space-age civilization, heaven on earth. The reason being is that our earth in ancient times had an active population of two interplanetary systems which lasted until the fall of Atlantis. As a result, the founders of our galaxy decided to grant earth her original glory as a population two system as it was before the fall of Atlantis. However in normal conditions regarding all of the other terrestrial planets in our galaxy, a planet similar to the evolutionary phase of our current stage in which our earth is in, would have to first transition into a population one system before advancing to that of a population two system, by virtue of the concept of gradual ascent, providing a steady upward ascent of all evolutionary organic lie forms returning back to the source in which it came from.

# CHAPTER SEVENTEEN

## COSMIC CYCLES
## AND THE PRECISION OF THE EQUINOXES

Something to understand about our existence is that everything is cyclic by nature. From the moment of cosmic conception, everything proceeds in circular form. This circular form is an established rhythm that starts at the highest level of existence and descends involution outward and evolution inward as it perfects itself in never-ending infinite spirals, one space level at a time. In other words, at the point of this Immaculate Conception, when the always existing Omni-Verse decided to divide and fractal itself there was only space and no time. Time began as a result of its expansion (involution), for a time became a construct of measuring where a point begins and another point ends, the alpha the Omega. This alpha and omega are just one cycle or one gigantic mega-hertz and at the end of an alpha omega- cycle a new alpha, omega-cycle begins.

We may compare this cycle to one universal round which expands our always existing central universe one space level at a time. In this sense, time becomes a measuring devise or tool designed by the always existing central universe as a way to determine all its points and conjunctions that mark all events that will ever transpire and have ever transpired as it expands forever outward. From a higher perspective, in the celestial spheres it's all happening at once, and from a lower perspective, in the material spheres is all relative, happening in sessions, segments or fractals, which is the whole dividing itself in order to experience more of itself as it explores every level of its own being.

However, let it be known that before the great beginning of space and time (involution) there was an only pure potential force. This unqualified absolute began the process of dividing itself so it set out to complete what is known in esoteric studies as one universal round of the cosmic process known as the descent and ascent of the great God force. This is a process that is ultimately controlled by a cosmic Meta central sun and the great central suns of all universes who are the timekeepers on every level of existence. This process repeats again and again as the grand central universe rotates like a clock in circular form, and that is why it is always spinning new universes into existence, as we expand one outer space level at a time into infinity.

Cosmic time is a governing force just like gravity and it is controlled by rotation and spin which is what produces all the forces that hold and bind universes together. Cosmic time is, therefore, a circle rather than a line; in fact, our entire cosmos is one big rotating circle within circles, down to the atoms. A circle like a clock begins at the top making its way round the clock, full circle to repeat the same cycle again and each time it does it gathers more experience. This is backed by the Urantia Material and all other spiritual resources, not to mention by the Mayan Calendar, which has been the keeper of the great cosmic spin behind all sacred time that harmonizes all living things in our cosmos.

Sacred time is the measurement and relationship between all living things as it harmonizes into one great symphony as everything is interconnected with everything else. It is neither linear nor limited but a force that is everywhere at once and infinite. Divine time is also the harmony of all things as opposed to man-made time which is a disharmony of all things. These cosmic cycles of time and the harmony of the cosmos, from the macro to the micro, have always been understood and acknowledged, by the ancient spiritually advanced cultures that flourished before the flood.

For instance, based on the understanding of divine time, the ancients knew more about astronomy than what we have barely discovered today in the twentieth-first century. They not only understood our heliocentric model that the earth with other planets revolves around our sun, but that our solar system itself revolved around a greater sun in a cycle of 25,000 years. Even the Greek philosopher, Plato referred to this cycle as the platonic year which is the revolution of our solar system around the central sun of its parent source Alcyone as it travels around the Zodiac. Today this greater revolution known as the precision of the equinoxes is gaining more ground within our scientific community, as astronomers' peek deeply farther into our skies.

By understanding what is now referred to as The Precision of the Equinoxes the ancients would know where we were in the grand scheme of things. Since they knew about the zodiac they understood our solar system's relationship with all-stars and constellations within our galaxy as it traveled a circular path throughout space in greater revolutions. Since the ancients were in tune with cosmic time, they were able to plan beforehand everything before it happened.

They know when to grow crops, for example, when the next solar or lunar eclipse would occur, and most importantly when a new age would begin and where we were heading in every moment of time based on precise mathematical astronomical conjunctions. In general, they are new that everything happening in our world was directly influenced by the movements of the earth in the heavens. This also provides more evidence that our universe is holistic, everything is interconnected so what happens above in the macro also reflects below in the micro.

Equally important to understand in reference to sacred time is that all celestial bodies from planets to stars are vibrators of frequencies and depending on where our solar system is located in the heavens, it takes on new energies as certain intercrossing points generate different vibrations that influence our world. Even among the esoteric circles, it is well understood that each age brings in a new energy field that determines the quality and what kind of world it will be.

According to mystical traditions, each age is governed by a constellation and each constellation has its own frequency and all frequencies are produced by the cosmic transmission that resonates at the center of our galaxy. In other words, all celestial bodies get their spin and frequency from the central sun of our galaxy, for it is well understood now that the central sun of our galaxy generates and transmits cosmic energy outward from its center influencing all stars and planets, as indicated by the theory of centrifugal force, which is energy going outward from its center.

In this sense, time is related to Astrogeny, the ancient science that astrology is derived from, as a method of keeping track of our planet and solar system in RELATIONSHIP with other stars, planets, and most important with the great central sun of our galaxy. We may therefore conclude that the ancients had an unerring mathematical system that tracked all events and turning points and lived in harmony with it. Maybe that is why they experienced the golden ages, as they understood the harmonics of life and strived to live in harmony with all living things.

In truth, it is this resonance that determines all conditions in existence. For example, all solar systems in our galaxy including the millions of worlds are vibrating to the frequency transmission that is emanating from our central sun at the center of our galaxy. So, when our galaxy's central sun transmits a new frequency which is what is happening now, all solar systems change to match its new resonance.

This is done via what is known as super galactic photon fields of light, that emanate from the central hub of our galaxy. The Pleiadeans refer to these high-energy fields as super galactic highways of light and it's the source of spontaneous evolution happening everywhere in our galaxy.

It appears, that our solar system is emerging in one of the various super galactic photon fields, that is shifting the resonance of our solar system into a new spin a new vibration, a NEW HEAVEN ON EARTH. Considering this we may conclude that a new emanation of higher energy is shifting reality in our world and our solar system.

It is now confirmed by all celestial intelligence that indeed this photon field resonance that emanates from the galactic center is what causes great and sudden changes in all living things throughout the galaxy. The changes are detectable not only in the planets, our sun, and most importantly in our DNA as our scientists began noticing these unexplained anomalies. According to the Mayan scholars, our earth and its solar system are poised to once again enter one of these high resonating fields of supercharging energy as it does twice every 25,000 years. Moreso, our cutting-edge science has also confirmed the idea of a rare galactic alignment with the center of our galaxy that is taking place now in these days and has to do with the completion of a 230,000-million-year cycle.

Now in turn, our galaxy's central sun and its many photonic galactic fields are vibrating to the frequencies of our local universe great central sun in which our galaxy and eleven other galaxies revolve around. In turn, our universe's central sun is vibrating to the frequency of our super universe's great central sun as it is also vibrating to the cosmic pulse of the mother universe's cosmic great central sun.

All ancient cultures understood this and that is why their calendars which are precise measurements of these sacred cosmic alignments with photon fields were destroyed. However, one sacred culture preserved these alignments and their sacred calendars, knowing that a time would come when they would be unearthing and understood. This culture was the Mayans.

According to the higher restored knowledge, the Mayans were directly seeded by the Pleiadeans, right before the fall of Atlantis, in order to preserve the sacred calendars.

These were the same sacred calendars that were given to the ancient Egyptians, Atlanteans, Lemurians, Romanians, and the Yu Culture, that flourished before the fall of Atlantis. As they were also given to the early Hebrews, the Dogan tribe of Africa, and the native indigenous cultures of the Americas, who were genetically related to the early Hebrews.

Apparently, the higher intelligence knew of the Atlantean decline and understood that the new powers that took over the affairs of our planet would eventually destroy any recollection of the sacred calendar. Again, these ancient sacred calendars kept perfect track of all the celestials and planetary movements, all solar and lunar eclipses with precise mathematical calculation, and all events that have ever transpired and events that are going to transpire, based on the understanding of all intersecting points in the cosmos.

In fact, the Mayans were named after the second-star system (Maya) of the

Pleiadean seven sisters were chosen to hide this prophetic code that would emerge when the time was right, in preparation for the transformation or restoration of our planet before DEC,-2022, which is the real completion of the Mayan calendar. It is no coincidence that the higher intelligence planed for the emergence of the great sacred calendar in our times 1970 A. D.

Just when the western world thought that they discovered the idea of our world as a sphere that revolves around our local sun with other planets, the Mayans as well as all the other ancient cultures understood the revolution of not only our solar system around Alcyone (Pleiadean central sun) but also knew about the revolution that our solar system and Alcyon make around the great central sun at the center of our Milky Way Galaxy.

It was precisely this greater revolution that our solar system along with Alcyone, around our galactic center, was recorded to be known, as one universal round marking the completion of the 206-225-million-year cycle, that our astronomers have recently discovered. As mentioned earlier we live in a holographic existence and the concept of twelve going around the one is repetitive on every level.

For example, according to astrological and astronomical knowledge, our solar system takes about 2160 years to travel through one of the twelve houses of the zodiac, The 25,000-year revolution is what is known as the Precession of the Equinox's and it further divided into shorter world ages of about 5,100 years, a total of five. It is this 5,100-year period the Mayans referred to as the long count or thirteen baktuns. According to the long count, the last world age began at around 3114BC and terminates in Dec. 21, 2012 AD, but really (2020- 22) non-Gregorian calendar, completing a long count world age cycle.

In understanding the Precession of the Equinoxes or what Plato called the great Platonic year, we may now see how a Toroid shape field, discovered by our astronomers called the photon belt is the reason why the earth recycles herself every 25,000 years or so. It turns out that as our solar system enters one of the many Photon Belts for a period of two thousand years, corresponding to the rise of all golden ages that have ever existed. It is believed that when we are in the photon belt our earth experiences ages of light and balance, due to the high resonance that vibrates with the galactic center. Apparently, all photon fields automatically transmute all vibrations into higher frequencies of vibrating light, allowing humans to connect with their light bodies, which link us to the central sun.

Since our solar system enters it twice in a 25,000-year cycle, our solar system experiences two ages of light, a total of 5000 years of peace when it is in the photon band and as it travels through the long dark nights, outside of the photon band it reflects dark ages, for a period of 20,000 years, a ten thousand year interval between two periods of light. For instance, when our solar system travels furthest from the band at apogee, it experiences the lowest vibrations. In like manner, as it travels close or in the photon band at perigee point, it experiences the highest vibrations, which correlate to the ages of light being within the higher energy field that emanates from the Ecliptic of our galactic equator.

It was well understood by all ancient sacred cultures that the platonic year of the Precession of the Equinox is divided by what all ancient traditions call the five world ages. In India, they are known as the five Yugas.

The first world age is known as the Golden age which corresponds to the time period our solar system spends inside the radiation zone of the Photon Band.

As it leaves the photon band, it ends a half phase of the first world age, a period of two thousand or so years, then it begins the silver age, another 2160 years, which is still producing a fairly peaceful benign society though however with a bit ¼ of darkness beginning to lurk.

Together the golden and the silver make up what all ancient cultures call the first world age or KritaYuga that last about five thousand years or so.

Now as we finish what might seem a 5,000 or so year cycle, which is two 2,160-year cycles, we experience 1/5 of the 25,000-year great Platonic cycle.

As our solar system goes further out from the photon band of manasic high energy emission, finishing its first world age or a five-thousand-year period, it begins a new five thousand year period known as the second world age and now we are about 2/5 in the great platonic year entering the epoch of what is known as the second world age of Treta Yuga.

This world age is commonly known as the blending of silver and bronze and it is where we begin to fall from paradise, as darkness begins to gain ground.

When the second world age Tetra Yuga ends, the third world age begins also kwon as the Dwapara Yuga and this is a mixture of Bronze and Iron and marks a period where darkness increases to 3/5 and the beginning of tyranny begins to take root. Now by the time we enter the third world age, the golden-silver age begins to deteriorate because of the increase of evil 3/5 that has occurred due to our solar system being further from the Apogee of the menisci radiation zone.

In the final world age and last phase of the 25,000 Platonic year cycle, we enter the darkest period known to mankind. This is the Kali Yuga and in the esoteric west, it is the Iron Age, or as many have come to discover the age of hell on earth. In this age, our solar system is furthest from the messianic radiation at apogee point and when darkness is absolute.

The good news is that according to the sacred calendars of all ancient cultures, we are days away from ending the last world age Kali Yuga, as we are also ending the last few years of the Great Platonic cycle, of 25, 000 years. In other words, we have completed a full circle around the Pleiadean central sun Alcyone once again as we have 5,200 times before.

Therefore, once again, we are poised to enter the monastic field of highly charged energy. According to Mayan scholar Greg Braden it took our solar system 5,000 of 25,000-year cycles for our entire Pleiadean constellation to make a full circle around the great central sun of our Milky Way galaxy. In fact, since we are at the completion of this greater revolution, then perhaps our planet earth will continue ascending without repeating any more dark ages.

Mayan scholars, as well as a good number of spiritual people, believe that the convergence of the precision of the Equinoxes and the greater 230,000-million-year cycle of the Pleiadeans around our galaxy's great central sun marked the global event known as Harmonic Convergence in 1987. Indeed, we are living in the greatest times ever, as we approach the closing of all cycles in the grand cosmic clock. A NEW HEAVEN ON EARTH will commence on earth for all life and all eternity as described by John the revelator.

Furthermore, it could be possible that the completion of the 230,000-million-year cycle marks the ascension of our entire galaxy and perhaps the ascension of our local universe. After all, it was revealed by lord Michael that the entire twelve creation is now ready to come home particles, bringing us again into the first world age, that will bring a new golden age HEAVEN ON EARTH.. Again, the idea of living closer to the menisci fields of the central sun also corresponds to living in a higher dimension, in like manner the further we are from the menisci fields of the central sun, we embark on darkness. It appears that all worlds experience the same phenomena as we are all influenced by the positioning we take in the heavens relative to the great central sun, and their offspring the central suns of the constellations themselves. That is the good news the Mayan calendar brings to our world, not gloom and doom.

Now in light of the higher restored knowledge, we can conclude that the events leading towards the end of the great cycle are related to the idea that we are ending the age of Pieces, a 2,160, cycle as well as a world age 5,000 years cycle, a 25,000-year cycle (platonic year) and a 230,000,000 million year cycle, which is a grand cycle that our solar system along with the Pleiades and Sirius system take around the center of our galaxy.

Perhaps the completion of the seventh super universe of Orvonton would be final when all its local universes ascend. In light of this, could it be that not only are we ending a platonic 25,000-year cycle causing a planetary ascension, a 206 million year cycle, causing the ascension of the entire constellation of the Pleiadeans and further a greater cycle than the 230, million year one that marks the completion of our Milky way galaxy completing its revolution around the central sun of our local universe, causing the entire ascension of our universe?

In summary, in these days to come not only are we ending the 2160 year of Pieces as we begin Aquarius but also ending the 13 baktuns long count of the Mayans that began 3113BC, as well as ending the 25,000-year cycle, as well as ending the greater 230, million years cycle, and finally ending greater cycles that apparently have not been mathematically calculated by our earth scientist.

All these cycles are culminating in the ascension of not only our planet, our constellation, our galaxy, our local universe, our major universe sector and finally completing our super universe, which is one segment of the entire grand central universe (Meta-Verse) that is now ready to complete the construction and organization of the first outer space level.

After all, it was revealed in the Urantia material, that the Super universe of Orvonton was incomplete. While speculating further, we may assume that the completion of Orvonton is the greatest cycle completed, in the overall descent of the already existing grand central spheres that is expanding one space level at a time.

It was revealed by the creator himself, that the earth has been ethereally ascending into higher dimensions since 1998. For about almost twelve thousand years our planet has been stuck in the third dimension.

As of 1998, it graduated into the fourth dimension as a fourth-dimensional grid system begins to form. By 2000, our world move up into the fifth and sixth dimensions as a fifth and sixth etheric grid system began to form and by 2001 it moved into the seventh dimension and has been there until 2020-22 where we will be ascending into the eighth dimension A NEW HEAVEN ON EARTH. Bear in mind that it has been a gradual process until it hits turning points where the old-world age ends and the new world age begins.

Also, according to the esoteric knowledge, this reactivation of our junk DNA will open our seven chakras, which John the Revelator calls the opening of the seven seals in the Book of Revelation. This idea is supported by the higher council of Sirius, the office of the Christ, and the Galactic Federation of light who is monitoring the entire transformation process, that's taking place right now as we approach the Mayan galactic conjunction with the center of our galaxy.

Something to understand is that all research points to the fact that this trigger reactivating our junk DNA begins with a few humans and like a domino effect, it will gradually trigger the rest of humanity, or at least those that are going to be ready to shift into the fourth and fifth densities. This trigger also corresponds to the religious idea of the harvest of souls for not everyone would have a chance to be exalted.

Apparently, the wicked, sorcerers and warmongers, are going to burst and burn away in the photon belt, when this shift in dimensions takes place, for no negative energy or entity is allowed to exist in densities higher than the fourth after the ascension.

It's a fact, after the ascension, all humans on earth are going to live for hundreds of years but in these days to come, a new race of humans will emerge due to the shift in planetary density, that will be able to live for thousands of years. As mentioned, they are already living among us, for they are what are known to lightworkers, like the rainbow and crystal children and rainbow and crystal adults. These new earth humans are here now in the millions, as reported by gifted people who sense their high-level energy field (aura)

They are incarnating from the higher dimensions as proposed by the new science. The spiritual community believes that they are the returned angels that are helping to anchor the eighth-dimensional energy for the ascension of our entire planet into the fifth and up dimensions, heaven on earth. Some call them the star people who are now incarnating among us from the higher realms, as our planet ascends into higher densities.

It is believed that when our planet ascends, all the star people will become transformed into physical angels. They will be utilizing the power of their light body as in the case of our celestial parents the Pleiadean - Nibirians, and most importantly they will be the way-showers and beacons of light for the rest of humanity to follow.

Perhaps from a Christian perspective, this would be the many people who will become like Christ, performing miracles, walking on water, healing the sick, etc. "For isn't it written in your own law that yea is", gods said, Jesus.

Throughout history, this new breed of higher evolved humans has been coming one at a time. They were mainly the prophets, sages, philosophers, and of course the suppressed benevolent line of priest-kings and queens who came from the direct line of the Pleiadean Nibirians. Now thanks to the times that we are living in, the star people are incarnating in the masses and are living among us. In fact, they are going to be heroes in assisting other humans through the changes.

They are not ADD, ADHD, or autistic; please don't label them, for they are the forerunners of a new race of superior beings, who have come to show the rest of us a higher way of living as we all prepare to transform into what our new science considers a population two stellar system space-age civilization. Unfortunately, a lot of the star children have been drugged to suppress their superior abilities, however, due to their superior DNA and the effects of the photon belt, it's not affecting them at all.

In conclusion, the ancient prophecies that talked about the return of celestial beings in human form is the same emerging phenomena our scientist use to describe the emergence of the next phase in our evolutionary ascent, the rise of Homo Nauticus, which will be the next stage in our evolutionary ascent into the higher realms. For we are at the culminating point in our evolution, our DNA is changing to accommodate our new reality HEAVEN ON EARTH, as we prepare to become part of a multi-dimensional existence. The final leap for mankind draws near; mankind is becoming exalted and death shall be no more.

# CHAPTER EIGHTEEN

## A VISION OF THE TWO THOUSAND YEARS

One of the most important things to expect in the coming new world age is the sudden transformations of governmental systems, social structures, economies, and the rise of inter-planetary and galactic culture.

Our world and humanity are scheduled to take the greatest quantum leap ever, transitioning into what our new science considers a POPULATION TWO interplanetary Steller SYSTEM space-age civilization. We are becoming galactic again, as we were before our planet become quarantine from the rest of our galaxy, during the fall of Atlantis.

And when this occurs we will be switching our genetic material from DNA strands to RNA strands.

Since universal divine order begins at the highest levels and makes its way down to the lower dimensions, and since we are at the end and synchronization of all cycles, then the externalization of the divine order that has been restored by the emissaries of light for the past million years in our galaxy, is scheduled to also manifest here in our world now.

It is important to understand, that the great white brotherhood/sisterhood from all dimensions has been working endlessly for the restoration of A NEW Heaven on Earth.

In politics, they are known as the white knights who are not only guarding the constitution of the United States (Zion) government against total abolishing by the dark knights of the Jesuit- Illuminati new world order clan, but are also working closely with the higher intelligence of the Federation of Planets and the spiritual hierarchy of earth angels for the establishment of a worldwide constitution that recognizes, honors and serves all nations.

This new system of governments that is materializing in our planet is being executed by the order of Michael of the council of twelve and supported by all councils of the Galactic confederation. This new system will initiate a worldwide commonwealth that is known as the governments of the world or the Commonwealth of Nations. It is a system that will be both divine and democratic at the same time.

According to the restored Yanihian script and the higher intelligence; the NEW world system has already been established but in the eighth dimension where the earth is heading by 2023 It is official, the NEW world system would be headed by the office of Christ, the office of cosmic fusion, the office of power and rulership, the office of culture and civilization and finally the office of universal justice, as revealed in the Yanihian Script. These NEW world foundations are commonly known as the office of the four arms, or the great vehicle.

The new Commonwealth of Nations is to be formulated under a universal constitution called The Five-Pointed Star serving the mandate of the five petals.

The Head of the New world council is Lord Maitreya, Surya Vishnu, who is of the direct line of king David. It has been revealed through the restored records transmitted by Lord Michael, that those new governments of the world or the Commonwealth of Nations are to include all national identities or states within a global structure of 20 and 2 Federated regions, each with its own leadership and independent infrastructure.

These infrastructures will in turn act in harmony with all the governments of the world producing a great vehicle of global infrastructure that will secure the rights of all mankind. It will be a global democratic network for the people and by the people, while overseen by the new celestial council of twelve.

However, according to the Script restored by Lord Michael, they are now the thirteen adepts of the thirteen solar rays. Lord Gabriel Franchela, who was Michael's firstborn and apprentice become promoted and are adept at the thirteen-ray replacing Samana and now the ray is known as the Franchala ray of sound that deadens the noise of war.

These thirteen celestial beings, who are already among us will make their appearance right before the Galactic Federation (angels) establishes the first contact with our planet. In fact, the commanders of the Federation will serve the mandates of the thirteen adepts. When these great lords and ladies of light make themselves known, the people of the earth will have a sense of serenity due to the great love generates from these beings.

All this will transpire the moment our solar system is fully emerged in the photon belt, catapulting our collective density into a higher collective energy field, vibrating all matter at fifth, sixth, seventh, and eighth density frequencies. It is in these higher planes of existence that our humanity will once again walk with the higher evolved beings of light.

These sons and daughters of light will head the new planetary spiritual council also known as the restored council of twelve and their 144, 000 helpers who will have all the support of the galactic Federation guardians of councils overseeing all matters in the NEW HEAVEN ON EARTH.

These thirteen adepts will be the most powerful beings in the universe and have chosen Earth as their new home. Serving the new council of thirteen will be the council of 144,000 who will oversee the affairs of the entire new world structure of 20 and 2 federated regions of the interplanetary new earth system.

In this NEW world structure, everyone will be provided for, health care, housing, education, food will be basic human needs that will be met and will include everyone, Now, since we are becoming part of a greater galactic community, we will meet and learn also to co-exist in harmony with other beings of non-humanoid physic, kind of like in Star Wars. We will learn higher universal values and since we will have taped the power of our local sun, we will be able to visit and interact with other planetary and stellar systems in our galaxy. After all, since 2001 our planet has had a full membership in the Galactic Federation of planets and will operate under the galactic tribunal council, by no later than 2022.

By then the theory of everything will be mathematically explained and the idea of tapping into what science calls, Zero-point field allowing our technology to match that of a population two-star system civilization will be achieved. Also, the rise of our collective consciousness into the fourth, fifth and sixth dimensions will allow all people to also understand the oneness of everything as the unified field theory merges the gap between spirituality and science, art, and philosophy.

In other words, since the celestial kingdom of light has always existed and since the etheric levels have fallowed, then the time for the kingdom of light to manifest in the lower levels of the material realms has brought the opportunity for earth humans to ascend to even greater levels of existence, beyond the material spheres.

Following the restoration, some of the star people (from stellar civilization) who are here in the millions now, will leave the earth and advance directly into the higher dimensions of the celestial realms in the grand central universe.

They were called upon by the guardians of councils from Sirius to incarnate on the earth plane to assist in the transformation of our planet. These were the waves of higher evolved souls that have been incarnating since the fifties and have helped gradually shift the density of the earth by merely existing on the earth plane. They were volunteered souls who are waiting to return to the worlds where they came from.

For example, since there are three major levels or planes of existence, then some souls will be advanced to the highest level of the celestial realms, corresponding to the heavenly spheres of the central universe.

As revealed, the celestial realms are the highest level of existence and even those spheres are divided into different sublevels of celestial glory.

Some will be advanced into realms within the spheres of the etheric levels of existence, commonly known as the middle heavens or Morontia worlds of etheric matter as revealed by the Urantia material.

Some, of course, will be here on earth for the next two thousand years to assist the rest of ascending earth beings into higher levels of existence, further than the fifth, sixth, seventh, and eighth densities. The three overall levels of heavens are the three overall levels of existence that comprise the many dimensions of reality.

As for our world here in the lower material realms which is now beginning to vibrate reality at the eighth density, will appear to split into three worlds after the great shift. This is known as the harvest of souls according to all religious traditions. As revealed, those souls that are not able to make the shift into the higher dimensional densities HEAVEN ON EARTH will be removed from our world to continue their existence in another third-density planet to eventually bring those planets fully into the light. Also for those that don't make the shift, there will be a moment of peace and enlightenment for a few minutes during the transition, as a reminder of what HEAVEN ON EARTH would be like so that they may have that imprint in their souls as they go off to another parallel third-dimensional world to continue learning there lessens.

Now for those that will remain on EARTH will continue to ascend along with its spiritualized citizens, into the higher dimensions never to repeat or experience a Dark Age cycle ever again. The reason is that our earth and solar system were the final phases in the closing of one universal round of descent and ascent completing the periphery of our super universe of Orvonton. In other words, the ascension of our planet marks the completion of a long descent of light into matter and the return or ascension of matter back into light that is now well in progress, bringing everything that partook in the descension, back to the godhead, creator source.

Eventually, those souls that get recycled into parallel earth will have a chance to choose oneness and harmony over division and separation at the closing of that planet's next cycle. This is done so that no soul may be left behind in the overall ascension of everyone who had their origin in the always existing spheres of the grand central universe/METAVERSE, /MOTHERVERSE.

For those that ascend or get a direct ticket to the celestial realms, the highest levels of existence are because they were originally from there or because they become the most advanced spiritual souls on the planet. Now for the rest of the remaining earth souls that make the transition into the higher densities, will be given an opportunity in continuing ascending even higher into the celestial realms of the central universe.

These three kingdoms of light could also be compared, to the idea proposed by the new physics, regarding the existence of a population of one, two- and three-star system civilizations.

At this point, it is frivolous to speak about the population three-star system because in our current earth stage they are millions of years ahead of us according to both scientific and spiritual sources. However, upon the ascension of A NEW Heaven on Earth, it would only take about one hundred thousand years to reach the level of population three statues.

However, since our earth is being restored back to its original glory, then we may focus at this time, on our inevitable transformation or ascension into a population two-star interplanetary system space-age civilization. As mentioned, all civilizations of a population one- and two-star systems, are all part of the confederation of planets, since they live in harmony, not only within their planet but with other planets and star systems in their respective galaxy.

For example, under normal circumstances, a Population One-star system is a planetary culture with full admission in the Federation of Planets that has been allowed to interact with a few star systems in their local cluster. The reason is that they just finished a long quarantined dark age and are at the beginning stage of advancing spiritually.

Now a Population Two-star system can interact with millions of star systems who are on their level, spread out, across an entire galaxy.

As mentioned in chapter two, a Population Three Star System, the most advanced, can interact with other galaxies. A population three system civilization is beyond our material realm, higher than the eighth density, is etheric-material, and functions above all Galactic Federations of planets in our galaxy and are part of an intergalactic alliance of many universes.

It is believed that a population three-star system civilization is what makes up the eternal fabric of the central universe spheres, of Havona.

Since our earth is advancing directly into a population two-star system planetary culture, we will only evolve spiritually upward into higher and higher levels of awareness, and densities. As mentioned, a few others will be more spiritually advance, as they take their ascension higher than the eighth dimension, but overall, we will all be multidimensional.

However, for the most part, most of the ascending earth humans (non-star seeds and returned celestial beings) will have to be educated in the proper way of using their light bodies since it has been dormant for thousands of years.

Therefore, for the next two thousand years, temples and great academies of higher spiritual education will be dotting the earth everywhere so that every single human continues to receive higher initiations into higher levels of consciousness and awareness. Great cities of light will exist once again as in the times of Atlantis.

Also, it is believed that the old continent of Atlantis and Lemuria will rise again, as they were before their collapse, with all their cities and temples intact, as if they were never destroyed.

Upon our ascension, our world will once again be reunited with the inner earth people who have lived for thousands of years in great cities within the earth. As revealed earlier these are the ancient Lemurians and Atlanteans who remained loyal to the light and have been waiting patiently for the restoration of our surfaced world.

In the days to come, our planet will once again shine like a jewel in the heavens and become the intergalactic exchange center for cosmic transmission pertaining to our entire super universe segment which is 1/7 of the entire mother universe.

It will truly be a showcase planet as prophesied by the Pleiadeans, as beings from all universes will once again visit earth, and earth beings will visit other planets in the galaxy as well.

Also, there will be a few highly even more so advanced souls that will experience even higher dimensions than the eighth capable of materializing an eighth density vehicle at will or of lower density, while experience a population three-star system here in our planet. They will also interact simultaneously with the rest of the galaxy and other universes as well. It is believed that beings of these levels can coexist and consciously embody all dimensions in our galaxy.

The possibility of all three types of civilizations co-existing side by side on our planet is possible because our earth will not only be operating with one magnetic field but with multiple bands of electromagnetic fields allowing the merging of all dimensional densities (vibrations) into one planetary energy field.

However, only seventh density beings will be able to perceive eighth density beings while eighth-dimensional beings in turn will seek the council of the higher ninth, tenth, eleventh, and twelve-dimensional beings, who will also be here but on the higher frequency bands since our earth was originally designed to exist in twelve dimensions.

Earth will once again exist simultaneously in three places in relation to the central sun of our galaxy.

The first earth will be anchored in all twelve dimensions and exist near the center of our galaxy within the first concentric circle.

That is where the Lords and Ladies of light, the council of twelve will be stationed overseeing the evolution of billions of worlds as we

begin the colonization process of the entire galaxy. The earth embodying dimensions Ninth, Eighth and Seventh will exist in the second concentric circle orbiting around the Sirius were the first earth existed prior to the first galactic war that destroyed the first earth known as Avyon in Lyra. The earth embodying dimensions Sixth, Fifth, and fourth will continue existing in the Pleiades in the third concentric ring where we are heading.

It appears, however, that our planet has a total of twelve other unseen fields of energy. In the esoteric records, these other non-active electromagnetic fields that our science has not discovered yet, because they exist in higher frequencies, hold together what is known as the earth's grid system. It is this Crystalline grid system that during the times of Atlantis and Lemuria became the living energy field, the living matrix that allowed beings from the higher dimensions to co-exist with the beings of the lower dimensions. This was recorded in our bible as a time when the angels walk with man. It is believed that this living energy field known as the crystalline grid system, will be reactivated upon fully merging into a photon belt allowing for the interaction and coexistence of all intelligence from the multiply levels (dimensions) of existence. In the Urantia material, this is known as the re-activation of the systems life circuits that reconnect our world back into the Jerusem system and Jerusem/Plaiedians of which our planet is part.

Since all beings on earth will be of a spiritual nature in the new world age, there will be an increase of interaction and love between the human kingdom, the animal kingdom, and the device kingdoms or the elementals of the Telluric realm. In fact, in the coming millennium, all animals will be as kind as the deer and rabbits are, they will be communicating telepathically with people and people will actually be able to have hours of conversations with plants and trees and all of nature since we will all acknowledge that they two are sentient beings. Also, new technologies of light will be replacing our outdated Stone Age technologies that only pollute our world. We will not only be using advanced Pleiadean, Syrian and Arcturians technologies of light but our enlightened scientists are also going to learn the secrets of interdimensional travel, through the proper use of our light body, since there will be a unification taking place between science and spirituality.

In this NEW WORLD AGE, all the advanced knowledge of the ancients will be available for everyone because unlike the times of Atlantis, a good number of evolving earth humans have finally reached a mature level of spirituality making them eligible for the forbidden knowledge that at several times in the past almost caused the destruction of our human race.

Overall, all, the technologies in the next two thousand years are going to be used for the benefit of all beings allowing for a perpetual upward spiritual ascension into the higher never-ending realms of light.

As far as work is concerned, it will be fun because people are finally going to be doing what they were born to do in fulfilling their heart's desire. Everyone will have a chance to contribute to the greater whole by virtue of their talents, and no one will be left behind.

In fact, education of a higher nature will be the cornerstone and foundation of our NEW world system.

All talents will be cultivated and people will have the opportunity to excel in whatever field of study they want. Since all levels of study are going to fall under the union of science, religion, and philosophy, everyone will have an equal chance to contribute to the whole.

The new motto will be for the greatest benefit of everyone and everything. Our fundamental philosophy will be that we are all one.

If they're to be any misunderstanding or conflict that might erupt, there will be an arbitrator who will hear both sides and since the arbitrator will be a twelfth-dimensional being, he or she will be able to see right through the fourth and fifth-density humans and determine who is right. Though situations like this will be rare, for most if not all, people will be of a loving nature, due to the high charge electromagnetic fields that our solar system will engage in.

Also, the way the new economic system will be set up will be based on how much love and compassion people generate from their hearts.

The more love and compassion one generates, the more abundance will come their way, and since most if not all, people will be of a compassionate loving nature then everyone will have abundance.

There will be no more haves and have naught; no more centralized governments controlled by private interest groups.

No more oligarchy or caste system that only looks out for the interest of the privileged few. In the NEW world system, everyone will be privileged and the idea of inequality will cease to exist and the rise of perfect balanced egalitarianism will be the new social norm. We will go back to a system of bartering and money will cease to exist as a paper form. We will have a world treasure overseen by the restored council of Twelve who will issue trust funds for every individual issued by a collective world treasury, that will be known as the bank of universal abundance.

No more loans and credit, or centralized banking, or currency but a world treasury that will provide and administer endless funds for all in the form of units.

This transformation in world economics is already in progress through the Nesara law and the prosperity programs that were implemented by the white knights in the political arena. In fact, our entire world government is currently shifting into the new Commonwealth of Nations who will be serving all the governments of the world. This NEW system with all other changes will be fully implemented by no later than the end of 2018. By 2022 our world will have already been adapted to the new changes well in full swing as both a population one interplanetary and population two stellar systems space-age spiritual culture, at the same time. our earth will be once again connected to the core of the union of galaxies in all nine dimensions Cures for everything will come forward through the avenues of natural and Holistic medicine.

Since the body-mind-spirit connection will be understood by all, great breakthroughs will bring powerful technologies that will synthesis cutting-edged science with ancient spirituality, into a wonderful tool for regenerating and healing anything including our environment. Great amusement parks that will make Disneyland look primitive, will be built allowing individuals to experience alternate realities in virtual reality like games. These would allow people to experience any world or role they want, without hurting anyone. Since we will be at the level of a population of two interplanetary systems and part of a greater galactic family we will be training in space travel as some will get recruited into the Galactic Federation for interplanetary service.

As far as the third dimension is concern, it was a constructed temporary reality created not to entrap our spirit in the matter but to allow a greater evolution for our spirit, since we are spiritual beings experiencing a temporary limited human expression.

As mentioned, as we ascend, into the higher dimensions, we will be taking our bodies with us except they will be of a more refine matter vibrating at a higher frequency.

They will be transfigured into bodies that will live for hundreds of years. Some humans will appear to live for thousands of years as the mythological gods of pre-historic times.

They will be the higher-density humans who will have full access to their light bodies and appear to be immortal because of the constant regeneration of matter.

These higher dimensional humans will mostly live off universal life force energy, as they harness higher vibrations of spiritual energy from their light body.

This being will also have the ability to lower its frequency down an octave in order to project a vehicle of a lesser density form in order to interact with the rest of the evolving humans from the fourth-density earth.

As far as death is a concern there will be non, for all humans in the NEW HEAVEN ON EARTH from the fourth dimension and up to the Sixth are going to be eternal beings' children of God, as we engage in the ascension process.

For the light body, open activation is what the Bible calls our celestial bodies, what we all have been waiting to achieve.

It is important to understand, the new and exalted humans of the fourth-density and up will be sustained by a universal life force coming through their chakras. Health will no longer be an issue for everyone will be healthy.

This will be a world with no more diabetes, heart problems, or any other illness, a world where there is no more injury but laughter, learning, and fun.

Our new educational system will fall under the guidance and direction of the great academies of higher learning that in turn are going to be under the leadership of the restored sacred temples.

For children, instead of attending a school with other children, they will be educated individually by a few teachers per child to make sure that every individual gets all the attention they need in order to excel in anything their hearts desire. All education will be based on universal cosmic principles since our world will be evolving only spiritually and will no longer experience survival mode.

Meaning that in the NEW WORLD AGE, there is to be no more living to work and working to live, for that was the old program of slavery. In fact, in the millennium, people will finally have rest from struggle and everything will be provided for so that they may only focus on their education and spiritual evolution. The season of physical survival or physical evolution is over. Now we will utilize natural healthy technology to do all the work for us so that we only focus on our perpetual ascension into even higher realms.

All of this or at least the turning point, that will lead to this type of world, is to come to pass in the days ahead of us because of the great acceleration of time as explained through the Fibonacci ratio. This is a mathematical formula that clearly maps out all the lengths of sequences in the universe down to the t.

According to the theory of time acceleration, as revealed through the Fibonacci ratio and Mayan calendar, and because we are approaching a rare and most unique galactic alignment, we are about to take the greatest quantum leap ever in the evolutionary process of our world and species.

Therefore, due to accelerated evolution, everything will speed up, a hundred times faster and after going through the eye of the needle then everything will continue to exist but on a different frequency. We are entering an ERA where we have come to the final and closing of the greatest human chapter, one that marks the completion of our involution (descent) and the beginning of a greater evolution (ascend) towards higher realms. We are merely passing from one phase of energy field into another as energy is neither created nor destroyed and only those with enough love and compassion will partake of A NEW HEAVEN ON EARTH, for these are the prophesies.

Everyone that goes directly into heaven upon the earth will be experiencing love beyond anything they ever knew, and they will never be in want of anything whatsoever. They will be in a place where only love resides at all given times.

The family is now residing in the pure heaven upon the earth. And will be enjoying everything that comes with heaven on earth. And they will always be in God's favor eternally.

Now that the truth is clear it is best to live life accordingly and to always go about your day with a spiritual understanding of things and most importantly, as of this day forward always give a moment of your time every day and praise to our great creator of all that is through quite a time, prayer meditation or any kind of devotion that you see fit. Everything else will fall into place and the kingdom of God will open for you. Peace be with you in HEAVENS ABUNDANCE.

As far as the coming earth changes, they will only take effect in the third-dimensional earth. For it has been revealed, that the earth changes are necessary because mother earth will need to go through a purification process before she ascends into the higher densities. Also, it has been reported that the earth changes are only to affect those people whose energy fields are not matching the new earth structure.

However right before the earth changes, planet Nibiru will be seen as a clear huge object in the sky, by all as it comes close into our earth's proximity and since we will fully emerge in the photon band, the chosen 144,000 beings along with the twelve adepts will be activated into physical angels.

They will emerge as heroes and help in the rebuilding of the new world. When the time comes for these events to transpire the chosen elect of the 144, 000 will take their post and bring the right knowledge, tools, and wisdom to enough people in order to prepare them for the coming earth changes. Do not be afraid, for this is the harvest of souls, not the destruction of all. There are safe zones in the planet and when the time is right the elect will guide only the good to safety.

# CHAPTER NINETEEN

## A CLOSER LOOK AT THE COMING WORLD

In days to come, we will no longer be a world with over three hundred countries, all independent and separated from one another. As revealed we will integrate our world into 20 to 2 Federated regions known as The Governments of the World and the Commonwealth of Nations. This information was revealed by the one who heads the office of the planetary Christ, known as Lord Maitreya, acting under the head of the current planetary spiritual hierarchy, Lord Sanut Kumara. Lord Maitreya has already signed for the convergence of the United Nations into the NEW Commonwealth of Nations and the Federated regions that will align with the Galactic Federation. With no further said, here is a look at the coming new world structure.

**THE RUSSIAN FEDERATION** will be in the Russian region, and it will include St. Petersburg, and all present provinces, regions, and sea territories.

**THE OLD ASIAN FEDERATION** will include China, Mongolia, South Korea, Taiwan, Japan, including a small portion of Russian territory, Uighur land, inner

Mongolia Ningsi Hui, and Guanxi Zhuang.

**THE VEDIC FEDERATION** will include, India, Sri, Lanka, The Maldives, and Bangladesh, a decision about the northwest and northeast Frontier will be made after further analysis on the ground.

**THE BOHEMIAN FEDERATION** will include, Czech Republic, Finland, Estonia, Latvia, Lithuania, Poland, Slovakia, Byelorussia, Ukraine, Austria, Hungary, Slovenia, Croatia, Bosnia, Herzegovina, Albania, Yugoslavia, Kosovo, Macedonia, Greece, Bulgaria, Romania, Liechtenstein, and Moldova.

**THE VIRACOCHA FEDERATION** and will consist of Peru, Ecuador, Brazil, and Bolivia.

**THE WHITE ELEPHANT FEDERATION** will include Myanmar, Thailand, Vietnam, Malaysia, Singapore, Cambodia, and Laos.

**THE EASTER ISLAND FEDERATION** and will include, Chile, Argentina, Uruguay, and Paraguay

**THE QUETZALCOATL FEDERATION**, and it will consist of Guatemala, Belize, el Salvador, Cuba, pana, Nicaragua, Honduras, Costa Rica, Colombia, Venezuela, Guyana, Surinam, Bahamas, Jamaica, Haiti, Dominican Republic, St. Kitts Nevis, Antigua, and Barbuda St, Vincent, Barbados, Trinidad and Tobago, Puerto Rico. Guadeloupe, Martinique, Netherlands Antunes, Grand, Cayman, French Guyana, margarita, St. Lucia, Grenada, Virgin Islands.

**ABYSSINIAN FEDERATION** Ethiopia, Eritrea, Somalia, Kenya, Tanzania and Seychelles, Djibouti, Malawi, Burundi, Rwanda, The islands of Zanzibar, Pemba, and Mafia.

**THE REFLECTIVE FEDERATION** includes the Antarctic, Islands, and Sea territories.

**THE HIMALAYAN FEDERATION** will include Tibet, Kashmir, Nepal, Bhutan, and historic Sikkim.

**THE OCEANIC FEDERATION** will include the aboriginal Nation Australia, New Zealand, Indonesia, Brunet, Borneo, The Philippines, Papua New Guinea, and Irian Jaya, Fiji, Solomon Islands, Tonga, Kiribati, Nauru and New Caledonia, Tuvalu, Mariana is Timor, Marshal Is, Wallis and Future, Vanuatu, Samoa, Polynesia, Micronesia, Palau, Niue, Pitcairn.

**THE PEACOCK THRONE FEDERATION** will include Afghanistan, Pakistan, Turkmenistan, Uzbekistan, Kazakhstan, Kyrgyzstan, Tajikistan, Iran, and Azerbaijan.

**THE ATLANTIAN FEDERATION** will consist of Madagascar, South Africa, Swaziland, Botswana, Namibia, Mozambique, Lesotho, Zimbabwe, Zambia, Angola, Mauritius, Reunion Island, and Comoros.

**THE BABYLONIAN FEDERATION** will include Turkey, Syria, Iraq, Lebanon, Cyprus, Georgia, Armenia, and Kuwait.

**THE FREEDOM FEDERATION** will include Cape Verde, Senegal, The Gambia, Guinea Bissau, Guinea sierra leone, Liberia, Cote D Ivoire, Ghana, Togo, Burkina Faso, Benin, Nigeria, and Cameroon.

**THE EUROPEAN FEDERATION** will include, France, Portugal, Spain, Monaco, Italy, including the Vatican and San Marino, The islands of all these lands including the isle of man, Jersey, and Guernsey, Malta, Switzerland, Luxembourg, Germany, Holland, Belgium, England, Iceland, Ireland, Scotland, Wales, Norway, Sweden, Andorra, and Gibraltar.

**THE EL COSO FEDERATION** will include Morocco, Algeria, Mauritania, Niger, Mali, Tunisia, and the Canary Islands.

**THE JERUSALEM FEDERATION** Will include Jerusalem and other specific interconnected locations.

**THE HOLY FEDERATION** will include Saudi Arabia, Yemen, Oman, United Arab Emirates, Bahrain, Oater, Jordan, and Palestine.

**THE YANIHIS FEDERATION** will include Egypt, Sudan, Libya, Chad,

Uganda, Central African Republic, Democratic Republic of Congo, Sao Tome, and Principe, Gabon, Republic of Congo, Equatorial Guinea.

**THE JABOUCAS FEDERATION** will include Canada and Islands, USA, Mexico, Alaska, Greenland.

Afterthoughts. The premise of this work is to remind people that there is more to reality than the obvious. We are in the midst of the greatest transition ever and we need to prepare by learning to change our limited belief systems so that we may expand into other levels of reality, that is only opening up to those that are becoming more balanced integrated, and whole. In order to survive this coming shift and harvest all we need do is open our hearts and become more compassionate towards others and learn how to love one another. This is a time where the golden rule is to be respected and practiced by all

...............................................................................

...............................................................................

...............................................................................

THIS BOOK WAS WRITTEN BY
AN EMISSARY OF LIGHT WORKING FOR THE MOST HIGH.

# GLOSSARY

**Adam/Michael**: the first incarnating fifth and fourth-density descending son of light that occupied the vehicles of the homo sapiens sapiens species, the strand that humans today came from.

**Aln**: the original home planet of the fallen angels, the reptoids.

**Andromeda**: our sister galaxy and closest to the milky way.

**Draco Orion Empire**: the galactic organization that opposed the galactic federation of free worlds, serving as the axis forces for the Draco reptilians, who have represented the dark side in our galaxy.

**Anu**: the prior sixth-dimensional commander of Nibiru and the galactic human that became the progenitor of our planet's current human race through his children and grandchildren, the benai-ha elohim- anunaki-Pleiadian-librarians. ascension: the process of integrating all our vehicles in a union of matter (body) and spirit avyon: the original home of the descending angelic humans in our galaxy.

**Alpha Centauri**: the closest star system to our solar system and a system associated with the galactic federation of light.

**Alpha Draconis**: the second stronghold of the fallen angels known as the draco reptilians.

**Ancient astronaut theory** is the belief that an advanced race of humans from another planet came to our world and seeded the current human race.

**Atlantis**: the third seeding of our planet and the third root-race that existed for half a million years as an advanced space-age civilization. this once great civilization was ruled by the Pleiadians of the federation in a benevolent way. its decline was a result of reptilian influence during its second golden age approximately fifty thousand years ago.

**Bellatrix**: star system in lower orion associated with the original home planet aln of the reptilians. b. c. before Christ Cappella: star system associated with the forces of light the federation of free worlds.

**Cathars**: a spiritual community that flourished in the middle of the dark ages, a Millenium ago in southern France, thanks to the templars.

**Catholic church**: the revealed modern-day harlot (Babylon Rome) as revealed in revelation.

**Celestial realms**: the highest level of existence and our common origin. the always existing meta-verse that has no beginning and no end as confirmed by our new science.

**Central sun**: the central core of our galaxy and the great central which is at the center of our local universe.

**Centropy**: the concept of an existing central core to everything from macro meta-galaxies to the micro.atom divine or divinity: pure-eternal- celestial essence.

**Cosmos**: everything in existence, all universes, the omniverse, meta-verse or central universe of Havona; see Urantia book for more info on Havona see Urantia book...

**Cycle**: one universal round, hertz per second, one full circle, completion, infinite radius. study science for more info.

**Cyrus**: the Persian conqueror who carried a high concentration of the Babylonian reptilian-human bloodline in 500 B.C. demi-god: half galactic nibirian half ascending earth human. the new strand that gave rise to the homo- sapiens dimension: one of many planes of vibrating light-energy-matter., range of vibration in the light wave spectrum.

**Energy**: converted light into multiple expressions of spectral-spectra radiations. everything that exist is made up of this spectral spectrum or combinations of all matter is congealed energy physics.

**Epsilon Eridani**: one of the various star systems that are part of the confederation of planets serving our galaxy on the side of our heavenly father and mother...

**Epsilon Bootes**: star system associated with the anchara alliance of the draco reptilians.

**Enki**: galactic fifth-dimensional human. firstborn of former commander plaiedean-nibirian anu of the battle star-planet nibiru. earth builder (ea) and rival of lord enlil his half-brother, second born of anu and known as the lord of the mountain. see. zacheriah zitchin on the ancient translated sumerian tablets for more info. also see the nibirian council com site for more accurate info.

**Enlil**: galactic fifth-dimensional human. The second born of former commander anu. half brother and rival to earth lord enki. enlil is known as the lord of the mountain according to all ancient records. he corresponds to zues of ancient Greece and to. Jehovah of ancient israel and to indra of ancient india. leader of the gods in all pantheon traditions.

**Entropy**: the process of decay or the ultimate end

**Evolution**: the process of eternal progression, to move upward as opposed to moving downward as involution in the higher spiritual understanding of returning back to source through the process of ascension-evolution.

**Fith dimension**: a higher refined level of existence where matter is easily manipulated by energy mind and a place where all opposites are reconciled which is the next level of vibration we are moving into.

**Galactic Federation of free worlds**: a galactic peacekeeping vehicle that protects life in our galaxy serving the higher dominions or councils of light beyond our galactic system.

**God**: all that is, everything that was, and all that will ever be., higher power, creator source, and eternal source.

**Giza**: pyramid used by earlier pre-historic civilizations for advanced interplanetary activity and power plants..

**Hathor**: the planet was most of the pre-historic galactic humans (mistakinly known as gods) fled before the cataclysm of Atlantis.

**Helios envesta**: the name of the deity that resides as head of the council in our solar systems spiritual hierarchy, solar logos, serving the great central sun Kolob on the side of light and life.

**History**: a collection of stories that explain events in the past. ¾ of history has been deleted, especially dating to the times before the flood.

**Hyboria**: the first great seeding and the first intergalactic space-age civilization that existed on our earth about two million years ago. the first root-race according to theosophy.

**Igigi**: a group of galactic human astronauts stationed in one of our terrestrial planets during the days of Atlantis when the nibirians came to take over the affairs of earth.about half a million years ago.

**Illuminati**: financial monopoly of power brokers who work for the Vatican in the `takeover of the world's economic system in order to initiate a one-world government.

**Isis**: name of one of enkis twins, Osiris and isis his sister/wife. mother goddess in ancient egypt, female carrier and representative of the sacred divine feminine in the ancient order of melchizedek, after the fall of Atlantis. known in ancient cultures under different names. A state in Phoenicia, Athena to the greeks, venus to the Romans.

**Isle of paradise**: the central core of all that is and eternal isle of the central universe of Havona. see Urantia book for info.

**Jaboucas federation**: one of the federated regions in the coming new world structure, including the regions of America, Canada, Mexico, and Greenland.

**Jahova**: the Hebrew name of the galactic human known as Enlil to the Sumerians and Zeus to the greeks.

**Jesus**: the great silver son and firstborn of heaven, as revealed in the yanihian script.

**Jesuits**: the core of the antichrists that rules today's dark brotherhood

**Judah**: the line of messianic descent of galactic humans in our world that carried the highest concentration of human galactic bloodline. it came from our biblical Abraham, through his children, and was the line that Jesus the christ incarnated in.

**Kelpert belt**: the outer belt of asteroids that was once a planet known as maldek that was used by the reptilian forces during the earhts first seeding about two million years ago.

**Lanonandek**: according to the urantia papers, it is the second-order of descending sonship after the order of Melchizedek.

**Lemuria**: the second seeding of the earth by the federation of a type two space-age civilization. corresponding to the second root-race of theosophy and according to all sources, the first garden of Eden.

**Lyra**: the first constellation where all humans in the milky way galaxy originated from as the first steller human civilization.

**Lyran**: the first full conscious humans that hail from the Lyran constellation.

**Masons freemason**: a fraternity associated with the legendary knight's templars and a lost art that goes back to Egypt. it is an arm of the brotherhood of light design to restore the republic and to guard it against the infiltration of the Bavarian Illuminati who works with the Jesuits as co-conspirators in the destruction of the u.s. constitution. they are the white knights of freedom against fascism.

**Mikaal**: christ Michael according to the urantia papers., archangel Michael, lord mikaal, adept and creator son of the twelve major universes of compassion, as revealed by the yanian script.

**Melchizedek**: the highest order of divine sonship and the celestial administration known in all universes as the cosmic order of Melchizedek. a teacher of light. see Urantia and keys of Enoch for more info.

**Meta-verse**: the mother universe that is constantly giving birth to endless membrane universes, all evolving parallel to one another. the always existing central universe of Havona that has no beginning or end.

**Metatron**: a high-ranking celestial being who operates beyond the confines of our local universe of Nebadon.

**M- theory**: the concept of many universes existing as single membranes. m-theory along with string theory and unified field theory are higher ways of explaining laws in the higher dimensions all these theories fall under the idea of a grand theory of everything as proposed by Einstein and many physicists today.

**Mothership**: huge space fleets utilized by the galactic federation in a type two-star population star system, design for all purposes. colossal space vehicles with built-in cities as well as different landscape environments for the different types of species that exist throughout our galaxy.

**Millennium**: the Christian interpretation of the coming golden age.

**Nibiru**: the planet of the crossing according to ancient text. the battle star planet of the galactic federation was used by played a galactic human to patrol and secure many star systems and planets from the invading reptilians.

**Nabu**: son of Marduk and second in command as the leader of the dark forces after the fall of Atlantis.

**Nihma**: aka Ninhursag or the lady of the mountain according to all traditions. giver of life and enkis partner in the genetic upgrade of homo Erectus.

new age: the idea of a coming new world age based on spirituality. the idea for a new age has nothing to do with the Illuminati all information herein was confirmed by the ascended beings many call the masters and ladies of light, serving the great central sun of our galaxy and the one creator.

Made in the USA
Las Vegas, NV
12 August 2022

53119027R00157